VOLUME TWO

The

SPIRITUAL

MAN

WATCHMAN NEE

Living Stream Ministry

Anaheim, California • www.lsm.org

First Edition, March 1998.

ISBN 0-7363-0269-7
(three-volume set)

Published by

Living Stream Ministry
2431 W. La Palma Ave., Anaheim, CA 92801 U.S.A.
P. O. Box 2121, Anaheim, CA 92814 U.S.A.

Printed in the United States of America

05 / 12 11 10 9 8 7 6 5

CONTENTS

SECTION FOUR

THE SPIRIT

CHAPTER ONE

THE HOLY SPIRIT
AND THE BELIEVER'S SPIRIT

The knowledge most lacking among believers today concerns the existence of the human spirit and its function. Many believers do not know they have a spirit in addition to their mind, emotion, and will. Even after hearing that there is a spirit within man, they either think that their mind, emotion, or will is the spirit, or they are puzzled and do not know where their spirit is. This ignorance is a very serious matter. Because of this, believers do not know how to cooperate with God, control themselves, and fight against Satan, since all these three things require the work of the spirit.

The most important thing that a believer should know is that there is a spirit within him besides the thought, knowledge, and imagination of the mind; the feeling, love, and desire of the emotion; and the ideas, opinion, and determination of the will. The spirit is deeper than the mind, emotion, and will. A believer should know that he has a spirit; he also should know the feeling of the spirit, its working, its power, and the principle of its activity. Only in this way will a believer be able to know how to walk according to the spirit, not according to the fleshly soul or body.

An unregenerated person's spirit and soul are constituted together. Naturally, he only knows the feelings of the soul, which are strong and powerful, and does not know the existence of the spirit, which is dead and dormant. This ignorance started when he was a sinner and continues even after he becomes a believer. Although a believer has life in his spirit and the experience of overcoming "fleshly things," he sometimes walks according to the spirit and sometimes according to the soul. He does not know what the spirit demands, how the spirit initiates, or how to nourish the spirit.

He does not know the feeling of the spirit and the meaning that these feelings represent. Naturally, he restricts the life of the spirit and lets the natural life of the soul continue to act as the principle of his living. This matter is very serious; it is beyond the common believer's imagination. There are some believers who faithfully seek higher and deeper spiritual experience. After they have the experience of overcoming sins, they no longer go forward because they do not know the work of the spirit. Instead, they pursue after "spiritual and biblical knowledge" in their mind; they seek after the Lord's presence in their feelings and a kind of burning feeling in their members; and they mostly behave and walk according to the power of their own will. This causes the believer to be deceived and over-emphasize his own (soulish) experience, thinking himself to be super-spiritual. This will cultivate his "self" life (soul) to a great extent. He subjectively thinks that his experience is spiritually solid, which will keep him from progressing in the spiritual path. Therefore, God's children should humble themselves before God, subject themselves to the Holy Spirit and biblical teachings, and gradually examine the function and work of the spirit in order that they may walk according to the spirit.

THE REGENERATION OF MAN
(COMPARE WITH SECTION ONE, CHAPTER FOUR)

Why should a sinner be regenerated? Why should he be born from above and have a regeneration of the spirit? Because man is a fallen spirit. As a fallen spirit, man needs a regeneration of the spirit to receive a new spirit. Satan is a fallen spirit and man is also a fallen spirit, except that man has a body. Satan's fall was before man's fall. By knowing Satan's fall, we may know our fall. Satan is a spirit who was created by God to have a direct fellowship with God Himself. However, he fell, became the leader of the authority of darkness, and was separated from God and all the virtues of God. Nevertheless, Satan did not lose his existence because of his fall; rather, he just lost his normal relationship with God. Similarly, man, like Satan, fell into darkness and was separated from God, yet man's spirit still exists. Now his spirit is separated from God and cannot fellowship or reign. Spiritually speaking, man's spirit is already dead. Just as the sinful archangel's spirit exists forever, sinful man's spirit also exists forever. However, man has a body, and his fall caused him to become a fleshly man (Gen. 6:3). No religion, ethics, culture, or law in this world can improve this fallen human spirit. Since man has now fallen into the position of flesh, nothing can enable him to become a spirit again. Therefore, regeneration—the regeneration of the spirit—is a must. Only God's Son, who shed His blood to cleanse us from our sin and give us a new life, can bring us back to God.

When a sinner believes in the Lord Jesus, he is regenerated. God gives the sinner His own uncreated life to enliven the sinner's spirit. The regeneration of a sinner is a matter in the spirit. All God's work begins within man, from center to circumference, unlike Satan who works from the outside to the inside. God's purpose is, firstly, to give life to man's darkened spirit, where man should receive God's life and fellowship with God, and to cause it to be regenerated. Then He works from there, spreading out to man's soul and body.

Regeneration causes man to receive a new spirit on one hand and, on the other hand, causes his old spirit to be resurrected. Concerning regeneration, Ezekiel 36:26 says, "And a new spirit will I put within you." John 3:6 says, "That which is born of the flesh is flesh, and that which is born of the Spirit is spirit." The "spirit" mentioned in these two verses refers to God's own life, because this is not the spirit which we had originally but that which is given to us by God at the time of regeneration. This new life is "divine" (2 Pet. 1:4) and "cannot sin" (1 John 3:9). The spirit which man originally had, although it has been enlivened, may still be defiled (2 Cor. 7:1) and needs to be sanctified (1 Thes. 5:23).

When God's life (which also is called the "Spirit") enters into our human spirit, it enlivens our spirit which was in a state like a drunken stupor. Formerly our spirit was "alienated from the life of God" (Eph. 4:18), but now it has been made alive. Therefore, "the body is dead because of sin, the spirit is life because of righteousness" (Rom. 8:10). What we lost in Adam was the spirit which died; what we receive at regeneration is this dead spirit which has been enlivened. However, we not only obtain what we had lost in Adam, we also receive a new spirit with God's life which Adam never had.

As a result of seeing this, we understand the vanity of self-improvement, exhortations to do good, revival, repentance, etc. No matter what man does on his own, he cannot enliven his spirit, nor can he receive a "new spirit." Regardless of how he improves, that which is dead is dead. Regardless of how he repairs, that which is old is still old. Unless man receives a new life from above, no matter how diligently he studies religion and practices morality, he will not be able to make his spirit alive and new. Only the new Spirit of God can enliven man's old spirit. Those who want to make their spirit alive but do not receive God's new Spirit of life will be dead forever. A man without regeneration has absolutely nothing to do with Christ (Rom. 8:9); therefore, every so-called believer should ask himself whether he has been regenerated. Only those who receive God's surpassing life are God's children. Being His children and yet not being born of Him is an absurdity.

God's life is most often called "eternal life" in the Bible. This word "life" is *zoe* in the original language, which means higher life or spiritual life. Everyone who believes in the Lord Jesus is regenerated and receives eternal life as soon as he believes. What is the function of the eternal life? "And this is eternal life, that they may know You, the only true God, and Him whom You have sent, Jesus Christ" (John 17:3). Therefore, eternal life is not only a later blessing for believers' enjoyment but also a spiritual ability. Without eternal life we do not know God, neither can we know the Lord Jesus. Knowing the Lord by intuition comes after man receives God's life. This tiny bit of God's life within man can eventually develop and grow into a spiritual man.

After man's regeneration, all of God's purpose is that many, through His Spirit, may remove everything that belongs to the old creation; all of God's work in man is also in the spirit.

THE HOLY SPIRIT AND REGENERATION

At the time of man's regeneration, his spirit receives God's life and becomes enlivened. It is the Holy Spirit who actively accomplishes this work. It is the Holy Spirit who reproves man of sin, righteousness, and judgment. He prepares man's heart, causing him to willingly believe in the Lord Jesus as his Savior. The work of the cross is accomplished by the Lord Jesus. However, it is the Holy Spirit who applies this upon the sinner and within his heart. We must understand the relationship between the cross of Christ and the work of the Holy Spirit. While the cross has already accomplished everything, the Holy Spirit accomplishes within man what has been accomplished before. While the cross causes man to have the position, the Holy Spirit causes man to have the experience. While the cross achieves the "fact" for God, the Holy Spirit gives man the experience. While the work of the cross creates a position and achieves a salvation so that the sinner may have the possibility of being saved, the work of the Holy Spirit reveals to the sinner what the cross has created and accomplished so that he may receive and obtain it. The Holy Spirit does not work alone; rather, He works through the cross. Without the cross, the Holy Spirit has no ground to work. Without the Holy Spirit, the work of the cross is dead. Although it has already been effective toward God, it has no effectiveness toward man.

Although salvation is entirely accomplished by the cross, it is the Holy Spirit who works directly to cause people to receive. Therefore, the Bible says that our regeneration is the work of the Holy Spirit. "That which is born of the Spirit is spirit" (John 3:6). In verse 8, the Lord Jesus said again that regeneration is being "born of the Spirit." It is the Holy Spirit who applies the work of the cross to the believer and imparts God's life into the believer's spirit; thus, the believer is regenerated. The Holy Spirit is the executor of God's life. We "live by the Spirit" (Gal. 5:25). If man merely understands in his mentality and there is no Holy Spirit to regenerate him within his spirit, his understanding cannot help him. If what man believes in is of man's wisdom, not of God's power, he is merely stimulated in the soul and cannot last long, because he is not regenerated. Only those who believe with the heart (Rom. 10:10) can be saved and receive regeneration.

In addition to enabling believers to receive life at the time of regeneration, the Holy Spirit has another step of work. From the point of regeneration, He dwells within the believers. How poor that man keeps forgetting about this and does not care for it! Ezekiel 36 puts together the matter of a believer's receiving the new spirit and receiving the Holy Spirit.

"A new heart also will I give you, and a new spirit will I put within you....And I will put my Spirit within you" (vv. 26-27).

"And a new spirit will I put within you." This means that a believer will receive a new spirit, have his own spirit renewed, and receive life. After speaking about receiving, it continues, saying, "And I will put my Spirit within you." This means that the Holy Spirit wants to dwell within our renewed spirit. A believer receives at the time of regeneration, not only a new spirit, but also the Holy Spirit (a person) dwelling within him. Unfortunately, just as a believer does not understand that the spirit which he has received is new, he also does not understand that when he receives a new spirit, he also receives the Holy Spirit who dwells within him. The Holy Spirit is not sought out and received by the believer due to revival a few years after his regeneration; rather, at the time of regeneration, the entire person of the Spirit begins to dwell in the believer, not just visit him. The apostle said, "Do not grieve the Holy Spirit of God, in whom you were sealed unto the day of redemption" (Eph. 4:30). "Grieve," not "anger," is used since this concerns the love of the Holy Spirit. "Grieve," not "leave," is used since "He abides with you and shall be in you" (John 14:17) "unto the day of redemption." Every regenerated believer has the Holy Spirit dwelling in him permanently. However, the condition of the Holy Spirit within every believer varies; He may be either grieving or rejoicing.

We must understand the relationship between regeneration and the Holy Spirit's abiding within believers. Without a new spirit, the Holy Spirit has no place to abide. The holy dove had no dwelling place in the judged world. It could not abide until the new creation emerged (see Gen. 8). Regeneration is absolutely necessary because without it the Holy Spirit cannot possibly abide within believers. At regeneration, a believer receives a new spirit and, at the same time, receives the Holy Spirit to abide in him forever. Since the new spirit and God, who begot it, are eternally inseparable, the abiding of the Holy Spirit is also forever unchangeable.

It is rare for believers to realize that they have been regenerated and possess a new life. It is even rarer for them to realize that as soon as they believe in the Lord Jesus, the Holy Spirit indwells them to be their guidance, power of life, and the Lord of everything. The reason many newborn believers are slow in progress and growth may be due to either the foolishness of their leaders or their own unbelief and unfaithfulness. Unless the Lord's servants abandon their preconceived opinion that "the truth of the indwelling of the Holy Spirit is for spiritual believers," it is difficult for them to guide others to a spiritual position.

The work of the Holy Spirit in regenerating us is to reprove us of our sins and lead us to repentance that we may believe and know the Savior; thus, He gives us a new nature. This is the fulfillment of God's promise that He will put a new spirit in us. But this promise does not end here. The second half of the promise is as good as the first half. The promise of the indwelling of the Holy Spirit comes right after the promise of receiving a new spirit. The Holy Spirit's work, which causes believers to know sin, believe in the Lord, and receive life, is only His initial preparatory work in order for Him to dwell within them. The Holy Spirit's indwelling of the believers to manifest the Father and the Son is a special glory in the dispensation of grace. God has already given His Spirit to His children. Now is the time for them to confess by faith and obey with faithfulness. The day of resurrection and the day of Pentecost are both over; the descension of the Holy Spirit has been accomplished. If a believer only knows the regenerating work of the Holy Spirit and does not know the reality of the indwelling of the Holy

Spirit, he is just like a person in the Old Testament. Truly, many believers are living on the other side of the day of resurrection and Pentecost!

Even if a believer is so foolish that his experience never goes one step beyond the first half of God's promise, and he is not aware that the Holy Spirit of God is a person dwelling in him, it is an unchangeable fact that God has given him the Holy Spirit. He is regenerated and is a holy temple qualified to be indwelt by the Holy Spirit. If he would draw upon the second half of God's promise with faith, then the second half of God's promise will be fulfilled just as gloriously as the first half of God's promise. If a believer only pays attention to regeneration and is content with receiving a new spirit, he will not have the strong and joyful life that he is entitled to. If a believer does not know or understand the mystery and work of the indwelling Holy Spirit, it is difficult for him to receive all the blessings God has prepared for him in the Lord Jesus. If he is willing to receive God's promise with faith, considering that God has not only given him a new life in regeneration but also the Holy Spirit, as a person, dwelling in his spirit to be his Lord, then his life will make great strides in the path of God.

If a child of God is willing to believe and be faithful, he will have the experience of the Holy Spirit's indwelling on the same day his spirit is renewed. After a believer's regeneration, the Holy Spirit dwells in him to lead him into a spiritual state, to manifest Christ in his life, teach him, and sanctify him. But very often a believer does not even know the position of the Holy Spirit, despises His indwelling, and walks according to his own will. A believer should humble himself in this light, respect His holy presence, allow Him to work, tremble with fear before Him because of love and respect, not daring to act on his own, and consider what an exaltation it is that God indwells him. If we want to abide in Christ and have a holy life as Christ's, we should use our faith to receive God's provision. The Holy Spirit is already in our spirit. The problem is whether we will let Him work out of our spirit.

THE HOLY SPIRIT AND THE HUMAN SPIRIT

Since we have seen that the Holy Spirit indwells the believers at the time of their regeneration, we should see in more detail where the Holy Spirit dwells so that we can understand His work within us.

We must remember that the real meaning of regeneration is not an outward change or the soul and the body being stimulated, but it is the spirit receiving life. Regeneration is a new event which takes place within the human spirit. It is the enlivening of the deadened spirit. The reason the deadened spirit can be made alive is due to receiving a new life. But the most important point is that when we receive a new spirit, we also receive the Holy Spirit of God to dwell within us. The phrase "put within you" occurs twice in Ezekiel 36:26-27 and indicates that the place where the Holy Spirit dwells is the human spirit.

We have seen that our whole being is just like the holy temple. "Do you not know that you are the temple of God, and that the Spirit of God dwells in you?" (1 Cor. 3:16). What the apostle means is that because believers are the temple of God, the Holy Spirit dwelling in us is just like God dwelling in the holy temple in the old days. Although the entire temple signifies the presence of God and is the dwelling place of God, the actual place of God's dwelling is in the Holy of Holies. The Holy Place and outer court are only places for God to work and move according to His presence in the Holy of Holies. Our spirit is signified by the Holy of Holies. According to this illustration, the Holy Spirit indwelling our spirit is a very clear matter.

The nature of the dweller and the dwelling place are the same. After man's regeneration, only man's regenerated spirit is an adequate dwelling place of the Holy Spirit—not his mind, emotion, will, and body. He is the Builder and also the Dweller. He cannot dwell before He builds. He builds because He wants to dwell. He can only dwell in the place which He has built.

As we have mentioned, the holy ointment cannot be poured upon man's flesh. We have also mentioned that everything of man before his regeneration, regardless of which part, in its totality is called "flesh" in the Bible. Therefore, the Holy Spirit cannot dwell in man's flesh. This also indicates clearly that the Holy Spirit cannot dwell in man's mind, emotion, will, or body. Not to mention that the Holy Spirit cannot dwell in any part of man's soul or body, He cannot dwell even in man's unregenerated spirit. Just as the holy ointment cannot be poured upon the flesh, in the same way, the Holy Spirit cannot dwell in any part of the "flesh." The Spirit can only lust against the flesh (Gal. 5:17); He has no other relationship with the flesh. Therefore, unless something different from the flesh exists in man, there is no way for the Holy Spirit to dwell in man. Therefore, the regeneration of the spirit is very important because the Holy Spirit dwells in the new spirit, which is different from the flesh.

The Holy Spirit indwelling man's spirit is a very important thing. If a believer does not know that the dwelling place of the Holy Spirit is in the deepest part of his whole being, which is deeper than his mind, emotion, and will, he will surely seek the guidance of the Holy Spirit in his mind, emotion, and will. If we understand this, then we will know that we were deceived before and were wrong in looking outward, outside the spirit in the soul, or inside or outside the body for guidance. The Holy Spirit is indeed dwelling in the deepest part of our being. Therefore, His work can only be expected to be seen there; His guidance can only be found there. Our prayer is toward the "heavenly Father," but the heavenly Father is within us leading us. Our Comforter is within our spirit. Therefore, His guidance also issues from there. If we seek a sign from a dream, vision, voice, or feeling outside of our spirit, then we will be deceived.

Many believers often look inwardly, searching into their own thinking, feeling, and opinion to see whether they have peace, how much grace they have received, or what kind of progress they have made. This is not of faith, and it is very harmful. This causes the believer to turn his eyes away from Christ to himself. But there is another kind of inward looking which is different from the one just mentioned. The greatest deed of faith is to look to the guidance of the Holy Spirit, who dwells in the spirit. The believer's mind, emotion, and will cannot sense the things within him, yet even in darkness he must believe that God has given him a new spirit, within which dwells the Holy Spirit. Just as God who dwelt behind the dark veil was believed, feared, and yet not seen by man, the Holy Spirit indwelling man's spirit also cannot be sensed by his soul and body.

After seeing this, we know what is the real spiritual life. It is not many thoughts and visions in the mind; neither is it many enthusiastic, joyful, and happy feelings in the emotion; nor is it sudden shakings, penetrations, and contacts brought by outward forces upon the body. Rather, it is a life issuing from the Spirit which is in the deepest part of a man. A real spiritual life is deeper than the mind, the feelings, and the consciousness of the body. It is in the deepest part of a man. Truly walking according to the spirit is knowing the moving of the innermost spirit and following it. No matter how wonderful experiences in the mind, emotion, and will are, if they are just outward, not even deeper than feelings, then these experiences are not of the spirit. Only the effect produced by the work of the Holy Spirit in man's spirit can be counted as a spiritual experience. Anything else is just thought and feeling. A spiritual living needs faith.

Romans 8:16 says, "The Spirit Himself witnesses with our spirit"—not the heart or the soul—"that we are children of God." Man's spirit is the part where man works together with the Holy Spirit. How do we know that we have been saved through regeneration and are the children of God? We know because our spirit has been made alive and the Holy Spirit lives in our spirit. Our spirit is a regenerated and renewed spirit, and He who dwells in, yet is distinct from, our spirit is the Holy Spirit. He bears witness with our spirit within us.

APPENDIX

In the Chinese Union Version of the Bible, it is difficult for us to tell when the word *spirit* refers to the Holy Spirit and when it refers to the human spirit. According to the translators of the Bible, whenever the original text used only

the word *spirit* and not *the Holy Spirit,* they thought it
actually referred to the Holy Spirit, and they added the word
Holy before the word *Spirit* to indicate that it referred to the
Holy Spirit.

The Bible, word by word and sentence by sentence, is God's
inspiration. Why does God not say *Holy Spirit* but rather
spirit in many places? Is not what God does not say as
meaningful as what God says? In many places God clearly
says *Holy Spirit.* But why in some places does He only say
Spirit? Yet, according to the Bible translators, it refers to the
Holy Spirit. We all know that in many places where only the
word *Spirit* is used, it refers to the Holy Spirit, such as *the
Spirit of Christ, the Spirit of God,* etc. But in many verses
when the *spirit* is not mentioned as the Holy Spirit, what
exactly does it refer to?

In 1913 a monthly journal which specialized in Bible
studies put out six messages concerning the Holy Spirit by
a person by the name of Fullest (?). They were all studies of
the original text. When he mentioned the word *Spirit,* he
explained the many ways that this word had been used in
the Bible. Later on he pointed out the mistake of considering
the word *Spirit* as the *Holy Spirit* without regard to the
context. He said it is wonderful that knowledge seems not to
be very useful concerning this big subject because there is
no indication whether or not this word *spirit* should be
capitalized when the Holy Spirit was writing the New
Testament. Therefore, all the capitalized words *Spirit* in the
English Bible are just the translator's interpretation. All the
New Testament experts still hold differing opinions concerning when the word *spirit* should be capitalized and when it
should be lower case.

The capitalized word *Spirit* indicates the Holy Spirit and
spirit indicates that it is not the Holy Spirit but a spirit
besides the Holy Spirit, such as the spirit of man, etc. After
reading this, do we not understand? In the original text there
is no indication that it refers to the Holy Spirit or human
spirit whenever just the word *Spirit* is used. Of course, the
answer to this question is not so simple. We still need to read
the word preceding it and after it, and determine if there is

an article in the original language, before we can determine whether it refers to the Holy Spirit.

However, for our present necessity we may say that the word *holy* which is before the word *Spirit,* in some cases in the New Testament, is really the translator's interpretation rather than his translation. Whenever we come across this kind of situation, although we dare not think that it only refers to the human spirit, at least we may say that it sometimes refers to the human spirit.

After seeing the above, we know that the Holy Spirit and the believer's regenerated spirit have a relation which is very difficult to separate. Since the Holy Spirit is working in man's spirit in order to control man's whole being, in some places in the Bible the Holy Spirit and the human spirit are mentioned as one. A person's spirit should dominate his whole being; yet not the spirit alone, but the spirit indwelt by the Holy Spirit should dominate his being. The part of man which can work with the Holy Spirit is his spirit, and the part of man where the Holy Spirit can work is also his spirit.

CHAPTER TWO

A SPIRITUAL MAN

A regenerated believer, with his spirit enlivened and the Holy Spirit indwelling him, can still remain a carnal or fleshly believer, with his spirit still oppressed by his soul or body. There is a specific path that a regenerated believer should specifically take in order to succeed in becoming spiritual.

Briefly, there can be at least two great changes in the life of a human being—changing from a perishing sinner into a saved believer and changing from a fleshly believer into a spiritual one. Just as a sinner can, in fact, become a believer, a fleshly believer can, in fact, become a spiritual one. God can cause a sinner to become a believer and have His life; God can also cause a fleshly believer to become a spiritual believer and have His life more abundantly. Once a man believes in Christ, he becomes a regenerated believer; once he obeys the Holy Spirit, he becomes a spiritual believer. When a man has a normal relationship with Christ, he becomes a Christian; and when a man has a normal relationship with the Holy Spirit, he becomes a spiritual man.

Only the Holy Spirit can make a believer spiritual. The work of the Holy Spirit is to make a man spiritual. In the arrangement of God's way of redemption, on the negative side, the cross carries out a destructive work, destroying everything that is from Adam. The Holy Spirit, on the positive side, carries out a constructive work, building up everything that is from Christ. The cross makes it possible for the believers to be spiritual, and the Holy Spirit makes believers spiritual. Being spiritual means belonging to the Holy Spirit. The Holy Spirit strengthens the human spirit so that He may rule over the whole person. Therefore, if we pursue being spiritual, we should not forget the Holy Spirit and not put the cross aside, because the cross and the Holy Spirit work as the left and right hands. Neither can be spared and neither of these two work independently. The cross always guides man to the Holy Spirit and the Holy Spirit always guides man to the cross. A spiritual believer must have experiences in his spirit with the Holy Spirit. If he wants to become a spiritual man, he must have several steps of experience. Paying attention to these steps does not necessarily mean proceeding from step one to step two and from step two to step three. For the sake of writing, however, they have to be written in sequence, although in actual experience they often occur simultaneously.

Although there are many things we want to mention about how believers progress to become spiritual men, believers should not forget previous teachings (Section Two, Chapters Four and Five). Believers should know that what hinders a man from being spiritual is the flesh. Therefore, if a believer can assume the final attitude that he should have toward the flesh, then he will progress easily. It is marvelous that the more a man is spiritual, the more he knows the flesh and discovers about the flesh. If a man does not know the flesh, he is not spiritual. All of the things previously mentioned about the flesh (Section Two, Chapter Five) are the foundations for one to pursue being spiritual and cannot be neglected by anyone. If we do not pay attention to the flesh, no matter what kind of progress there may be, it will all be vain, superficial, and unreal. Actually, when a believer knows how to deny the flesh and its activities, abilities, and opinions in all things, we can say that this man is spiritual. But, we would again like to mention something positive which is directly related to the spirit.

THE DIVIDING OF SPIRIT AND SOUL
(COMPARE WITH SECTION THREE, CHAPTER FIVE, "THE DIVIDING OF THE SPIRIT AND THE SOUL")

The main point in Hebrews 4:12 is whether we are living according to the guidance of the intuition in the spirit or under the influence of our (soulish) natural likes and dislikes. God's word will judge us on such matters, showing us what belongs to the spirit and what belongs to the soul. Only God's sharp sword can clearly discern the source of our living. Just as man's knife can divide bone and marrow, God's sword can divide the most closely knit spirit and soul. This dividing is only knowledge in the beginning and must become experience later. Actually, believers can only know by experience how the spirit and soul are divided. The believer must experience allowing the Lord to divide his soul and spirit. Not only should he desire, pursue, consecrate himself, pray, and allow the Holy Spirit and the cross to work in him, he must also gain and possess this kind of experience. The spirit of a believer must be freed in reality from the embrace of the soul. The soul and the spirit must be clearly divided, like the Lord Jesus whose spirit and soul are not mixed at all. The spirit of intuition should be entirely free to be the *sole* dwelling place and office of the Holy Spirit and not allow the soul (that is, the mind and emotion) to have the slightest influence. The spirit must be freed from every entanglement of the soul.

The work of the cross on the soul-life must be very real, and the restriction imposed by the cross on the soul-life very definite. The soul-life must suffer loss in experience. The faculty of the soul must maintain a position under the rule of the spirit.

A believer must have experiences of the soul and the spirit being divided to the point where the spirit is no longer surrounded by the soul. Only then can he become a spiritual believer. A spiritual believer differs from other people in that his entire being is ruled by his spirit. The rule of the spirit is not only the rule of Holy Spirit over the soul and body. A believer's own spirit rises up to be the head of his entire being by the Holy Spirit's working through the cross; instead of being ruled by the soul and the body, the spirit has the strength to fully control the soul and body.

The dividing of the soul and spirit is an indispensable work on the negative side in order for a believer to enter into spiritual life. This is a spiritual preparation. Without this, the believer will always be influenced by the soul, and the spirit and the soul will often be mixed in his living. Sometimes he has a spiritual living, but sometimes he is governed by the mind and emotion, or he may even live by the natural life. The expression of life is not pure. A mixture of the spirit and soul is the life principle of a believer who does not have a pure spiritual life. This keeps the believer in the position of being soulish. His own life will suffer loss, and God's Holy Spirit will be unable to use him to do important work.

If there is an actual dividing of the believer's spirit and soul, and he walks according to the spirit, not according to the soul, then whenever his soul reacts, he will sense it immediately, as if he is being defiled, and struggle to break the soul's power and influence. The natural life is truly defiled and can defile the spirit. After the dividing of the spirit and soul, the intuition of the spirit will be very sensitive. Whenever the soul acts, it immediately suffers pain and resists. Even when others act in their soul, it immediately feels unpleasant. Even when it is the object of the soulish love or emotion of others, it will be annoyed as if it cannot bear with them. Only when the dividing of the believer's spirit and soul becomes very real will he have clean feelings and intentions that are genuine. Only then will he have an actual understanding of the meaning of being "clean." Only then will he know that not only are sinful things defiling, but everything natural is defiling and should be rejected as well. He knows and feels in the intuition of the spirit that all contact with that which is of the soul—regardless of whether it is his own or others—is defiling and should be cleansed immediately.

THE KNOWLEDGE OF BEING JOINED
UNTO THE LORD AS ONE SPIRIT

Paul said, "He who is joined to the Lord is one spirit" (1 Cor. 6:17), not one soul. The resurrected Lord is the life-giving Spirit (15:45); therefore, His union with the believers is His union with the believers' spirit. The soul is only the personality of a man and is natural; it should only be used as a vessel to express the results of the union between the Lord and the spirit of the believer. In the believers' soul there is nothing that matches the nature of the Lord's life; only the spirit can have such union. Since the union is a union of the spirit, there is no place for the soul. If the soul and the spirit are still mixed, it will make the union impure. As long as our living has any trace of walking according to our thoughts, of having our own opinion in anything, or of having our emotion stirred in any way, it is enough to weaken this union in our experience. Only things of a similar nature may have a fitting union. Mixture will not do. Just as the Spirit of the Lord is pure and without a trace of mixture, our spirit should also be pure so there can be a real and actual union. If the believer is unwilling to let go of his own wonderful thoughts, unwilling to get rid of his own likings, and unwilling to lay aside his own ideas to obey God's will, it is impossible to express this union in experience. This is a union of the spirit; anything of the soul cannot be allowed to be mixed in.

Where does this union come from? It is from our death and resurrection with the Lord. "For if we have grown together with Him in the likeness of His death, indeed we will also be in the likeness of His resurrection" (Rom. 6:5). This verse explains the meaning of our being joined to the Lord, which is to be joined to His death and resurrection. What does it mean to be joined to the Lord in death and resurrection? It simply means that we are completely one with the Lord. We accept His death as our death and the joining with Him in death as the beginning of our being joined to Him. Having died with Him, we also accept His resurrection as our resurrection. If we accept this way by faith, we will experientially stand together with Him in the position of resurrection. The Lord Jesus was resurrected according to the Spirit of holiness (Rom. 1:4) and made alive in the spirit (1 Pet. 3:18). Therefore, when we are joined to Him in resurrection, we are joined to Him in His Spirit of resurrection. This is very clear. We die to all that belongs to ourselves and live to His Spirit. This is the meaning here. All these are accomplished through the exercise of our *faith* (see Section Three, Chapter One, "The Way to Be Delivered from Sin"). When we are joined to His death, having lost all that is sinful and natural, and joined to the Lord in resurrection life, then our spirit is joined to the Lord to be one spirit. Romans 7:4 and 6 say, "You also have been made dead to the law through the body of Christ so that you might be joined to another, to Him who has been raised from the dead...so that we serve in newness of spirit." We are joined to Christ by the death of Christ, and we are also joined to His resurrection life. The result of this kind of union is that we serve in newness of spirit, without any mixture.

How wonderful! The cross is the foundation of all things. The goal and result of the work of the cross is that a believer's spirit would be joined to the resurrected Lord as one spirit. The cross must work deeply on the negative, destructive side to make the believer lose everything sinful and natural. Only then can the believer be joined to the Lord's positive, resurrected life as one spirit. The believer's spirit must cause all that the believer has to pass through death, so that everything natural and temporal will be lost in death, allowing the spirit, in the freshness of resurrection, to be joined to the Lord to be one spirit in a pure way, without any mixture. The believer's spirit is joined to the Spirit of the Lord, and the two spirits being joined are one spirit. The result of this union is the capacity to serve the Lord in "newness of the spirit." There is nothing of the natural self or any natural liveliness mixed in with the living and work. From this time on, the soul and the body are used only to express the Lord's own life and work. In this way the life of the spirit will manifest its own nature in everything, and there will be frequent experiences of "flowing out" the Lord's Spirit.

This is the ascension life. The believer is joined to the Lord who is at the right hand of God. The Spirit of the Lord on the throne flows to the believer's spirit that is in the world, but not of the world, and the life on the throne is lived out on the earth. The Head and the Body have the same flowing life. After the believer is joined to the resurrected Lord, the believer must daily keep "reckoning" and "yielding." The Lord can then pour out His life-giving power through the believer's spirit. Just as a water hose connected to a fountain flows out living water, the believer's spirit, which is joined to the Spirit of the Lord, also gushes out life. This is because the Lord is not only the Spirit but the "life-giving Spirit." There is nothing that can hinder such a believer. His spirit is full of life and nothing can limit this life because his spirit is closely joined to the life-giving Spirit. We need life in our spirit so that we may always have victory in our daily life. We can gain all the victory of the Lord Jesus by such union. We can know all of His will and mind by such a union. Such a union causes the believer to gain the Lord's life and nature and builds up the Lord's new creation in him. By death and resurrection, a believer's spirit will ascend, just as the Lord ascended; he will be in the "heavenlies" in experience, crushing everything worldly under his feet. By joining to the Lord as one spirit, the believer's spirit is no longer hindered by anything, and it can no longer be disturbed by anything. Instead, it soars toward the heavens above the clouds, always free and always fresh. It has a clear, heavenly view of all things. This is so different from temporal, emotional feelings; it is the heavenly life lived out on the earth. Such a living always has the heavenly nature inside it, and it is spiritual.

THE KNOWLEDGE OF THE HOLY SPIRIT'S INDWELLING

The Holy Spirit is inside a believer; but the believer either does not know it or he fails to obey Him. Therefore, he must know the Holy Spirit who indwells him and completely obey Him. The believer must know that God's Holy Spirit, being a person, indwells him to teach, guide, and give the "reality," the truth, in Christ to the believer. This work of the Holy Spirit can be done only after the believer acknowledges how ignorant and dull his soul is, and he decides that, even though he is foolish, he is willing to be taught. The believer must be willing to let the Holy Spirit take hold of everything and reveal the truth. When the believer knows that God's Holy Spirit dwells in the deepest part of his being, in his spirit, and waits for His teaching, then the Holy Spirit can work. When we do not pursue on our own and are completely willing to be taught, the Holy Spirit can teach us the truth in a way that our mind is able to digest. Otherwise, there is danger. When we know that within us there is a spirit, God's Holiest of all, which is deeper than mind and emotion and is able to fellowship with the Holy Spirit and when we wait for God's

Holy Spirit, then we know that He truly indwells us. When we confess Him and honor Him, He will manifest His power and work from that hidden place inside us and will allow the life of our soul and consciousness to have His life.

The Corinthian believers were fleshly. When Paul persuaded them to leave their fleshly situation, he exhorted them more than once that they were the temple of the Holy Spirit and that the Holy Spirit was indwelling them. Knowing that the Holy Spirit indwells a believer is a help in getting out of the fleshly situation. The believer must know by faith, know entirely, know clearly, and know constantly that the Holy Spirit indeed indwells him. The believer should not only know the doctrines in the Bible that speak about the Holy Spirit; he should know the Holy Spirit Himself. With this kind of knowledge, the believer should commit himself unreservedly to the Holy Spirit to be renewed and willingly submit the various parts of his soul and body to Him, allowing Him to guide and correct.

The apostle asked the Corinthian believers saying, "Do you not know that you are the temple of God, and that the Spirit of God dwells in you?" (1 Cor. 3:16). He seemed to be astonished at their lack of awareness of such a sure thing. He considered the indwelling of the Holy Spirit to be the very first result of salvation, yet they did not know this! It does not matter what the believers' level is, even a level as low as the Corinthian believers. What a pity it is that many believers may not be higher than them! They should clearly know this fact. Without knowing this, a believer will be fleshly and unable to be spiritual. If you have never experienced His indwelling, have you ever known in faith that He indwells you?

When we consider how the Holy Spirit is God, how He is one of the Triune God, how He is the life of the Father and the Son, and then further consider His honor and how He indwells us, who are fleshly, we will surely fear, honor, and praise Him. The Lord Jesus took the likeness of sinful flesh, and the Holy Spirit dwells inside the likeness of sinful flesh. What grace this is!

THE STRENGTHENING OF THE HOLY SPIRIT

The strengthening of the Holy Spirit is needed for the spirit of man to control the soul and body of man and to be the channel of the Holy Spirit flowing out life to the multitudes. Ephesians 3:16 says, "That He would grant you, according to the riches of His glory, to be strengthened with power through His Spirit into the inner man." These are the words which the apostle prayed for the believers. If it were not so important, the apostle surely would not have prayed in this manner. He asked God to strengthen the believer's inner man through His Spirit. The "inner man" is the believer's new man, which the believer has only after believing in the Lord. Therefore, this is the spirit of the believer, the regenerated spirit. The prayer of the apostle is for the spirit of the believer to be strengthened by the Holy Spirit so that it can become strong.

This verse tells us that some believers have weak spirits, while others have strong spirits. Whether a believer's spirit is strong depends on whether or not he has specially been given power by the Holy Spirit. The believers at Ephesus had long been sealed with the Holy Spirit (Eph. 1:13-14). Therefore, what the apostle prayed for on their behalf surely must have been a gift other than the Holy Spirit dwelling in them. The meaning of the apostle's prayer is that they would not only receive the Holy Spirit to dwell in their spirit, but they would also have the special power of the Holy Spirit poured into their spirit to enable their inner man to become strong. A believer may have the Holy Spirit dwelling in his spirit and still have a weak spirit.

A believer must realize the weakness of his own spirit. Then he will pray for the Holy Spirit to fill his spirit with power; being filled with power in the spirit is the need of the believer. Many times the body of a believer is in excellent condition, but he feels a little lazy. At such times, working for the Lord seems unbearable, and his heart is most unwilling. This shows that his spirit is weak and unable to control the emotion. Sometimes the believer may feel very excited, but his body is a little lazy. At such times, laboring for the Lord also seems impossible. In the garden of Gethsemane, the disciples indeed had this kind of experience. What was the reason for this? It was because "the spirit is willing, but the flesh is weak" (Matt. 26:41). To be willing in the spirit is not enough; the spirit must also be strong. When the spirit is strong, it can overcome the weakness of the flesh. Sometimes when a believer is preaching and working on someone, it seems as though he is unable to do anything and has no way to manage him. This is because of the lack of power in the believer's spirit. If the situation were the opposite, when the believer could not save him, it would not be due to a lack of power but because that person did not want to be saved. This is also the case in regards to the environment. Due to outside confusion, the believer may also feel that he is affected. If the spirit is strong, then he can manage the most confused situations in a calm and composed manner. Prayer is the greatest test of the spirit's strength. Those whose spirits are strong can pray much and will not quit before the prayer is answered. Those whose spirits are weak will find it difficult to petition God for several years or several decades without being tired and discouraged. This is the case in all matters. Only those with a strong spirit have the energy to go forward continuously without regard to the environment or feelings. Otherwise, they soon feel that they cannot bear it any longer. In regard to fighting with Satan, there is even more need of power in the spirit. Only those who really have power in the spirit will know how to exercise the power of the spirit to resist and attack the enemy. Without power, all the fighting is just a dramatic struggle. If it is not from the mind's imagination, then it is from the excitement of feelings, and sometimes it may even be the natural strength of the flesh.

Therefore, in order for the believer to receive this power of the Holy Spirit, some works must be accomplished on his side. He must have a specific surrender; he must get rid of all the dubious things and actions in his life; he must be willing to fully obey the will of God; he must believe that God will pour the power of the Holy Spirit into his spirit;

and he must pray for this matter. If there is no obstacle on the side of the believer, God will immediately accomplish what he hopes for. The believer does not need to wait for the Holy Spirit to come and fill him, because the Holy Spirit has descended long ago. The believer only has to wait for the cross to work deeply enough within him to fulfill the necessary condition for the Holy Spirit's filling. If the believer is faithful, obedient, and believing, then in a very short time the power of the Holy Spirit will be poured into his spirit, making him strong and providing the strength to live and work. For some believers, just one instance of surrendering to the Lord may enable them to immediately receive this filling without any delay, because they have fulfilled the necessary condition for the Holy Spirit's filling.

The pouring of the Holy Spirit's power into the believer—it may also be called the believer's being filled by the Holy Spirit—is a matter which occurs in the spirit, the inner man. The Holy Spirit does not fill man's feeling or body, rather He fills the spirit of man. The "inner man" is aroused and becomes strong with energy from the Holy Spirit, not the outward man. This is most important, because it will keep us from seeking for physical feelings, such as shakings, spasms, and falling down, when we seek the filling of the Holy Spirit, rather than simply applying faith (Gal. 3:14). However, a believer must be careful never to regard his faith as an excuse for not needing the inward strengthening of the Holy Spirit. The conditions must be fulfilled, and the attitude must be firm. God will accomplish His promise.

If we read what the apostle said in the subsequent passage concerning how to apprehend, know, and be filled, then we will realize that the strengthening in the spirit causes the consciousness of our spirit to become very clearly manifest. The spirit, like the body, has its functions and consciousness. When the believer has not yet had the power of the Holy Spirit poured abundantly into his spirit, it is very difficult for him to perceive the intuition of his spirit. Once he has had the new experience of being strengthened in the spirit, his spirit's intuition becomes clearly manifest. Consequently, many believers will more easily know the intuition of their own spirit because their inner man has become strong. When this happens, they will be more able to feel the slight movements of their spirit.

A spirit that is full of the power of the Holy Spirit can control the soul and body and make them completely submissive. Regardless of whether it is thought, desire, feeling, or intention, everything must be controlled by the spirit. This will keep the soul from acting independently; rather, the soul will be the steward of the spirit. This will also enable the Holy Spirit to flow out the life of God through the spirit of the believer so that He may water and revive those who are dried up and dead. This is different from the baptism in the Holy Spirit. This strengthening emphasizes life or living (it also affects the work); however, the baptism in the Holy Spirit is particularly for the purpose of the work.

WALKING ACCORDING TO THE SPIRIT

We have already seen how a soulish believer becomes a spiritual believer. This does not mean, however, that he will no longer walk according to the flesh. On the contrary, he is always in danger of falling into being fleshly. Satan is always on the watch. Whenever he has a chance, he will cause the believer to lose his high position and be brought down to a low living. Therefore, it is very important for a believer to always be watchful and walk according to the spirit; then he can always be spiritual.

Romans 8 clearly speaks about the importance of walking according to the spirit. Verses 4 through 6 say, "That the righteous requirement of the law might be fulfilled in us, who do not walk according to the flesh but according to the spirit"; "those who are according to the spirit, [mind] the things of the Spirit"; "the mind set on the spirit is life and peace." Walking according to the spirit is in contrast to walking according to the flesh. If a believer does not walk according to the spirit, he walks according to the flesh. Sometimes he may walk according to the spirit and sometimes according to the flesh. But he should *only* walk according to the spirit. A believer must learn to walk *only* according to the spirit, only according to the intuition of the spirit, without walking for a moment according to the soul or body. A person who walks according to the spirit will consequently be "spiritually minded." Being spiritually minded like this makes his whole being "life and peace." Therefore, the result of walking according to the spirit is life and peace.

Living according to the spirit means walking according to the intuition (see Section Five, Chapter One). Living according to the spirit is to live, work, and act in the spirit. It is also using the strength of the spirit and being governed by the spirit. Thus, life and peace will always be maintained. If a believer does not walk according to the spirit, he cannot maintain his spirituality. Therefore, he should know the various functions of the spirit and its law, so that he will know how to walk.

Walking after the spirit is a daily task for believers which must not be forsaken. We should know that while we live on this earth, we do not live according to our good feelings, doing whatever we feel we should do. Neither should we live according to the good thoughts in our mind, either suddenly or constantly, doing whatever we think. We should act and behave according to the guidance in the intuition of the spirit. The small consciousness of the spirit is where the Holy Spirit expresses His thought. The Holy Spirit does not work directly on our mind to make us suddenly think of something. The work of the Holy Spirit is always done in our spirit. Therefore, if we want to understand the mind of the Holy Spirit, we should walk according to the intuition in our spirit. Sometimes our spirit has consciousness but we do not know what it means, what it demands, and what it expresses. Then we must spend much time in prayer so that our *mind* may understand the meaning of the intuition. After understanding it, we must walk accordingly. The mind may suddenly understand what the intuition means. However, if there is no intuition, the sudden thought from our own mind should not be followed. The teaching of the intuition is the thought of the Holy Spirit. We should follow only this.

This kind of walking according to the spirit requires *dependence* and *faith*. We have already seen that all of the good behavior of the flesh is independent of God, rather than dependent on God. The nature of the soul is independence. If a believer wants to walk according to his own thoughts, feelings, and desires, he does not need to spend time waiting on God, praying to God, and depending on God to guide him. "Doing the desires of the flesh and of the thoughts," (Eph. 2:3) does not need dependence. Only when a believer wants to seek God's will, knowing that he is useless, unreliable, and weak beyond repair, does he have a heart to depend on God. If he wants God to guide him in his spirit, he must wait for God in his spirit and not arbitrarily take his own feelings and thoughts as his guide. The believer must remember that whatever is done and can be done without depending on, waiting on, and trusting and seeking God is walking according to the flesh. Only trusting in a trembling manner for God to guide in the spirit is walking according to the spirit.

Walking also needs faith. Faith is in contrast to seeing and feeling. The feeling of the soul is always to demand, grasp, and desire everything that can be seen and felt as a guarantee in order to act and behave. If a believer walks according to the spirit, he does not walk according to the soul. In other words, he walks by faith and not by sight. Therefore, one who walks according to the spirit, on the one hand, will not feel disheartened if there is no help from man, and on the other hand, will also not be moved when there is opposition from man. Because of faith, he can believe God in darkness and not depend on his own resources; he can trust in the unseen power more than his own visible power.

Walking according to the spirit has two parts: one is to begin working and the other is to do this work with power. Many times, the believer lacks the revelation to do certain things in the intuition of the spirit, but he asks God to give him spiritual power to do this work. This is impossible, because that which is born of the flesh is flesh. Sometimes, what the believer does is based on the knowledge of God's will through revelation in the spirit, but then he uses his own power to do this work (see Section Two, Chapter Four). This is also impossible, because what has begun in the spirit cannot be perfected by the flesh. For a man to follow the Lord, he must be broken by the Lord to the extent that he has absolutely no self-confidence; he must realize that no good thought can originate from him; and he cannot have any power to complete the work started by the Holy Spirit. He must forsake all thoughts, cleverness, knowledge, capabilities, and gifts; he must completely depend on the Lord. The world worships and superstitiously trusts those things. But moment by moment, we should confess that we are undone, worthless, incapable, and useless. We dare not do anything before God does command; even in something that God does command, we dare not have the slightest amount of self-reliance.

If we want to walk according to the spirit in this way, we should follow the small consciousness in the *intuition* in the spirit to begin to work, and we should depend on the *power* of the spirit to do the work revealed by the intuition. Not walking according to thoughts, ideas, feelings, and tendencies, but only according to the intuition, will cause us to begin well. Not depending on our own talents, power, and abilities, but only on the power of the spirit, will cause us to continue to be perfected. We must remember that as soon as we cease walking according to the spirit, we immediately begin walking according to the flesh and minding the things of the flesh, allowing death to operate in our spirit. Only when we do not walk according to the flesh can we walk according to the spirit. "For those who are according to the flesh mind the things of the flesh...for the mind set on the flesh is death" (Rom. 8:5-6).

Our purpose is to be a spiritual man, not a spirit. This distinction will prevent our spiritual life from becoming one-sided. We are men, and will be men forever, but the highest attainment of being a man is to be a spiritual man. Angels are spirits, and not men. They have no body and no soul. Man has a soul and a body. We are to be spiritual men, not spirits. Therefore, we still have a soul and a body. A "spiritual man" is not a person who only has a spirit, with no soul and no body; in that case he would be a spirit and not a man. Being a "spiritual man" simply means man is subject to the rule of his spirit. The spirit is the highest part of the whole person. We should pay considerable attention to this point; otherwise, we will misunderstand. The functions and faculties of man's soul and body are not cancelled because a man is spiritual. A spiritual man still has a soul and a body.

A spiritual man still has the will, mind, and emotion of his soul. Even though these are various parts of the soul-life, these functions are the essentials of man being man. Therefore, although the spiritual man does not live by them, he does not destroy them. On the contrary, they have died, been renewed, and are resurrected. Therefore, they are now completely united with the spirit to be the instruments to express the spirit. The spiritual man does have an emotion, mind, and will, but they are completely subject to the guidance of the intuition of the spirit.

The spiritual man has an emotion, but his emotion does not act independently as it once did; it is completely under the control of the spirit. Now his emotion no longer has its own likes, its own love, and its own feelings which once impeded the spirit and opposed every move of the spirit. Now it only likes what the spirit likes, only loves what the spirit chooses, and only feels what the spirit allows. The spirit is its life, and it responds at once to the move of the spirit.

The spiritual man also has a mind, but his mind is not as loose as it once was; it co-works with the spirit. The mind does not oppose the revelation of the spirit by its reasons and arguments. It does not disturb the quietness in the spirit by confusing thoughts. It does not boast in its own wisdom and disobey the revelation of the spirit. It is of the same mind as the spirit and cooperates with the spirit to go forward in the spiritual journey. If the spirit has a revelation, it will think through its meaning. If the spirit is "depressed" because of fighting, it will support the spirit to fight. If the spirit wants to teach some truth, it will help the spirit to think and understand. The spirit has the power to stop the mind's thoughts and also has the power to make the mind think.

The spiritual man also has his will, but his will is not as self-centered as it once was; it is not independent toward God but rather obeys or refuses according to the yes or no of the spirit. It no longer has its own will nor disobeys God's will. It is no longer hard and unable to be softened. It is completely broken; it no longer resists God, no longer works against God, and no longer is wild and difficult to harness. As soon as it has the spirit's revelation and understands God's will, it will, on behalf of the spirit, decide to follow as if it is the spirit's minister, standing at the spirit's door and waiting for the spirit's order.

The spiritual man's body is also subject to the spirit. It does not, by its lusts, draw the soul to commit sins as it once did. Now it is cleansed by the precious blood, its lusts were dealt with by the cross, and it is entirely a servant of the soul which takes orders from the spirit. It responds quickly to complete authority to control it by the renewed will. It no longer oppresses the weak spirit. The spirit of the spiritual man has been strengthened, and the body is under its power.

The apostle mentioned the actual condition of a spiritual man in 1 Thessalonians 5:23: "And the God of peace Himself sanctify you wholly, and may your spirit and soul and body be preserved complete." This verse speaks of a spiritual man as follows:

(1) He has God dwelling in his spirit to sanctify him wholly. The life of the spirit, poured into his whole being, causes every faculty to live by the life of the spirit and walk by the power of the spirit.

(2) He does not live by the soul-life. His mind, imagination, feeling, ideals, love, and opinion have all been renewed and cleansed by the Holy Spirit. These are completely under the rule of the spirit and no longer act independently.

(3) Although he still has a body and is not a disembodied spirit, the tiredness, pain, and other demands of the body have absolutely no influence on the spirit to cause it to lose its ascended position. All the members of the body are instruments of righteousness.

Therefore, a spiritual man is a man who belongs to the spirit. His whole person is ruled by the spirit, and all the faculties of his person are completely under the spirit and regulated by it. His spirit is the characteristic of his life; everything comes from the spirit. He has absolute dependence: what he says and what he does are not freely done by himself. He always denies his own strength and draws strength from the spirit. A spiritual man is a man who lives by the spirit.

CHAPTER THREE

SPIRITUAL WORK

As a believer gradually progresses on his spiritual path, he will gradually see more clearly that living for himself is a sin, even the greatest sin. A believer who lives for himself is like a grain of wheat which is not willing to fall into the ground and die; therefore, he remains just one grain. A believer may seek the filling of the Holy Spirit and want to become a spiritual man with power. What is his goal, however? It is to make himself happy and feel more comfortable! If he is asked to live completely for God and God's work, regardless of his own happiness and feeling, he will shrink and not go on. This indicates that he misunderstands the meaning of being spiritual. In the deepest part of his heart, the self-love of the soul-life has not been forsaken. Every person who is a child of God is a servant of God. Everyone has received a gift from the Lord; no one is without a gift (Matt. 25:15). God places each believer in His church and gives each one a portion of labor which he must fulfill. God's intention, from the beginning to the end, is not that the believers' spirit should become a pool of spiritual life. If this were so, the water would begin to dry up. The regression of a believer and the decrease of spiritual power are probably mainly due to this cause. Once the life of God is blocked up in the spirit, a believer begins to feel the drought. Actually, the spiritual life is for spiritual work. Spiritual work is nothing less than the expression of the spiritual life. The secret of living a spiritual life is to let life flow out without interruption and reach the lives of others.

The food of the believer's spiritual life is to work the work of God (John 4:34). If a *spiritual* believer (beginners have not advanced sufficiently enough to be considered here) exclusively pays attention to his own spirituality, making his Bible reading and prayer his recreation, then as he cares for himself, the kingdom of God suffers a great loss. He must believe that God can sustain him, not only physically but also spiritually. If he is willing to bear the hunger, not seeking food when he is hungry, but seeking only to do what God wants of him, he will be fully satisfied. To obey and do the will of God is to eat spiritual food. In contrast, those who pay attention to things that nourish them will obtain nothing. But those who single-heartedly care for the things of the kingdom of God will be fully satisfied. When a believer does not care for himself, but only minds the Father's business, he will see that he is always full and satisfied.

A believer must never overly desire something new. What he really needs is to guard what he has gained so that it will not be lost, because what has not been lost has been gained. The way to guard is to use what he has gained, because burying it in the ground is a sure way to lose it. When a believer lets the life in his spirit flow everywhere, he not only gains other people, but he also gains himself. However, this gain is due not to wanting to gain himself but to losing himself to gain others. The spiritual life within the spiritual man must flow out by means of spiritual work without. If the spirit of the believer is habitually open—it must be shut to the enemy—then the life of God will flow out from it to save and build up many people. Once spiritual work stops, spiritual life is hindered. These two things cannot be separated.

No matter what worldly profession a believer may have, there is always a sphere of his work. The spiritual believer knows his place in the Body of Christ; therefore, he also knows the sphere of his own work. Every member has his usefulness, and fulfilling his usefulness is his work. Some gifts are for certain kinds of members, and some gifts are for the whole Body. The believer must know the sphere of his own gift and work within that sphere. Herein lies the failure of many spiritual believers. Either they withdraw from work so that the spiritual life does not have the possibility to develop, or they work outside their sphere so that the spiritual life is damaged. The harm from not using the hands and feet is the same as misusing the hands and feet. Retaining the spiritual life is the unique way to lose it, but working recklessly also hinders the release of spiritual life.

SPIRITUAL POWER

If we want to receive power to witness for Christ and fight Satan, we have no alternative but to seek the experiences of the filling of the Holy Spirit. It is true that at present more and more people seek the filling of the Holy Spirit. But to what end do they seek to be filled with the Holy Spirit and receive spiritual power? How many seek power to show off? How many are for making their own flesh more splendorous? How many hope to receive power which would enable people to fall before them, saving them the labor of searching and fighting? We have to see clearly what our motive is in receiving spiritual power. If our motive is not in accordance with God and is not out of God, we will not receive. The Holy Spirit of God will not rest upon the "flesh" of man. The place He rests upon is only on the spirit that God has newly created. This is not to say that we may let the outer man (the flesh) live while asking God to baptize our inner man (the spirit) in the Holy Spirit. If the flesh has not yet passed through dealing, then the Spirit of God will not descend upon the spirit of man, because giving power to a fleshly man will have no other result than to make him boast and become even more fleshly.

We have often said that the cross comes before Pentecost; the Holy Spirit will not give power to men and women who have not yet passed through the cross. Golgotha is the only road to the upper room of Jerusalem. Only those who follow this pattern have the possibility of receiving the power of the Holy Spirit. The Word of God says, "This shall be a holy anointing oil...upon man's flesh shall it not be poured" (Exo. 30:31-32). Regardless of whether it is the most filthy or the most cultured flesh, the Holy Spirit of God cannot descend upon it. If there are no nail prints from the cross, there can be no anointing oil of the Holy Spirit. The death of the Lord Jesus is the verdict of God upon all men in Adam: "All must die." God waited until after the Lord Jesus died; only then did He send down the Holy Spirit. Likewise, unless a believer experiences the death of the Lord Jesus and has died to all that belongs to the old creation, he cannot hope to see the power of the Holy Spirit. In history, Pentecost came after Golgotha; in spiritual experience, the filling of the power of the Holy Spirit also comes after bearing the cross.

The flesh is forever condemned before God. God wants it to die. A believer may not want the flesh to die, but may instead want to receive the Holy Spirit to adorn it and provide more power to work for God (of course, this is absolutely impossible). What is our motive in all this? Is our motive personal attraction, reputation, being welcomed by people, being admired by spiritual believers, success, acceptance by man, building up our own self? Those with unclean motives—"double-minded" motives—cannot receive the baptism in the Holy Spirit. We may think that our motives are very clean, but our great High Priest will let us know through the environment whether or not our motives are really clean. Without coming to the point where our present work completely fails and people despise and reject us, considering our name to be evil, it will be very difficult to know whether or not our motive is completely for God. Everyone who has *really* been used by the Lord has walked this path. Whenever the cross has accomplished its work, at that moment we receive the power of the Holy Spirit.

Are there not many believers who do not have deep experiences of the cross, yet they have the power to witness for the Lord and have been greatly used by the Lord? The Bible tells us that in addition to the holy anointing oil, there is an anointing oil that is "like" it (Exo. 30:33). It is similarly compounded, but it is not the *holy* anointing oil. We should not desire success and greatness; we should only observe whether or not our old creation—everything we have by birth—has passed through the cross. Without the flesh passing through death, the power which we have is *surely* not the power of the Holy Spirit. All believers with spiritual insight, who have arrived at the other side of the veil, know that such successes have no spiritual value.

When a believer has condemned his flesh and walks according to the spirit, he can truly receive the power of the

Holy Spirit. Otherwise, he wants his flesh to receive spiritual power. If the flesh does not pass through death, the spirit has no possibility of receiving power, because when the power of the flesh remains, the flesh still reigns and the spirit is oppressed. The power of the Holy Spirit only descends upon a spirit which is full of the Holy Spirit, because only then is there a possibility for the power of the Holy Spirit to flow out. When the spirit is full, the power that comes in will overflow. Therefore, on the one hand, the believer must die to the old creation, and on the other hand, he must learn how to walk together with the Holy Spirit in his living. Then he can receive power.

Every believer must seek for the power of the Holy Spirit. Understanding in the mind is not enough. The Holy Spirit must surround his spirit. Whether his work is effective depends on whether or not the believer has the experience of being baptized in the Holy Spirit. The Holy Spirit needs an outlet. What a pity that He cannot find an outlet in many believers. Some are hindered by sin, some are proud, some are cold, some are filled with their own opinion, and some trust in the soul-life. The power of the Holy Spirit has no place to exude! Besides the Holy Spirit, we still have too many sources!

In the matter of seeking the power of the Holy Spirit, we must keep our mind clear and our will active. This guards against the counterfeit of the enemy. Moreover, we must let God remove from our lives, one by one, everything that belongs to sin and everything that is unrighteous and doubtful. We must consecrate our whole being to the Lord. "Receive the promise of the Spirit through faith" (Gal. 3:14). Rest in God and consider that God will do according to His Word in His own time. Do not forget this matter. If God delays, we must allow His light to examine our own living even more. If God allows us to have some feeling when we receive the power, we may rejoice. If He does not, we still should believe that He has done it.

Just by looking at a believer's experience, we can tell whether or not he has received power. Whoever has received power will develop a very keen awareness of the senses of his spirit. He will receive eloquence (albeit not worldly) to witness for the Lord. His work will be effective and bear everlasting fruits. Power is the basic condition for spiritual work.

After a believer receives the power of the Holy Spirit, he will have a clear feeling concerning the senses of his spirit. In the work of God, a believer must keep his spirit free to allow the Holy Spirit to flow out His life after he receives power. To keep the spirit free is to keep the spirit always in the condition wherein the Holy Spirit can work.

For example, God may command a believer to lead a meeting. The spirit of this believer needs to be free. He should not come into the meeting with many burdens or loads still in his spirit. This will cause the whole meeting to have a burden and become "hardened" and unbreakable. The one who leads the meeting must not come to the meeting with his own burden, hoping that the congregation will function or assist him to be free of his burden. Depending on the response of the congregation to free the leader of the meeting from his spiritual burden will result in failure.

A believer's own spirit must be buoyant and without entanglement when he arrives at the meeting place. Many at the meeting are full of burdens when they come. The leader of the meeting must first release them by means of prayers, hymns, or the truth before he gives the message of God. If the leader of the meeting has a burden from which he cannot be freed, how can he hope that others would be free?

We must know that spiritual meetings are a fellowship between spirit and spirit. A speaker releases a message from his spirit, and the listeners receive the words of God with their spirit. Whether a believer is a leader or a listener, when his spirit has a burden and is not free, it is not able to open toward God and respond to God's words; therefore, a believer's own spirit must be free. Furthermore, the leader must first endeavor to free the spirits of the congregation before delivering a message of God.

We have to obtain the power of the Holy Spirit before we can do a powerful work. We have to keep our spirit free for the power to flow out from the spirit. The expression of the power upon a believer is in different measures. How much he experiences Golgotha will determine how much he will also experience Pentecost. If the spirit of the believer is really buoyant, the Holy Spirit will be able to work.

However, in working, especially with regard to an individual, there is sometimes the experience of the spirit's being closed. This may be caused by the other party. Perhaps the person you are meeting has a particular condition which makes your spirit feel closed. He may not have an open spirit and mind or the capability to receive the truth; he may have an improper thought in his mind that blocks the flowing out of the spirit. If others have these kinds of conditions, this will cause the spirit of the worker to feel closed. In many instances, we only need to look at the attitude of the one who comes to us to know whether or not we can do a spiritual work toward him. If we feel that our spirit has been closed because of him, we cannot spread the truth to him.

If our spirit feels closed and we force ourselves to work, the work will probably not be from the spirit but rather just a product of the mind. Only work done from the spirit has lasting and effective fruit. What is produced from the mind will always lack spiritual power. If we do not first remove a person's hindrances by prayers and preparative labor so that our spirit will be free to spread the Word of God, our work will lose its effectiveness. Believers must learn to walk according to the spirit so that they can work in the spirit.

THE INITIATION OF SPIRITUAL WORK

It is not a small matter to initiate anything. A believer should not rashly do something just because it is good, needful, and profitable to others. These are not sufficient reasons to prove that a work is according to the will of God. Perhaps God wants to raise up others to do the work, or He may prefer to allow the work to stop temporarily. Although it may be hard to let go from the human point of view, God knows how to take care of it. Therefore, goodness, necessity, and profitableness are altogether insufficient to be the guidelines to our work.

The book of Acts is the best pattern for our work. In Acts

we do not see someone "consecrating to be a preacher," "deciding to do the Lord's work," "becoming a missionary," or "becoming a pastor," etc. Rather, we see the Holy Spirit Himself appointing people and sending people to work. God does not recruit men to give themselves for the work; God only sends the persons whom *He* wants. We do not see anyone choosing to do a work himself; only God selects the laborers for His work. There is no place for the thought of man's flesh. If God wants something, even a Saul will not be able to resist. If God does not want something, even a Simon will not be able to buy it with money. As the Lord of all, God controls His own work, not allowing even a little part of man to be mixed in with it. Man does not come to work; rather, God "sends out" the laborers. Therefore, spiritual work must begin with a personal calling from the Lord Himself. One must not go forth to work because of the entreaty of preachers, the urging of relatives and friends, or the affinity of his own nature to the holy Word. Only those who are not wearing fleshly shoes can stand upon the holy ground of God's work. Much failure, waste, and confusion happen because man himself *comes* to work rather than being *sent* to work.

Even if a man is selected, he cannot then begin to act freely. From the viewpoint of the flesh, no other work in the world is more constricting than spiritual work. We read in Acts phrases such as: "the Holy Spirit said," "the Lord said to him," "the Holy Spirit said to him," "sent out by the Holy Spirit," "forbidden by the Holy Spirit." Other than obeying, the worker has no authority to offer any opinion. At that time the work of the apostles was nothing other than knowing the mind of the Holy Spirit in their intuition and then following it. How simple this was! If spiritual work needs a believer to somehow use his own effort to devise, calculate, maneuver, and worry about it, then only those who are naturally gifted, intelligent, and educated will be able to work. However, God has completely put aside everything which is of the flesh. As long as a believer's spirit towards God is holy and clean, lively and full of power, he will be able to follow the Lord's direction and do a very effective work. God has never given believers the authority to control the work; He only wants them to listen to what He says in their spirit.

Samaria had a "great revival," but Philip was not responsible for the continuing work of nourishing. He had to leave immediately and go to the wilderness to save a Gentile eunuch. Ananias had never heard of Saul's conversion, and according to his reasoning, it meant death to go and intercede for him; however, he did not decide for himself. The Jewish rule prohibited Jews from going to a Gentile home to associate with them, but when the Holy Spirit spoke, Peter could not resist. Paul and Barnabas were sent by the Holy Spirit, but the Holy Spirit still had the authority to forbid them from going to Asia and the authority to later lead Paul to Asia to establish the church in Ephesus. All the work is in the hands of the Holy Spirit; a believer should just obey. If the work was according to human thought, likes, and dislikes, then in the early days, they would not have gone to many places where they should have gone, and they would have gone to many places where they should not have gone. These experiences show us that we should not follow our own thought, reason, preferences, and decisions; rather, we should follow the leading of the Holy Spirit in our spirit. They also show us that the Holy Spirit does not lead through our thoughts, preferences, and decisions; on the contrary, our thoughts, preferences, and decisions are completely opposite to the leading of the Holy Spirit in our spirit. If the apostles could not work according to their mind, emotion, and will, how can we?

All the work that God calls us to do is revealed in the intuition of the spirit (see Section Five, Chapter One). When a believer acts according to the thoughts of the mind, the activities of the emotion, and the ambitions of the will, he goes outside of the will of God. Only that which is born of the Spirit is spirit; all the other things are not. All of a believer's work must only come from receiving revelation in the spirit after trusting and waiting upon God; otherwise, the flesh will come in. God will surely give us the spiritual power to do everything that He calls us to do. Therefore, there is an important principle of never working beyond the strength in our spirit. If we work beyond our spirit, we will draw on our own power for assistance. This is the beginning of misery. Overstretching in the work will prevent us from walking according to the spirit and from doing real spiritual work.

Almost everyone today uses rationality, thoughts, reasons, emotions, feelings, likes, wishes, desires, etc., as the standard for work. But all of these are from the soul and have no spiritual value. We should know that these things are good servants, but they are not good masters; if we follow them, we will fail. Spiritual work must come forth from the spirit. God will not reveal His will in any place other than in the spirit.

Furthermore, when people need spiritual help, the worker should never allow soulish feelings to overcome the spiritual relationship. Besides a completely pure desire to help their spirituality, other soulish feelings are damaging. This is often a danger and snare to a worker. Love, affection, concern, worry, interest, fervency, etc., must all be completely guided by the Holy Spirit. When they do not obey this law, some workers for Christ have moral and spiritual failures. On the one hand, we may let natural attraction and human desire control our work; on the other hand, we may let natural hatred and a lack of human affection control our work. In both cases the result will be failure, and the life of the worker will be desolate. Many times, even regarding the loved ones who are most dear to us, a relationship based upon the flesh must be placed in a secondary position, sometimes even completely disregarded, before spiritual results can be obtained. Our intentions and wishes must be completely consecrated to the Lord.

We should work only when we know in the intuition that the work is according to the leading of the Holy Spirit. The flesh does not have a possibility of joining in God's work. The extent of our spiritual usefulness depends on how deeply we let the cross cut our flesh. Superficial accomplishments matter little; only the work that is done by God, through men and women who have been crucified, matters. Even works that are done in the name of the Lord Jesus with fervency and labor, for the sake of some good cause or for the mission of the kingdom of the heavens, are not sufficient to cover up the flesh. God only wants Himself to do the work; He does not want the flesh to interfere with Him. We should realize that even in the matter of serving God, there is the possibility of offering "strange fire" and of being "not spiritual." This will stir the wrath of God. All of the fire that is not kindled in our spirit by the Holy Spirit is strange fire and sin in the eyes of God. Every work which is done for God is *not* necessarily the work of God. Doing something for Him is not enough. The real question is who is doing it? If God Himself does not work from the spirit of the believer, and there is only the activity of a believer using his own strength, then the work cannot count before God. Everything out of the flesh will decay with the flesh. Only that which comes from God will last forever. Only doing the work which God commanded will not be in vain.

THE GOAL OF SPIRITUAL WORK

The goal of spiritual work is nothing other than the spirit of man receiving life and building up the spirit which has life. If the aim of our work does not pay attention to the spirit in the deepest part of man, then our work will not have any spiritual value and result. Sinners do not need some sort of beautiful thought; rather, they need life. Believers do not need more knowledge of the Bible; rather, they need something which can feed their spiritual life. If all that we have is just excellent paragraphs, clever illustrations, deep meanings, wise words, or clear reasonings, then we can only give the mind of man one more thought, the emotion one more stimulation, and the will one more decision. After so much effort, we still allow the person upon whom we have worked to go away just as he came—with a dead spirit. A sinner does not need better reasonings, more tears, or a firmer resolve; he needs the resurrection of the spirit. A believer does not need the building up of the outward man; he needs the more abundant life which can make his spirit grow. If we pay attention only to the outward man and forget the inner man, the spirit of man, then all our work, even though it is complete and absolute, will eventually be empty. This work is the same as not working and may even be worse because time is wasted!

A person may be emotionally touched, shed tears, confess his sins, understand doctrines, admit the reasonableness of redemption, be interested in religion, resolve, repent, sign his name, read the Bible, pray, be "revived," rejoice, and testify. However, his spirit may still not have received the life of God and may be just as dead as before. The soul of man can do all these things regardless of whether his spirit is dead or alive. We do not despise them, but we know that if the spirit is not made alive, these things are just sprouts with no roots and will dry up when the sun shines on them. In the regeneration of the spirit, there may be these expressions outwardly in the soul; however, in the deepest part of his whole being he has received a new life, enabling him to know God and Jesus Christ whom He has sent. If the spirit has not resurrected so that he can know God in the intuition, none of the work will have any spiritual result.

We must realize that it is possible to have a "false faith" and a "false regeneration." Many have confused "apprehending" with "believing." To apprehend is just to understand in the mind that this doctrine is reasonable and believable. To believe, in the biblical sense, is to be united. To believe that the Lord Jesus died for us is to unite ourselves in the death of the Lord Jesus. A person may understand the doctrine, but he may not believe in the Lord Jesus. We should pay attention to the fact that man is not saved by his own doings but by receiving eternal life through believing in the Son of God. Man must believe in the Son of God. Many have "believed the doctrine of redemption" but have not believed in the redeeming Savior. Many have put the blood of the Lamb in the container but have not applied this blood on the door of their heart. Regeneration may also be false! The living of many so-called Christians seems to be the same as that of the genuinely regenerated. They are very clean, pious, and willing to help others; they know how to pray, often read the Bible, often come to meetings, and are very loving! They exert a great effort to lead others to believe in Christ. Although they have all these things and even say that the Lord Jesus is their Savior, they have a basic lack. They do not know God in their intuition. They may hear and talk about God, but they do not know God, nor do they have a personal knowledge of God. "My own know Me...and they shall hear My voice" (John 10:14, 16). Those who do not know the Lord and do not know the Lord's voice are not the Lord's genuine sheep.

Since the relationship between man and God begins at regeneration and is all in the spirit, all our works should focus on this point. If one only wants superficial success and his goal is just to make people fervent and excited, he will find that there is nothing of God in his work. Once we know the position of the spirit, our work must have a fundamental change. Rather than working aimlessly, following what we think is good, we should have a clear goal to build up the spirit of man. While we previously emphasized natural things, now we must stress the things of the Spirit of God. The meaning of spiritual work is nothing other than working by the spirit to enliven the spirit of others. All other work is not genuine spiritual work.

If we truly know that all that we have cannot give life to others, we will see how useless we are. If we truly do not rely on or use anything of ourselves, then we will see how weak we are. Then we will see how much power our inner man, our new I, and our spiritual life really has. Because we ordinarily live by the soul, we do not know how powerless our spirit is. Once all the other help from our soul is eliminated and we solely depend on the power of the spirit, we will realize that the life in our spirit is so small. When we no longer want others to understand in their mind, when we no longer want them to be moved in their emotion, and when we no longer want them to decide in their will, and instead only want their spirit to receive life, we will see that we absolutely cannot give life to others unless the Holy Spirit uses us. "Who were begotten not of blood, nor of the will of the flesh, nor of the will of man, but of God" (John 1:13). If God does not beget them, truly we cannot beget them. Then we will realize that all the work must be done by God and that we are just empty vessels. Within us there is nothing which can beget people, and within a man there is nothing which can beget himself. Rather, it is God who pours out His life from our spirit. Therefore, spiritual work is nothing other than the work which God does Himself. Everything that is not done by God cannot be regarded as spiritual work.

We must ask God to reveal this to us, to let us know the nature of His great work and that we need His great power in order to do His work. Then we will realize that our opinions are truly foolish and our self-reliance is truly laughable; all our works are nothing but "dead works." Although many times God grants us special mercies and lets our work have results beyond what we deserve, we must not think that we can do even more. Any work from ourselves is useless and dangerous. The work of God cannot be accomplished in a fervent atmosphere and attractive environment, by romantic thoughts, poetic imaginations, idealistic viewpoints, rational suggestions, impassioned persuasions, or by occasionally arousing the will to encourage people to have a lasting zeal. If spiritual work was based on our imaginations and not on reality, these methods could be used. But if spiritual work truly causes the spirit of man to be regenerated, resurrected, and receive new life, it can only be done through the power of God, through which He raised the Lord Jesus from among the dead.

If we do not give people the life of God, then there will be no praise in the heavens. Regardless of whether our work is full of reasonings, emotions, and words which can cause people to resolve in their will, or even if our work is completely against reasons, feelings, and stimulations, if it does not issue from the spirit in which the Holy Spirit dwells, our work will not cause man to receive life. Although counterfeit spiritual power may produce similar results, the dead spirit of man can never genuinely receive life from it. Many things may have been gained, but the goal of spiritual work has not been obtained.

If our goal is truly to impart life to others, then the power we use must be the power of God. If we utilize the power of the soul, we will encounter failure. The soul may be living (Gen. 2:7), but it cannot give life; "it is the Spirit who gives life" (John 6:63). The Lord Jesus is "the last Adam [who] became a life-giving Spirit" (1 Cor. 15:45). "He poured out

His soul unto death" (Isa. 53:12). Those who are channels for the life of the Lord Jesus must also deliver their soul-life to death and work by the life of the spirit so that people can be regenerated. Otherwise, even though the soul-life may be beautiful, it has no power to give birth. Drawing real power from the natural life to do any spiritual work is impossible. The old creation never helps the new creation. If we have revelation from the Holy Spirit and work through the power of the Holy Spirit, our audience will be self-reproved and will allow God to enliven their spirits. Otherwise, the sermon we preach will become an excellent ideal which can stir people up temporarily, but nothing spiritual will subsequently happen. The one who depends on the power of the spirit may use the same words, but these words will become life to the spirit. The words of the one who depends on the power of self will become human ideals. Moreover, the work that is done by utilizing the power of the soul will cause these people to demand these feelings and ideals more and more. Therefore, they will stay around whoever can give them these things. Someone who is ignorant will consider this to be spiritual success because many people have been gained. However, someone who has spiritual knowledge will realize that they have no life in their spirit, because their spirit still cannot move. This kind of work in the religious realm is like opium and alcohol to the physical body. Man needs life, not ideals and stimulus. Therefore, a believer has no responsibility other than to consecrate his own spirit as a vessel for God's use and to commit to death all that is of his self. God could greatly use His children to be channels of life to enable sinners to receive salvation and saints to receive edification, but they block their own spirits on the one hand, and on the other hand, they give to others only what they have in themselves. All that the audience receives are the thoughts, reasons, and emotions of the worker. After all the speaking, the audience does not receive the Lord as their Savior so that their dead spirit can be made alive. If we understand that our goal is to let the spirit of others receive life, then we ourselves must have considerable preparation. If we really lose our soul and depend on the spirit, we will see that the words which the Lord speaks from our mouths "are spirit and are life."

THE CESSATION OF SPIRITUAL WORK

Spiritual work often flows with the current of the Holy Spirit without any constraint and without the need for the strength of the flesh. This is not to say that there is no opposition from the world or attack by the enemy; rather, it means that in the Lord there is always the sense of having the Lord's anointing. When a believer's work is needed by God, he will feel the flow of the Holy Spirit no matter what kind of difficulty. The Holy Spirit has always been for the expression of the life of the spirit. This kind of work is very spontaneous. It is expansive, and it expands the life in the spirit.

However, many of God's servants who are urged by the environment (or other reasons) unconsciously let the work they are doing become mechanical. Whenever a believer feels this way, he must search to see whether this kind of "mechanical work" is still needed by the Holy Spirit or if it has accomplished His purpose so that now God is calling His own vessels to go on. The servants of the Lord must know that what is begun as a spiritual work, a work of the Holy Spirit, may not always continue to be spiritual. Many works originally come from the Holy Spirit, but subsequently He, not man, may not need this work. Yet man still continues, thinking that what the Holy Spirit has begun must be spiritual forever. This will cause what is spiritual to become fleshly.

A spiritual believer will never see the anointing oil of the Holy Spirit in a mechanical work. God may no longer need a certain kind of work. If a believer continues to do that work because of the outward organization (which may not necessarily be visible), then he must draw on his own power, apart from the power of the Holy Spirit, as the supply to meet the demand of the work. When spiritual work needs to stop and the believer does not stop, he has to use his soulish strength and physical strength to work. In true spiritual work, the believer must completely reject his own mental power, natural ability, gift, etc., before he can do a fruitful work for God. But a work which is not led by the Holy Spirit will fail immediately unless the believer exercises his mental power, natural ability, gift, etc.

A worker must be watchful to see on which part of his work the Holy Spirit is applying the ointment. Then he will know how to co-labor with the Holy Spirit and work according to the flow of the Holy Spirit's power. The responsibility of a believer is to fix his sight on the "flow" of the Holy Spirit and then follow that flow. If a work no longer has God's application of the ointment, if it is outside of the flow of the Holy Spirit, if it causes the worker to have a feeling of depression and obstruction, and if he is able to obtain the flow apart from this work, the work must be stopped. Those with spiritual discernment will discern faster than others. The question is: where is the "flow" of the Holy Spirit and where is it flowing? Any work which suppresses the life of the spirit, fails to support the expression of the life of the spirit, or hinders the Holy Spirit from flowing out in life and victory is a hindrance, no matter how it was in the beginning. If the work is not completely abolished, then either it must be corrected to let it obey the life in the spirit, or the relationship of the believer to this work must be changed.

In the spiritual experience of believers, there are many people who can serve as examples of being entangled in the "organization," both those with form and those without, until they have damaged their own life. At the start a servant of God receives the power of the spirit, and God greatly works. Many are saved and edified. Then there has to be a kind of "organization" or "method" to preserve the grace. Because of needs, requests, and maybe even commands, the servant will have to do the labor of "nourishing." Consequently, he is bound by the environment and can no longer follow the Holy Spirit freely. His spirit's life gradually recedes, but the outward work with organization still continues very prosperously. This is the story of failure for many persons.

Today among spiritual works there is a distressing situation in which the worker considers his work to be a heavy burden. Many people often say, "I am so busy with things and with work that I have only a little time for fellowship with the Lord. I hope that I will have an opportunity to stop the work temporarily to have a time for some spiritual nurturing, and then I will come back to work." This is really dangerous. Our work must be the result of the fellowship of our spirit with the Lord. All the work must be a joy; it must all be the overflow of the life of the spirit. If the work becomes a tiresome thing, separating the life of the spirit from the Lord Jesus, then this work must be stopped immediately. Since the flow of the Holy Spirit has changed course, one must find out where it is and follow it there.

The Holy Spirit's stopping of our work is very different from Satan's blocking of our work. Yet people often confuse the two. If God has said to stop and the believer still continues, then he will fall from working by the spirit to using his own mental power, ability, and effort as support. Even though he may resist the enemy, there is no anointing of the Holy Spirit. He cannot overcome because this battle is actually false. As soon as a believer sees that there is a blockage in the nature of the spirit, then he should discern whether in fact this comes from God or from the enemy. If the blockage is from the enemy, then he can resist the enemy in the spirit and go forward together with God through prayer, releasing his own spirit. If this is not the case, God will cause the believer's spirit to be more oppressed and to feel heavy laden and without freedom if he goes forward.

Therefore, at the present time the servants of God must get rid of all the work which God has not given, the work which he should have left long ago, the monopolizing work, the work which does not come from the Holy Spirit, the work which suppresses the spirit, the work which causes the believer to depart from the spirit, and the work which may be good, but which keeps the believer from being more noble.

CHAPTER FOUR

PRAYER AND WARFARE

SPIRITUAL PRAYER

All prayers must be spiritual. A prayer that is not spiritual is not a prayer and will not see a result. If all the prayers on earth today were spiritual prayers, believers would have many spiritual achievements. However, fleshly prayers are numerous! Self-will in one's prayer renders a prayer spiritually useless. Today many believers consider prayer a tool to accomplish their own purposes. If they had more knowledge, they would realize that prayer is just man speaking God's will to Him. The flesh must be crucified no matter where it is found. Even in prayer one must not allow the flesh to exist. God's work precludes any possibility of being mixed with human ideas. Even when the motive is good and the work is beneficial to men, God will not permit man to initiate anything that requires Him to follow the lead of man. Believers have only one right, to do what God tells them to do. They have no right to tell God what He ought to do. Other than following God's leading, believers can contribute nothing to God's work. God will not participate in any works that are initiated by self-will, no matter how much man prays for them. Self-will only makes prayers fleshly.

When a believer truly enters the spiritual realm, he realizes how empty he is, and that he has nothing of life to give to others and nothing in himself that can oppose the enemy. He spontaneously takes God as his source, and prayer then becomes indispensable. A real prayer is one that expresses the emptiness of the one praying and the riches of the One answering. If the flesh has never been dealt with by the cross to the extent that a man becomes a "vacuum," what use and purpose does his prayer have?

A spiritual prayer is nothing other than a prayer that is not from the flesh. It is not something that a believer thinks of, something that he desires, or something that he decides to do. Rather, it is something that he practices according to God's will. A spiritual prayer is a prayer in spirit. This means that a person first understands God's will in his intuition and then prays about it. "By means of all prayer and petition, praying at every time in spirit" (Eph. 6:18). This is the command of the Scripture. If we are not praying in spirit, we are praying in the flesh. We should not open our mouth the minute we come to God. Instead, we should first ask God to show us what He wants us to know and show us how to pray. We have already tried repeatedly to pray for what we wanted. Why do we not now pray for what God wants? In prayer the flesh has no place. It is not what you want, but what God wants. Those who are not truly spiritual will not have truly spiritual prayers.

All spiritual prayers originate from God. God shows us what we should pray. He shows us a need and causes us to be intuitively burdened for that need. An intuitive burden is our call to prayer. But many times, due to negligence, we miss many of the small feelings in our intuition. We should never pray more than the burden in our intuition. Any prayer that is not initiated and inspired by the intuition is a prayer that originates from the believers themselves and is of the flesh.

If believers desire to see their prayers becoming effective in the spiritual realm and if they desire that their prayers would not be fleshly, they should confess their weakness, acknowledging that they do not know how to pray (Rom. 8:26), and ask the Holy Spirit to teach them to pray. They should then pray according to the instruction of the Holy Spirit. If God grants words for preaching, He will surely grant words for prayer. The need for the latter is the same as that for the former. We must acknowledge our own weakness and power-lessness before we can utter His prayer through the operation of the Holy Spirit in our spirit. In the work it is vain to put one's trust in the flesh. In prayer it is equally useless to put one's trust in the flesh.

However, we must not only pray with the spirit, we must "pray also with the mind" (1 Cor. 14:15). When we pray, the spirit and the mind must cooperate. A believer receives the answer to his prayer in his spirit and understands what he has received in his mind. The spirit receives the burden to pray, and the mind prays out the prayer sentence by sentence. Only after this kind of cooperative work by the spirit and the mind can a believer's prayer be perfected. Many times prayers are only the exercise of the mind; they do not have the inspiration of the spirit. When this happens, the believers themselves become the origin of their prayer. Real prayer should originate from God's throne and should be felt in the believers' spirit, known in their mind, and prayed through the power of the Holy Spirit. Prayer and the human spirit cannot be separated from one another.

If a believer wants to pray in spirit, he must first learn to walk in spirit. A man can never walk during the day according to the flesh and pray in the spirit when it is time to pray. The way he prays cannot be very different from the way he lives. The spiritual condition of many people shows that they are not qualified to pray. The quality of a person's prayer is determined by the way he lives. How can a fleshly person pray a spiritual prayer? Even a spiritual person may not necessarily pray a spiritual prayer because if he is not watchful, he will fall into the flesh. However, if a spiritual person continually prays in spirit, his prayer will maintain his spirit and mind in a state of harmony with God. Prayer is an exercise of our spirit, and our spirit is strengthened through exercise. If we become negligent in prayer, our spirit will shrivel. Nothing can substitute for prayer. Even work cannot substitute for prayer. Many of us do not spend much time to pray because we are too busy with our work. Consequently, the demons are not cast out. Prayer allows us to first overcome the enemy within, before we deal with him outside of us. Whoever fights the enemy on their knees will find the enemy defeated when they rise up to meet him face to face. Through this kind of exercise, a spiritual man gradually becomes strong.

If believers pray all the time in the Holy Spirit, their spirit will be greatly developed, they will have very keen feelings in spiritual matters, and all of their spiritual drowsiness will be removed.

The present need of a spiritual believer is to detect the senses in his spirit. He should know how the enemy attacks, what God has revealed, and should express through his prayer the things that he has understood one by one. Believers should quickly realize any move in their spirit so that they can accomplish in prayer what God wants them to accomplish. Prayer is a kind of work. The experience of God's children proves that prayer accomplishes greater results than any other kind of work. Prayer is also a kind of warfare because it is the one weapon in our battle against the enemy (Eph. 6:18). Nevertheless, only the prayers that are prayed in the spirit are effective.

Prayers in the spirit are the most effective means of attacking the enemy and withstanding his wiles. Prayer can destroy and also build. It can destroy everything of sin and Satan and can build up everything of God. Therefore, prayer is the most crucial thing in our spiritual work and warfare. The success of spiritual work and victory in warfare both hinge on prayer. If a believer fails in prayer, he fails in everything.

SPIRITUAL WARFARE

Generally speaking, before a believer has experienced the baptism of the Holy Spirit, he is like the servant of Elisha, who was very unclear about the realities in the spiritual realm (2 Kings 6:15-17). Although he may have received the teachings of the Bible and some instructions, he only understands them according to his mind and has no revelation in his spirit. The intuition in his spirit becomes quite keen only after he has experienced the baptism of the Holy Spirit. In his spirit, a whole spiritual world will be opened up before him. When a believer passes through the baptism of the Holy Spirit, he comes in contact with God's supernatural power and touches a personal God.

At this point real spiritual warfare begins. First, the power of darkness will disguise itself as an angel of light and imitate the person and work of the Holy Spirit. Second, the intuition in the spirit will become truly aware of the existence of the spiritual realm and will know the reality of Satan and the evil spirits. The apostles did not receive the expounding of the Scripture by the Lord until after Golgotha. They saw the reality of the spiritual realm only after Pentecost. The baptism of the Spirit is the beginning of spiritual warfare.

After a believer has experienced the baptism of the Holy Spirit and comes in contact with a personal God, after his spirit is released and freed, and he realizes the reality of matters in the spiritual realm, he will engage Satan in warfare if he has the knowledge. (We should remember that although a spiritual man has knowledge, his knowledge does not come all at once, but is acquired through many testings.) Only a spiritual man knows the reality of the spiritual enemy, and only he will fight with such an enemy (Eph. 6:12). This warfare is not with fleshly weapons (2 Cor. 10:3-4). Since the warfare is spiritual, the weapons must also be spiritual. Hence, this kind of warfare is a warfare between man's spirit and the enemy's spirit. This is the warfare of spirit with spirit.

If a believer has not reached this spiritual state, he will neither understand nor be able to engage in such a warfare in the spirit. He understands the way to "wrestle" with the enemy with his spirit only when the Holy Spirit strengthens the power of his spirit. Believers see the reality of Satan and his kingdom and then know how to withstand and attack him with their spirit only when they become spiritual.

There are many reasons for such warfare. The greatest reason is the enemy's attack and obstruction. Satan always applies his tactics to assault spiritual believers. Sometimes he assaults the emotion. At other times he assaults the body. There are also many obstacles that he places in the believers' work and environment. Another reason for spiritual warfare is to fight for God. Satan has countless works in this world and has designed countless schemes in the air. His works and schemes are all for the purpose of opposing God. When we are for God, we fight against Satan with our spiritual strength, destroy his schemes, and work with the words of our prayer. Although at times we do not know what he is scheming or doing, we fight against him anyway because he is always our enemy.

In addition to the above reasons, another reason for fighting with Satan is to be delivered from his deceptions and to deliver those who are deceived by him (see Section Eight, Chapter Three and Section Nine, Chapter Four). Although believers become keen in their spirit's intuition when they experience the baptism of the Holy Spirit, this is not sufficient to protect them from the wiles of the enemy. They can still be deceived. After one has spiritual feelings, he still needs spiritual knowledge. If he does not understand the leading of the spirit and remains in a passive position, he will become a prisoner of the enemy. At this time, believers very easily fall into the error of ignoring the leading in their spirit and following irrational feelings or experiences, thinking that these are from God. After a believer has been baptized in the Holy Spirit, he enters into a supernatural realm. If he does not realize his own weakness and that he is no match for supernatural things, he will be deceived.

A believer's spirit can be affected by two sources: (1) the Holy Spirit and (2) evil spirits. If a believer thinks that his spirit can only be directed by the Holy Spirit and not be affected by evil spirits, he is very wrong. A believer should understand that besides the Spirit from God, there is also "the spirit of the world" (1 Cor. 2:12). This is the spiritual enemy mentioned in Ephesians 6:12. Unless a believer closes his spirit to reject them, evil spirits will take hold of his spirit through deceptions, disguises, and counterfeits.

When a believer is fully spiritual, he will be affected by the supernatural world. At this time, it is very important for him to know the difference between "spiritual" and "supernatural." Confusing these two things has led many believers into Satan's deceptions. Spiritual experiences are experiences that originate from the believers' spirit; supernatural experiences do not necessarily come from man's spirit. Sometimes they are felt in the senses of the body, and sometimes they are found in the realm of the soul. Believers should never take supernatural experiences as spiritual experiences. They should study their experiences and find out if these experiences come from the outward senses or the spirit within.

Things that come from outside may be supernatural, but they are not spiritual.

Believers should never accept anything supernatural without first questioning it. Besides God, Satan can also perform supernatural things. Whatever feeling, appearance, or declaration there may be, a believer has to study the source. *One must practice the teaching of 1 John 4:1.* The counterfeiting efforts of Satan are often beyond the believers' expectation. If a believer is willing to humble himself and acknowledge the possibility of being deceived, he will save himself from many deceptions. Because of these deceptions, spiritual warfare becomes unavoidable. In spiritual warfare if believers do not exercise their spirit to advance in attack, the enemy will come to them and suppress their spiritual power. Spiritual warfare is a battle between the believers' spirit and the evil spirits of the enemy. If a believer is under deception, his warfare is a battle for freedom. If a believer is free already, his warfare is a battle for the deliverance of others, for guarding himself and others against the enemy's attacks, and for taking an aggressive stand to oppose all of Satan's plans and works.

This kind of warfare is a warfare of spirits; spiritual strength is required for such warfare. A believer must understand how he can wrestle with the enemy by his spirit. Without the spirit working for him, he does not know how the enemy attacks and how God wants him to fight. If he walks according to the spirit, he will learn to work by praying unceasingly in his spirit and opposing the enemy in this way. Every time a believer's spirit goes through a battle, it becomes stronger. If he understands the law of the spirit, he can see that he not only overcomes sin, but Satan as well.

The most crucial aspect of spiritual warfare is to be empowered with strength. We can see this from the portion of the apostle's teaching concerning spiritual warfare. He said, "Finally, be empowered in the Lord and in the might of His strength" (Eph. 6:10). Then he mentioned the spiritual warfare (vv. 11-18). But how can one be empowered? The apostle's answer is Ephesians 3:16: "To be strengthened with power through His Spirit into the inner man." This is absolutely necessary. The inner man is the center of man, man's spirit. If the spirit becomes weak, everything becomes weak. Once the spirit becomes weak, there will be fear, and believers will not be able to withstand in the evil days. Believers need a strong spirit. The power of darkness is aimed at the human spirit. If believers do not understand the nature of the warfare, they will not be able to withstand *in their spirit* the principalities and powers.

Many believers feel elated in their spirit only when things are going smoothly. But when warfare comes, they are disturbed and become fearful, saddened, and depressed. They do not understand why they have failed. Believers must understand Satan's goal in the warfare before they can overcome. His aim is to take away the believers' position in ascension and to suppress their spirit in order that he can ascend. In warfare, position plays a key role. If a believer's spirit is depressed, his position in ascension is immediately lost. Therefore, believers must maintain a strong spirit and should not give any ground to the enemy.

Once believers realize that God has prepared the Holy Spirit to strengthen their spirit, they will realize the necessity of fighting with the enemy. Through assaulting prayers and wrestlings, their spirits are gradually strengthened. Just as those who wrestle with their bodies develop muscles through wrestling, the spiritual power of believers is increased when they fight the enemy. Evil spirits attack for the purpose of suppressing the believers' spirit and inflicting suffering to the soul. If believers realize the wiles of the enemy, do not draw back in anything, and withstand him, their emotions will be protected. Withstanding in spirit forces the enemy to take a defensive stand and neutralizes his attacks.

Withstanding is the most important work in spiritual warfare; the best means of defense is an attack. The withstanding that one experiences in the spiritual warfare is not accomplished just through the exercise of the will but through the exercise of spiritual power. Withstanding means to free oneself from the power of suppression. If one would "cut out a way" through the spirit, the enemy will be defeated. If one does not withstand the enemy, allowing him to attack, or if the enemy has already attacked without opposition, the believer's spirit will surely be suppressed and depressed. He will find it difficult to recover the transcendency in his spirit even after a few days. A spirit that does not withstand is often a spirit that is suppressed.

Our withstanding must be based on the word of God. This is the sword of the Spirit. When believers receive the word of God, it will become spirit and life to them. Only then are they able to use it as their weapon of defense. A heavenly person knows how to effectively use God's word to destroy all the lies of the enemy. This kind of warfare is going on even now in the spiritual realm. Although physical eyes do not see this warfare, all those who strive to press forward in their spirit realize and confirm this type of warfare. Those who are deceived and bound by the enemy must be set free. Other than being bound by sin and self-righteousness, the most common bondage for believers relates to supernatural experiences. Believers accept these experiences heedlessly because they are marvelous and give them happy feelings. Little do they realize that these supernatural experiences only make believers proud and self-justifying. They afford no help in holiness and righteousness in life. Neither do they produce any lasting and genuine effects in their work. Once evil spirits succeed in their work, they will gain a place in the believers, and they will advance further and further until the believers walk according to the flesh.

Those who are bound themselves cannot release others. Only when the believers themselves are fully delivered from the authority of darkness experientially can they win the battle to deliver others. Today believers are more aware of the importance of the personal experience of the baptism of the Holy Spirit. But the danger lies right here. I am afraid that as the days go by, the number of people possessed by evil spirits will increase in proportion to the number who have experienced the baptism of the Holy Spirit. The present need is to have a group of overcoming believers who know how to fight and deliver others from the deception of the enemy. If no one in the church of God knows the way to walk according to the spirit and the way to fight the enemy with their spirit, the church will be defeated! May God raise up men that He can use.

PRECAUTIONS IN SPIRITUAL WARFARE

In the life of a believer, each level has its own danger. The new life unceasingly wars against anything which is contrary to itself. While the saints live in the realm of the body, it wars against sins; while they live in the realm of the soul, it wars against the natural life; finally, while they live in the realm of the spirit, it wars against the principalities and powers. When a believer becomes *spiritual,* evil spirits launch an assault against his spirit. This is why it is called spiritual warfare, for it is a battle fought with spirit on both sides. However, unspiritual believers will not have, or will rarely have, such a danger. A believer should not think that once he reaches the spiritual realm, everything will be just fine and there will no longer be any need for war. We should realize that a Christian spends his whole life on the battlefield. It is impossible for him to lay down his arms until he appears before the Lord. While he is fleshly, he encounters danger and conflict in the realm of the flesh; while spiritual, he encounters spiritual danger and warfare. In the wilderness the Israelites only warred against the Amalekites. But after they entered Canaan, they started fighting against the seven tribes of the land. Before believers become spiritual, Satan and the evil spirits will not attack the believers' spirit; after believers become spiritual, all this will happen.

Because the enemy pays great attention to our spirit, it is necessary for spiritual believers to keep their *own* spirit in a proper state and constantly *exercise* their spirit. They should be very cautious about the sensations of their body. Any supernatural feeling and undue awareness of the natural affairs in the body need to be carefully distinguished. The believers' thoughts should be kept in perfect peace without any disturbance; their bodily senses also should be kept in complete calmness without being stirred up. They should reject anything that may cause their spirit to lose its peace, deny and oppose any falsehood with their will, and whole-heartedly pursue to walk only according to the spirit.

Otherwise, they will lose ground in spiritual warfare as they walk according to the soul. Additionally, there is another matter which needs our full attention: the saints must guard their spirit from being passive in spiritual warfare.

We have mentioned that all the guidance we have comes from our spirit and that we must wait for the leading of the Spirit in our spirit. This is absolutely true, but we should be very careful lest we be led into error. While we are waiting in our spirit for the moving and guiding of the Holy Spirit, there is a danger of letting our spirit and person fall into a state of passivity. Nothing can give more opportunity for Satan to work than such a passive state. On one hand, we should not use our strength to do anything and should only obey the Holy Spirit; on the other hand, we should take heed not to let our spirit or any part of our being become mechanical and tumble into passiveness. Our spirit should livingly govern our whole person and actively cooperate with the Spirit.

Once the spirit is in a passive state, the Holy Spirit will no longer have a way to use it because the condition under which the Holy Spirit operates in man's life is totally different from that under which Satan operates. The Holy Spirit *requires man to cooperate* with Him entirely and livingly. He desires man to actively work with Him. He never denies the personality of the believers. In contrast, Satan requires man to fully stop in order that he may *take over*. He wants man to receive his work passively and become his mechanism. We must be watchful not to go to extremes by misunderstanding spiritual doctrines. We need not be afraid of going to the extreme in obeying the Lord or in rejecting the works of the flesh, which we must put away thoroughly. However, we should be very careful not to go to the kind of extreme that results from misunderstandings. We have stressed the point that whatever belongs to man and comes out of man is vanity and that we should seek only after God's own work. Nothing will have spiritual value unless it is done by the Holy Spirit through our spirit. Therefore, we should wait for God's revelation in our spirit. All of this is true. How good it would be if the believers acted according to this truth! But here lies the danger of an extreme that comes from misunderstanding. Due to misinterpretation, believers assume that they should not do anything—that their mind should be "blank," letting the Holy Spirit think for them; that their emotion should not be allowed to have any affection, letting the Holy Spirit put His own affections in their heart; and that their will should not make any decision, letting the Holy Spirit decide for them. They accept whatever happens to them, assuming that they should not actively use their spirit to cooperate with the Holy Spirit, but passively wait for the Holy Spirit's move. Once there is any moving within, they think it must have come from the Holy Spirit.

This is absolutely wrong. God wants to do away with the action of our flesh, but He does not intend to destroy us *as a person*. He never eliminates our personality. He does not want us to become a lifeless mechanism; He wants us to cooperate with Him. He does not want us to become void of thoughts, affections, and judgment. He desires that we think, feel, and decide in accordance with what He thinks, feels, and decides. The Holy Spirit will not *replace* our thoughts, feelings, and decisions; *we* still have to think, feel, and make decisions in accordance with God's own purpose. (We will thoroughly discuss this later.) If our mind, emotion, and will become utterly passive, requiring an outside power to take their place, then the spirit will inevitably fall into a passive condition. When a believer is unable to use his own spirit and needs a power from without to "move" his spirit, Satan will take full advantage of him.

There is a fundamental difference between the work of the Holy Spirit and the work of an evil spirit. *The Holy Spirit motivates men to work by themselves, never denying their personality, but an evil spirit requires men to be entirely still, doing the work for them, so that their spirit becomes mechanical.* Therefore, passivity of the spirit (i.e., a passive state involving the whole person) not only gives an evil spirit opportunity to work, but also makes the Holy Spirit unable to function properly because He lacks the cooperation of the believers. The result is the domination of the evil spirits. If believers are not spiritual, they will not have the danger of coming into contact with evil spirits. After they become spiritual, however, evil spirits will come to attack their spirit. Only spiritual believers, not fleshly ones, have the danger of passivity in the spirit and counterfeit experiences of the spirit, etc.

Because believers misinterpret the nullifying of the flesh, they put their spirit into a passive state. This allows an evil spirit to pretend to be the Holy Spirit. In their ignorance believers think that any moving must come from the Holy Spirit, and they receive it unwittingly, forgetting that not only the Holy Spirit but also evil spirits can affect their spirit. Therefore, they give Satan the ground to attack them gradually in order to corrupt their morality, mental vigor, and health and make them suffer unspeakable pain.

This is what has happened to many believers who have experienced "the baptism in the Holy Spirit." It occurs because believers do not realize that once they have this kind of experience, they enter into a closer connection with the spiritual world (either God's or the devil's) and give the Holy Spirit or an evil spirit the possibility of influencing them. When they are about to experience this baptism, they consider any supernatural experience to be the baptism in the Holy Spirit. They are baptized in the spirit, but we must ask what kind of spirit they are baptized in, for a baptism in the Holy Spirit and in an evil spirit are both a "baptism in the spirit." Many believers want to experience the baptism in the Holy Spirit, but they do not know that the Holy Spirit needs the cooperation of their spirit, that their personality is not nullified, and that they still maintain their free will. Rather, they plunge into a passive state, giving up their own will and allowing a power from without to burn, twist, and cast them down. Thus, they are baptized in an evil spirit.

Some believers do have a genuine experience of the baptism in the Holy Spirit, yet they are subsequently deceived because they are unable to distinguish between the power of the spirit and the soul. Since they have had such a special experience, they think that they are under the full control of the Holy Spirit and should not make any decisions, thinking rather that they should remain in a passive attitude. Their spirit thus falls entirely into a passive state. Satan begins to give them extremely happy feelings with numerous visions, dreams, and other supernatural experiences. They do not realize that all these are due to their passive spirit. Instead, they consider them all to be from the Holy Spirit. Even though they have these experiences, they will still be able to tell the difference if they can distinguish their own feelings from the spirit and the supernatural from the spiritual. However, a mistake concerning the passivity of their spirit, compounded with a mistake in their lack of discernment, deeply entraps them in the enemy's deceit.

Once the believer's spirit is passive, his conscience spontaneously becomes passive as well. Once his conscience becomes passive, he thinks that he will be led *directly* by the Holy Spirit, either through a voice or through the Scriptures. He thinks the Holy Spirit will no longer lead him through his conscience or through the judgment of the intuition. Since he possesses the highest way of leading, he thinks that he only needs to listen to what the Holy Spirit is personally speaking to him or what He is speaking through the Scriptures. By not using his conscience and letting it slip into a passive state, he is defrauded in his daily living by the enemy. The result is nothing but obedience to the work of Satan. Since he no longer uses his own conscience, the Holy Spirit also, according to the principles of His work, will not employ his conscience on his behalf. Satan will take advantage of this situation to replace the leading of the believer's conscience and intuition with supernatural voices and other things.

As their conscience becomes passive and is led by evil spirits, some believers lower their moral standard. They no longer look at immoral matters as immoral. On the contrary, they think that they are living according to a higher principle. This hinders them from advancing in life and in their work. They stop using their intuition to sense the will of the Holy Spirit; neither do they use their conscience to distinguish right and wrong. They simply act as machines, following outward, superficial voices which they have mistaken for the voice of God. In this situation they ignore their reasoning, conscience, and other people's advice. They become the most stubborn persons in the world and will not be convinced by anyone because they think they are following a higher way than that of the rest of the believers. They are very close to what the apostle said: "Who are branded in their own conscience as with a hot iron" (1 Tim. 4:2). They are void of any feeling of their conscience.

In such a life of spiritual warfare, we must keep our spirit in an active state—fully obedient to the Holy Spirit, not in a passive state. Otherwise, we will inevitably be deceived by Satan. If our spirit is not active and reaching out, even if it is not attacked by the enemy, it will be locked in, and Satan will blockade it and shut off all of its outlets. Our spirit will be unable to work, serve, or war, as though it were being suppressed. Our spirit must be active and reaching out. It must always resist Satan, or else it will be attacked from every side by evil spirits.

In spiritual warfare, one very important principle is that we must keep attacking Satan constantly. In order to guard ourselves from being attacked, we must attack. To attack the evil spirits is the only way to prevent them from attacking us. Once believers have entered into the spiritual realm, if they do not have a daily attitude of resisting the enemy in the spirit, assaulting Satan with prayers in the spirit, and asking God to destroy all the works of Satan done through the evil spirits, they will soon see their own spirit fall from the heavens and become weak and powerless. In a short time these believers will lose their feelings and not even know where their spirit is. This is because their spirit has fallen into a passive state and is no longer aggressively attacking. Believers unknowingly allow the enemy to attack, block, and surround their spirit. If the believers "release" their spirit daily and always resist the enemy, they will see their spirit becoming active and growing stronger day by day.

A believer must rid himself of all misunderstandings concerning the spiritual life. Before he reaches the spiritual realm, he often dreams of how happy he would be if he too could become a spiritual believer like some of his brothers. He assumes that the spiritual life is ecstatic. He imagines that the so-called spiritual life is a life of perfect happiness, one of rejoicing all day long. In reality it is just the opposite; the spiritual life does not provide any happiness to him; rather, it is a life of daily fighting. If you try to separate spiritual warfare from spiritual life, you will soon find out that that life is no longer spiritual. A spiritual life is one of suffering, charged with vigilance, labor, fatigue, sufferings, heartbreak, and conflict. This is a life absolutely for the kingdom of God, and one which disregards one's own happiness. When a believer is fleshly, he lives to himself and for his own "spiritual" happiness. He has no real spiritual use in God's hand. He can be used by God only after he has taken the attitude of being dead to sin and his own life.

A spiritual life in the eyes of God is one with spiritual usefulness because it is a life of attacking God's enemy for Him. We should stir up our zeal for Him and war against the enemy constantly, never allowing our spirit, which is so useful, to become passive.

SECTION FIVE

THE ANALYSIS OF THE SPIRIT— THE INTUITION, THE FELLOWSHIP, AND THE CONSCIENCE

CHAPTER ONE

THE INTUITION

If we want to understand more clearly about spiritual life, we have to analyze the spirit thoroughly and understand all of its laws. Only after we have understood every function of the spirit can we comprehend the laws by which the spirit operates. Once we know the laws of the spirit, we will learn how to follow the spirit, that is, to walk by the laws of the spirit. These are vital to our spiritual life. We are not afraid of having too much knowledge concerning the spirit; our only concern is that we pursue it too strenuously with our mind.

The gospel of God tells people that fallen man can receive regeneration and that fleshly man can obtain a new spirit. The new spirit is the foundation of his new life. The spiritual life we normally speak about is just a life in which one lives by the spirit he received at regeneration. It is very regrettable that most believers know very little about the functions of the spirit and the things related to it. They may know in terminology the relationship between man and his spirit, yet they still cannot identify this spirit in their experience. As we mentioned before, either they do not know where their spirit is, or they reckon their own feelings and thoughts as the functions of the spirit. Therefore, an analysis of the functions of the spirit is needed because only then will believers know how to follow the spirit.

THE FUNCTIONS OF THE SPIRIT

We have mentioned before that the functions of the spirit can be categorized into three parts: intuition, fellowship, and conscience. Although these three are distinguishable, they are closely knitted together. It would be very difficult for us to talk about one without mentioning the other two. For example, when we talk about intuition, spontaneously we also include fellowship and conscience. Therefore, even though we are analyzing the spirit, we still need to make a close study of its tripartite functions. We have already seen how the spirit is categorized into intuition, fellowship, and conscience, and we will not repeat it here. However, we have to consider further what the intuition, fellowship (or worship), and conscience are, and what functions they have, in order to know how to walk according to our spirit. Since the spirit encompasses the work of intuition, fellowship, and conscience, we can say that walking according to the spirit is just walking according to one's intuition, fellowship, and conscience.

Intuition, fellowship, and conscience are just three functions of the spirit. We are not saying that the spirit includes only these three, neither are we saying that the spirit is just one of these three. According to the Bible, these are simply the three major *functions* of the spirit. The spirit is still the spirit; it is substantial, personal, and invisible. It is impossible for us to apprehend the inner essence of the spirit today. We can only realize what it is by the functions it manifests. We are not here to learn the wonderful mysteries of the future but to pursue a spiritual living. As long as we know the functions of the spirit and how to walk according to the spirit, it will be sufficient. Our spirit is not material, yet it can exist independently in our body as the human spirit. Therefore, although our spirit is not physical, it must possess its own "spiritual substance." Otherwise, it would be impossible for it to exist independently. This spiritual substance contains various functions which execute all the requirements that God has towards man. Therefore, we will only try to learn the functions of the spirit, not the substance of the spirit.

Man is like the holy temple, and our spirit is like the Holy of Holies. Going one step further, we can compare the intuition, fellowship, and conscience to the ark in the Holy of Holies. (1) God's law was in the ark to instruct the Israelites in what they should do. God revealed Himself and His will through the law. Similarly, God is making Himself and His will known to the believers through their intuition so that they can follow accordingly. (2) Upon the ark was the propitiatory cover with the blood sprinkled on its cover. This was the place where God manifested His glory and

received man's worship. Similarly, every one who has been
redeemed by the precious blood has his spirit regenerated.
In this spirit he worships God and fellowships with Him.
God could only fellowship with the Israelites over the
propitiatory cover of the ark. Similarly, He can only fellowship with the believers in their blood-cleansed spirit.
(3) According to the original language, the ark is the "ark
of testimony," and the Ten Commandments within it served
as the testimony of God to the Israelites. If they did well,
the two tablets in the ark would approve them. If they did
things improperly, the Ten Commandments would accuse
them silently from within the ark. Similarly, the Holy Spirit
has written God's law in our conscience so that it bears
witness to our conduct. It bears witness to those things that
are according to God's will and condemns those things that
are not according to God's will. "My conscience bearing
witness with me in the Holy Spirit" (Rom. 9:1)

Look how the children of Israel honored the ark! When
they crossed the Jordan River, they had no other guidance
except the ark. They simply followed the ark without any
doubt. When they fought against Jericho, they did nothing
other than follow the ark. When they could not stand against
the Philistines, they tried to utilize the ark according to their
own will. Was not Uzzah immediately killed when he tried
to hold the ark with his fleshly hands? How they rejoiced
after they had prepared a place for the ark! (Psa. 132). These
things ought to teach believers how to deal with the ark,
which is the intuition, fellowship, and conscience in our spirit.
There is life and peace when we follow these functions, and
there will be nothing but complete failure if we try to interfere
with them according to our fleshly will. Victory did not depend
on what the Israelites thought but on where the ark was
leading. Any spiritual usefulness depends not on our thought
but on the teaching of the intuition, fellowship, and conscience.

THE INTUITION

The body has its senses, and the spirit also has its senses.
The spirit dwells in the body and has a very close relationship

with the body; nevertheless, it is completely different from the body. The body has various senses, but a spiritual man can detect that which is beyond his physical senses. There is another sense in the innermost part of his being which can rejoice, grieve, fear, approve, condemn, determine, and discern. These are the senses of the spirit which are distinct from the senses of the soul expressed through the body.

The senses and functions of the spirit can be seen from the following verses:

"The spirit is *willing*" (Matt. 26:41).

"Jesus, *knowing* fully in His spirit" (Mark 2:8).

"He *groaned* deeply in His spirit" (Mark 8:12).

"My spirit has *exulted* in God my Savior" (Luke 1:47).

"The true worshippers will *worship* the Father in spirit and truthfulness" (John 4:23).

"He...was *moved with indignation* in His spirit" (John 11:33).

"When Jesus had said these things, He became *troubled* in His spirit" (John 13:21).

"His spirit was *provoked* within him as he beheld that the city was full of idols" (Acts 17:16).

"This man was instructed in the way of the Lord, and being *fervent* in spirit" (Acts 18:25).

"Paul *purposed* in his spirit" (Acts 19:21).

"I am going *bound* in the spirit to Jerusalem" (Acts 20:22).

"*Burning* in spirit" (Rom. 12:11).

"For who among men *knows* the things of man, except the spirit of man which is in him?" (1 Cor. 2:11).

"I will *sing* with the spirit" (1 Cor. 14:15).

"If you *bless* with the spirit" (1 Cor. 14:16).

"I had no *rest* in my spirit" (2 Cor. 2:13).

"Having the same spirit of *faith*" (2 Cor. 4:13).

"A spirit of *wisdom* and revelation" (Eph. 1:17).

"Your *love* in the Spirit" (Col. 1:8).

Now we can see how keen the sense of man's spirit is and how numerous its functions are. The Bible does not say man's heart senses and functions in this way, but his spirit does sense or function in this way. We must read the above verses very carefully to realize that the human spirit possesses all these functions. After thoroughly reading them, we will see that the functions and senses of the human spirit are as inclusive as those of the soul. Whether it is thoughts, decisions, or feelings, as long as it is something that the soul has, the spirit has it also. This shows us how important it is to learn to distinguish the spiritual from the soulish. As a believer passes through the deep work of the cross and Holy Spirit, he gradually becomes experienced and knows what is of the soul and what is of the spirit.

After a believer has embarked on a spiritual life, his spirit's senses and functions grow and fully develop. Before a believer's spirit is separated from the soul and joined to the Lord as one spirit, it is hard for him to notice the senses in his spirit. But once the power of the Holy Spirit is poured into his spirit and his inner man is strengthened, his spirit will possess the senses and functions of a full-grown man. Only then will he be able to understand the various senses of his spirit.

This sense of the spirit is called the *intuition* because it comes without any cause or reason. It comes "intuitively" without passing through any means. Our ordinary senses are aroused by specific means, which may be people, things, or events. These things give rise to certain feelings. If there is something to rejoice about, we rejoice. If there is something to be sorrowful about, we feel sorrow. All these senses are aroused by something; therefore, they cannot be called *intuition*. The sense of the spirit does not come from any means but comes directly from our inner being.

The soul and the spirit are quite similar. Believers should not follow their soul, which means that they should not follow their thoughts, feelings, or preferences. These are all from the soul. God's way for the believers is to walk according to the spirit. All other ways belong to the old creation and have no spiritual value at all. How, then, can we walk according to the spirit? Walking according to the spirit is walking according to the intuition in the spirit; this is because the intuition of the spirit expresses the thought of the spirit and of God.

Many times we intend to do certain things, and we may

have plenty of reasons for doing them. Our heart may desire certain things, and this desire may be very good. Furthermore, our will may decide to carry out the intentions of our mind and desire. However, in the deepest part of our being, there is something *unspeakable, silent, heavy, pressing, and lurking* which fights against our mind's thoughts, our emotion's desires, and our will's determinations. This complex feeling in our heart seems to tell us that we should not do these things. On other occasions this experience may be different. It may start with our innermost being having the same unspeakable, silent, heavy, pressing, and lurking feeling as we had before, which urges, presses, moves, or encourages us to do certain things. These things seem to us to be unreasonable and irrational and are contrary to our ordinary thoughts. These things are opposite to what we ordinarily desire, favor, prefer, love, and hold dear, and our will has no desire to perform them.

What is this thing which acts contrary to our mind, emotion, and will? It is the intuition of the spirit. The spirit expresses its thought through the intuition. Now we can see the difference between the intuition and the feelings of our emotion. Frequently, what we feel to do is just the opposite of the warning of this inward, silent intuition. This intuition is also completely different from our mind. Our mind comes from our head and is rational. However, the intuition is not located in our head and quite frequently is irrational. The Holy Spirit reveals His own thoughts through the intuition of the spirit. The "prompting" of the Holy Spirit is the work of the Holy Spirit in our spirit which causes our intuition to understand His will. Now we can distinguish between what is from the Holy Spirit and what is from the self and Satan. The dwelling place of the Holy Spirit is in our spirit, and our spirit is the center of our whole being. Hence, when the Holy Spirit reveals His will through our intuition, He does it through the innermost part of our being. The believers' own will, however, lies in the outer part of his being. Our thoughts come from the outside, and our feelings also lie in our outward parts. Once we see that our opinions come from our mind or emotion—our outward man—we will know that they are just our own thoughts and not the prompting of the Holy Spirit. The prompting of the Holy Spirit always comes from the deepest part of our being. The same distinction can be said for things from Satan (except those who are demon possessed). Satan does not dwell in the believer's spirit. His dwelling place is in the world. "Greater is He [the Holy Spirit] who is in you than he [Satan] who is in the world" (1 John 4:4). Satan can only invade the believers from the outside. He either works through the cravings and sensations of our body or through our mind and emotion, because the body and soul both belong to the outward man. Therefore, the believers should be very careful to discern whether or not their feelings come from the innermost part of their being or from their outward man.

GOD'S ANOINTING

The intuition is the place where God's anointing teaches us. "And you have an anointing from the Holy One, and all of you know....The anointing which you have received from Him abides in you, and you have no need that anyone teach you; but as His anointing teaches you concerning all things and is true and is not a lie, and even as it has taught you, abide in Him" (1 John 2:20, 27). This passage of Scripture very clearly indicates how the anointing of the Holy Spirit teaches us.

Before we consider this passage of Scripture, let us first differentiate between the meaning of "know" and "understand." The spirit "knows," while the mind "understands." A believer "knows" a thing by the intuition of his spirit. The mind can only "understand." Strictly speaking, the mind cannot "know." (Naturally, all this refers to the relationship between us and God.) Believers are so confused about the matter of seeking the thought of the Holy Spirit, because they do not know the difference between "knowing" and "understanding." According to the common usage of the words, there is not much difference between knowing and understanding. But in spiritual matters, knowing and understanding are as far apart as the heavens are from the earth. To know is the work of the intuition; to understand is the work of the mind. The Holy Spirit enables our spirit to know, and our spirit makes our mind understand. It is hard to distinguish between these two words, but in experience they are as different as wheat and tares.

Is it not true that many times we have an indescribable feeling in our inner being as mentioned above? This feeling enables us to *know* whether or not to do a certain thing. It is true that in our spirit we may know the thought of the Holy Spirit. However, in many cases, we *know* in our intuition what we ought to do, but our mind may still fall short of *understanding* the meaning and reason of it. In spiritual matters, it is quite possible for us to know but still not understand. Is it not true that many times our thoughts reach a dead end, but our spirit receives teaching from the Holy Spirit; at these times we cry, "I know it!" Many times when we deny the thoughts and reasonings in our mind and obey the thought of the Holy Spirit expressed in the intuition, we must wait for a long time before our mind is enlightened and before we understand the reason the Holy Spirit led us in a particular way. Only then are we able to cry out, "Now I understand!" These experiences tell us that we "know" the thought of the Holy Spirit in the intuition of our spirit, but we "understand" the leading of the Holy Spirit in the mind of our soul.

The apostle John tells us that the anointing of the Lord abides in us and teaches us so that we know everything and do not need any man to teach us. This refers to the functions of the intuition. The Lord gives the Holy Spirit to all believers; He abides in our spirit and leads us into all truth. How does He lead? He leads through the intuition of the spirit. In the spirit He expresses His thoughts. The intuition possesses an ability to know the meaning of the prompting of the Holy Spirit. Just as the mind enables man to apprehend the things of the world, the intuition enables man to apprehend the things of the spiritual realm. The anointing originally referred to the application of the ointment. The way that the Holy Spirit teaches, works, and speaks to us is in the human spirit. He does not speak from heaven with a loud voice and a flaming fire, or cast the believers to the ground with His power. Rather, He works silently in our spirit to make us sense something in our intuition. Just as an ointment gives the body a certain sensation when it is applied, the anointing of the Holy Spirit gives the believers' *spirit* a certain feeling when it is applied. When the intuition becomes aware of this feeling, it knows what the Holy Spirit is speaking.

If a believer wants to follow God's will, he does not need to ask others or even himself. All he has to do is to walk according to the direction of the intuition. The anointing will teach the believer "concerning all things." He will not leave him or allow him to make his own choice. Everyone who wants to walk according to the spirit must realize this. Our responsibility is nothing else but to be taught. We do not need to decide on our own way; actually, we cannot decide anyway. Anything apart from the leading of the anointing is just our own action. The work of the anointing is independent; it does not require man's help. It does not require the mind's searching or the emotion's stirring; the anointing expresses the Spirit's own thought independently. He works independently in the spirit and causes men to know His will in their intuition. After this, He causes men to carry out His instructions.

DISCERNMENT

If we read the context of this portion of the Scriptures, we will see that the apostle spoke about many false teachings and antichrists. He was saying that since the believers have received the anointing from the Holy One, who abides in them, this anointing will spontaneously teach them what is the truth, what is a lie, who is for Christ, and who is antichrist. There is no need for man to teach or speak anything; the anointing that abides within will teach spontaneously. This spiritual discernment is greatly needed today. We do not need to reference many theological books, reason, compare, research, observe, and think with our intellect before we can understand what is a lie and what is the truth. If we have to do this, no one except knowledgeable and intellectual believers would be able to save themselves from deceptions. God has no respect for man's old creation. Besides the spirit of the new creation, everything is dead in His eyes and should be done away with. Can the mental capacity, which God insists on abolishing, help man distinguish between right and wrong? No, absolutely not. Rather, God puts His Spirit in the spirit of every believer, regardless of how ignorant or foolish he may be, in order to teach him what is and is not of Him. Therefore, even though there are many times when we cannot find a reason to oppose a certain teaching, there is a sense of disapproving in the deepest part of our being. We do not know the reason, but our inner sense tells us that this is wrong. Sometimes we hear a teaching that is completely different from what we usually hold and which we do not wish to follow; yet within us there is a small voice persistently telling us that this is the right way and that we should walk in it. Although we may have many reasons to oppose it, and although our reasoning may win, this small voice of the intuition within is always speaking to us and always telling us that we are wrong.

These experiences show us that our intuition—the organ where the Holy Spirit works—is able to distinguish between right and wrong. It does not need any assistance from the observation and study of the mind. Regardless of a believer's natural upbringing, he can always be taught by the anointing as long as he is sincere, desirous, and faithful to follow the Lord. In spiritual matters the most educated doctor and most unlearned villager are equally foolish. Many times the educated one makes more mistakes than the unlearned one. Today false teachings are quite prevalent. Many people use guileful words to disguise their lies as truths. Hence, there is the need of discernment in the spirit concerning what is right and wrong. The best teachings, the most clever mind, and the most experienced advisors are all unreliable; only those who follow the teaching of the Holy Spirit in the intuition will be saved from being deceived by today's theological confusions and the many heresies, miracles, and wonders. We should continually ask the Lord to make our spirit more active and pure; we should also follow the small voice that comes from our intuition. We should not neglect its warning because some others have greater knowledge.

Otherwise, we will either be trapped into heresy or become fanatical. If we do not calmly follow the teaching of the anointing which comes from this small voice, we will be distracted by a confused emotion and clamorous mind.

DEALING WITH OTHERS

This anointing also teaches us to deal with people.

We should not criticize a person, but we should definitely know him in order to learn how to associate with him or help him. The common way to accomplish this is to examine a person by observing and studying him. But even this can often lead us the wrong way. We do not say that this is absolutely useless, but it is only secondary. A pure spirit usually brings the right discernment. Some of us can remember that as children, we could often make very accurate assertions about people we saw. A long time has passed, and our knowledge, experience, and power of observation have all increased, yet our ability to know people does not seem any better than before. At that time we did not know why we made those assertions; something seemed to be in our heart, but we could not utter it with our mouth. Time has passed, and everything has changed. Now the facts have proven that our "feeling" was correct. We did not make those assertions through drawn out investigations and inquiries; nor could we even give any evidence or reason for our assertions. This is the work of a pure intuition even though it is still natural. Nevertheless, the Lord wants us to regard the things of God in the same way. Our spirit should be converted, and we must become as little children. Only then will we have the clear knowledge from God.

Let us look at the life of the Lord Jesus. "And immediately Jesus, knowing fully in His spirit that they were reasoning this way within themselves, said to them..." (Mark 2:8). This verse shows us the operation of intuition. It does not say that the Lord Jesus had a thought or feeling in His heart, nor does it say that the Holy Spirit told Him so. The faculty of His spirit demonstrated its perfect ability. The sense of the spirit in the man Jesus Christ was very pure, sharp, and exalted; He knew in His spirit the reasonings of the surrounding people. He then spoke to them according to what He had perceived in His intuition. This should be the normal spiritual life of every spiritual person. The Holy Spirit dwells in our spirit; He enables our spirit to be fully operative and full of the power of knowledge. In this way, He regulates our whole being. Just as the human spirit of the Lord Jesus was working when He was on the earth, our spirit should be working through the Holy Spirit who indwells us.

REVELATION

The knowledge of things through the intuition is what the Bible calls revelation. Revelation means nothing less than the Holy Spirit revealing the reality of a matter in a believer's spirit and causing him to know such a matter. There is only one kind of knowledge, concerning either the Bible or God, that is worthwhile: it is the truth revealed by the Holy Spirit in our spirit. God does not explain what He is to man's intellect all at once, neither can man know God all at once through his intellect. No matter how wise a man's intellect is, and no matter how much he understands about God, his understanding is always veiled. He can only make inferences with his intellect about the things behind the veil; he does not see the actual things behind the veil. He has not yet "seen," so he can only "understand" and not "know." If Christianity is not a revelation—a personal revelation—it is worth nothing at all. Everyone who believes in God must receive His revelation in his spirit; otherwise, he will believe in nothing more than human wisdom, ideals, and words, and not in God Himself. This kind of faith will not stand in times of temptation.

Revelation is not a vision, a voice from heaven, a dream, or an external power which shakes one's body. All these may happen to a person without him receiving any revelation. Revelation is something in the intuition; it is quiet, neither slow nor quick; it appears to be a voice and yet not a voice. Many people call themselves Christians, yet what they believe in is just human philosophies, ethics, articles of truth, or some supernatural occurrences. Believing these things will not bring about a new birth; it will not give a person a new spirit. Although these kind of "Christians" are very numerous today, their spiritual usefulness is altogether nil. God gives grace to all those who have accepted Christ and causes them to see in their spirit the reality of the spiritual realm as if a veil has been removed from before them. Subsequently, what they *know* is far deeper than what they understood in their mind. The things they understood and perceived in the past seem to have a new meaning. Everything is transparent and known for certain because they have "seen" it in the spirit. "We speak that which we know and testify of that which we have seen" (John 3:11). This is Christianity. Intellectual pursuit will never save people; only revelation in the spirit will grant men genuine knowledge of God.

ETERNAL LIFE

Today many people speak about eternal life through faith. But what is the eternal life which we receive? While it refers to blessings in the future, what does eternal life mean for *today?* "And this is eternal life, that they may *know* You, the only true God, and Him whom You have sent, Jesus Christ" (John 17:3). Eternal life in this age is the ability to know God and the Lord Jesus. This is very real. Saying that everyone who believes in the Lord receives eternal life means that he receives an intuitive knowledge of God which he did not have before. "Eternal life through faith" is not a slogan. Rather, it is something that can be proven in this age. Those who do not have this life—the eternal life—may infer things concerning God, but they do not have a personal knowledge of God. Only after one obtains this new life and has been regenerated, can he *truly know* God through his intuition. He may understand the Bible, yet his spirit still remains dead. He can familiarize himself with theology, yet he is not regenerated in his spirit. He may enthusiastically serve "in the name of the Lord;" however, there is no regeneration of a new life in his spirit. The Bible tells us that man cannot find out God by searching (Job 11:7). Everything done through the mind cannot bring us to the knowledge of God. Apart from man's spirit, man cannot know God; he cannot know

God with his mentality. In the Bible we see only one kind of knowledge: the intuition in the spirit.

THE PROPER GUIDANCE

Not only should believers receive their initial knowledge through the spirit, they should continue in this way all the time. In the Christian life, other than the revelation one receives in his intuition, nothing else has any spiritual significance because none of the other things are of the spirit. Since they are not of the spirit, they are not the will of God; God only reveals the things concerning His will to us in our spirit. Anything that we think, prefer, and decide, apart from the revelation of the spirit, is dead in God's eyes. A believer may act according to sudden thoughts, ideas that come after a prayer, a so-called burning in the heart, natural inclinations, strong reasons, or his logical judgments. These are all just the activities of the old man. God's will is not known through such thoughts, feelings, or preferences. God only reveals His will in man's spirit. Anything not revealed through the spirit is self-activity.

God never reveals His will to man's mind. Revelation is of the Holy Spirit and in man's spirit. Man's spirit knows and receives God's will through the intuition. After this, it transmits the will of God to the mind for its understanding. The mind is where we can understand God's will, yet it can never be the source of God's will. God's will originates from God and is revealed to man's spirit by the Holy Spirit. The spirit, in turn, causes the outward man to understand through the mind what the inward man already knows. In this way, the outward man knows how to carry out God's will. If a believer does not seek after God's will in his spirit, but exercises his mind all the time, he will be lost all the time and not know what to follow. Our minds continually fluctuate. Those who walk according to their mind cannot, even for a moment, say from their heart, "I know *with certainty* that this is God's will." Only those who receive revelation in their spirit will have a *deep confidence;* only they *will know and be fully assured* of what they are doing.

God's revelation in our spirit can be of two kinds: one is

direct and the other is through searching. Direct revelation happens when God Himself has a will, and He charges the believers to carry it out. In this case, He comes into the believers' spirit and reveals His will to them. When the believers receive this revelation in their intuition, they carry it out accordingly. Revelation that comes through searching occurs when a believer has a need and does not know what to do; he comes before God and waits and seeks for His will. In answering the believer's searching, God operates in his spirit and reveals whether he should continue or stop. When a believer is young in his spiritual life, the revelation he receives is mostly of the searching kind. When he is more mature, he will have more direct revelations. However, this is not absolute; I only mean that searching is more typical than direct revelation at first. Nevertheless, this is where most young believers confront difficulties. Time is needed for them to wait before the Lord and eliminate their self-thought, self-preferences, and self-opinions; nevertheless, they often forsake waiting for God's revelation and substitute their own will instead. As a result, they are often accused by their conscience. Even when they truly desire to follow God's will, they foolishly walk according to the thoughts in their mind because of a lack of spiritual knowledge. Anything done without revelation will unavoidably lead to mistakes.

Now we can see what spiritual knowledge really is. Only that which is apprehended in the spirit is spiritual knowledge. Anything other than this is mere mental knowledge. How does God know things? By what means does He judge? What knowledge does He use to manage the universe? Does He reason with His mind like men do? Does He need to ponder things over before He can understand? Does He know things by logic, arguments, or comparison? Does He need to investigate and consider before He comes to a conclusion? Does the omniscient One also need to use His brain? Certainly not! God does not need to search in this way before He knows. All of God's knowledge and judgment is intuitive. Intuition is the faculty of every spiritual man or being. Angels follow God's will by knowing it intuitively. They do not ascertain it by the way of argument, reason, or thought. The difference between understanding God's will by the way of the mind and the way of the intuition is immeasurable. Spiritual success or failure is surprisingly dependent upon this distinction. If believers' conduct and work were based on their rationale, reason, and common sense, no one would dare to attempt the great spiritual works that have been done in the past and even presently. All the spiritual works are beyond human reasonings. Who would have dared to risk them if they had not known the will of God in their intuition?

Anyone who walks intimately with God, having secret fellowship with God and spiritual union with Him, receives His revelation in the intuition and clearly knows what moves he should take. This behavior receives no sympathy from men, for others do not know what he personally knows. According to the world's wisdom, his moves are totally meaningless. Have not many spiritual believers been opposed because of this? Have not the wise ones regarded them as crazy? Not only do the worldly people say this, but even their fleshly brothers criticize them in the same way. This is because the life of the old creation, whether in worldly people or in believers, is equally ignorant of the work of God's Holy Spirit. The more intellectual believers often label the ones who act contrary to common sense as "foolishly zealous." To them, their acts are soulishly enthusiastic. But actually, many so-called foolish zealots are very spiritual. They behave "foolishly" because they have received revelation in their intuition.

We must be careful not to mix up intuition with emotion. The zeal of an emotional believer may appear to be something spiritual, but it may not actually be from the intuition. The judgment of a rational believer likewise may appear to be something spiritual, but it also may not be a revelation from the intuition. Just as the emotional believer is soulish, the rational believer is also soulish. The spirit does have zeal. In fact, its zeal far exceeds that of the emotion. All of the actions of spiritual believers are "justified in the Spirit" (1 Tim. 3:16). They are not condoned by fleshly emotion or the mind. If we fall from the position of the spirit and walk according to our fleshly feelings or rational thoughts, we will immediately be at a loss as to what to do and where to turn. When this happens, we will be like Abraham, who went down to Egypt where help could be obtained from things which could be seen and touched. The spirit and the soul work independently of each other. If the spirit has not ascended and is not totally in control, the soul will always war against it.

When a believer's spirit is renewed, strengthened, and educated by the Holy Spirit, his soul loses its place and submits to the spirit. Gradually, the soul becomes a servant to the spirit, and the body is conquered to become the soul's servant for the execution of the spirit's will. The spirit then knows God's revelation through the intuition. This progress is without an end. Some have more things to be cast aside than others because their spirits are not as pure as others. They are filled with mental and emotional knowledge. Many people cannot have an open spirit to receive God's truth because they are already filled with prejudice. Before the intuition can receive anything from God, all these things must be removed.

Now we should be clearer than before about the difference between the intuition and the mind or emotion. Once we understand the intuition, we will be more clear about the spirit which is usually more mysterious to us. Now we should realize the basic difference between spiritual experience and soulish experience. A spiritual experience is spiritual because it begins from *God* and is known in our *spirit*. A soulish experience, on the other hand, begins from *man* himself and has never passed through the spirit. Therefore, one can be full of Bible knowledge and have a specific, accurate comprehension of Christian doctrines. He may be zealous and apply all of his talents to the work. He may have amazing eloquence and give absorbing speeches on subjects and topics about the Bible; nevertheless, his being may still be living in the realm of the soul. He may not have stepped beyond the soul for even one single step; his spirit may still be dead. People will not be brought into the kingdom of God through our encouraging, exhorting, arguing, inciting, attracting, and urging. They can only come through regeneration, which is just the resurrection of the spirit. This new life will come with various abilities, among the most important is the intuition to understand God, know God, and acknowledge God.

Does this mean that the human mind (brain) is completely useless? Of course not. Surely, there is use for the mind. However, we should remember that the intellect does not come first; it is secondary. We do not know God and the things of God by the intellect. If we did, eternal life would be useless. The eternal life (i.e., the new life) is nothing other than the spirit which is mentioned in John 3. We know God through our newly received eternal life and newly acquired spirit. The use of the mind lies in its ability to explain to our outward man what we see in our spirit and compose it into words for others to understand. We can see this in the example of Paul. In his Epistles, he emphatically pointed out that the gospel he preached is not of man; it does not come "wholesale" from man's mind, and it is not "sold in retail" to other minds. Instead, he received it through revelation. Though he may have had the best mental capability, his doctrine did not come from his thoughts, either suddenly or progressively. His mind was in union with his spirit, and it just communicated to others the revelation he received in his spirit. The mind (the soul) is never the organ for receiving spiritual knowledge; it is merely the organ for passing on spiritual knowledge.

Besides the spirit, there is no other place where God can communicate with us. There are no other ways for us to know God except in the intuition. Through the spirit, man enters into the eternal, divine, and invisible realm. We may say that the intuition is the "brain" of the spirit. When we say that man's spirit is dead, we are saying that his intuition has lost all feelings and is unable to know God and understand the things of God. When we say that the spirit is in charge of our whole being, we mean every part of the soul and every member of the body should completely follow God's will, which has been made known to us through the intuition. We have said previously that regeneration is absolutely necessary, but we will say it again emphatically. The human mind, emotion, and will cannot know God and substitute for the intuition. Unless man receives the life of God afresh, and unless his intuition is resurrected, he is forever separated from God.

Regeneration is very real. It is not just a term or a moral change but a definite entrance of *God's life* into our spirit, resurrecting our spirit and intuition. It is an absolute impossibility for man to do good and please God by himself because these activities are in the realm of the soul; they are not done through an intuition that has come alive toward God. It would be very difficult for a man to be born again by himself because he has nothing that can produce any new life. If God would not beget him, he would not be able to beget himself. Furthermore, no matter how much we understand doctrines, and how much we put our trust in them, they are altogether useless. Nothing can save man except putting himself in God's hand and asking Him to work. A man's spirit will remain dead forever unless he acknowledges that everything of himself is useless, that he is standing with the Lord Jesus in the place of death, and that he is receiving His life.

Man's way is not to receive the Lord Jesus as Savior; it is not the way of resurrecting the intuition (spirit). Instead, it is the way of substituting the intuition with the mind. Man considers, ponders, and comes up with different philosophies, ethics, or religions. But God says, "For as the heavens are higher than the earth, / So are My ways higher than your ways, / And My thoughts higher than your thoughts" (Isa. 55:9). No matter what thoughts man has, he is still of earth and not of the heavens. After our regeneration, God desires that we know His works and His will through our intuition so that we would walk according to them. But how easy it is for believers to forget what we learned at regeneration! How many believers walk according to their mind and emotion in their daily lives! When we serve, we still use our intellect, zeal, and ideas to move the mind, emotion, and will of others. God wants to teach us that neither our soul nor the souls of others have any spiritual usefulness and value. God wants to destroy our natural life together with its intellect, ability, and strength. Therefore, He allows us to fail, be disappointed, and become cold and useless in our spiritual work. This kind of lesson cannot be learned in one or two days. God will instruct us all of our lives and make us realize that other than walking according to the intuition, everything else is vanity.

Here lies the key issue: when the intuition proposes something totally different from what the soul proposes, which one will we follow? Now is the time to determine who will be in charge of our life and which way will we go. Now is the time for the decisive battle that decides who will be the head, our outward man or our inward man, the man of feeling or the man of the spirit. At the beginning of our Christian life, our spirit warred against our flesh. Today there is a war between our spirit and our natural life. Formerly we warred over the problem of sins; now it is not a matter of good or evil but of natural kindness or the goodness of God. Previously we were concerned about the nature of the things we did, but now, about the source of the good things. Today there is a war between the outward man and the inward man, a war between God's will and man's intention. Learning to walk according to the spirit is a lifetime job for the "new man." If one can fully walk according to the spirit, he will entirely overcome his flesh. Through the strengthening of the Holy Spirit into the spirit of the new man, he will entirely eliminate the mind of the flesh. A fleshly mind results in nothing but death in spiritual things, while a mind set on the spirit is life and peace.

CHAPTER TWO

FELLOWSHIP

Just as man has fellowship with the physical world through his body, he has fellowship with the spiritual world through his spirit. This fellowship with the spiritual realm is not through the mind or emotion but through the spirit. It is through the intuition of the spirit. Once we understand the functions of the intuition, we will understand the nature of the fellowship between God and man. For a man to worship God and have fellowship with Him, he must have a substance that is similar to God's. "God is *Spirit,* and those who worship Him must worship in *spirit*" (John 4:24). There cannot be fellowship between two different substances. Therefore, unregenerated persons, whose spirits are not resurrected, and those regenerated believers who do not worship with their spirits cannot have any real fellowship with God. Although a person may have some beautiful thoughts and strong feelings, he can never enter into spiritual reality and have personal fellowship with God. Our fellowship with God is in the deepest part of our being; it is in the part that is deeper than our mind, emotion, and will. We fellowship with God through our intuition.

First Corinthians 2:9 through 3:2 explains clearly how man fellowships with God through the intuition in his spirit and how he understands the things of God. Let us now look into this carefully.

THE HEART OF MAN

Verse 9 says, "Things which eye has not seen and ear has not heard and which have not come up in man's heart; things which God has prepared for those who love Him." This verse talks about God and the things of God. All of His acts are things which man's outer body (the eye and the ear) has neither seen nor heard. They are things which have never come up in man's heart. "Man's heart" is man's understanding, mind, or intellect. Man's thought can never fathom God's acts. God's acts are far beyond man's thought. Those who want to know God and have fellowship with Him can never reach God by simply using their mind.

THE HOLY SPIRIT

Verse 10 says, "But to us God has revealed them through the Spirit, for the Spirit searches all things, even the depths of God." The Spirit *searches* all things. The Spirit does not have to use the mind to *figure out* all things. The Spirit knows even the deepest things of God. The things which man does not know, He knows. He searches all things by His intuition. Therefore, through Him God can reveal to us things which have not come up in our heart.

This is "revelation." It is not the understanding which comes after an exercise of our mind. Since it is something that has not come up in our hearts, it is even more unlikely that it would come up in our thoughts. This is a "revelation" or an unveiling. There is no need for help from our mind. God does not reveal anything to us through our ears, eyes, or mind. How does revelation come? The next two verses answer this question.

THE SPIRIT OF MAN

Verses 11 and 12 continue, "For who among men knows the things of man, except the spirit of man which is in him? In the same way, the things of God also no one has known except the Spirit of God. But we have received not the spirit of the world but the Spirit which is from God, that we may know the things which have been graciously given to us by God." Only the spirit of man knows (not understands or apprehends) the things of man. Similarly, only the Holy Spirit knows the things of God. Both the spirit of man and the Holy Spirit know things directly, not by deduction or investigation. Therefore, they both know through the intuition, not through the mind.

Since only the Holy Spirit knows the things of God, we can only know the things of God when we receive the Holy

Spirit. The spirit of the world is a spirit which does not have any fellowship with God. Even though it is still a spirit, it is dead. Hence, it cannot bring us fellowship with God.

The Holy Spirit of God knows the things of God. Therefore, when we receive in our spirit what the Holy Spirit already knows in the intuition, we also know the things of God. This is why it says, "we have received...the Spirit which is from God, that *we may know* the things...given to us by God."

But how do *we know?* Verse 11 says that we know through our spirit. This makes the matter very clear. The Holy Spirit reveals to our spirit all that He knows in His intuition, causing our spirit's intuition to also know what He knows. Through the intuition we know the things revealed by the Holy Spirit. Furthermore, whenever the Holy Spirit reveals the things of God, He reveals them in our spirit. In God's eyes, other than man's spirit, there is no other organ in man which can know the things of man. Hence, the Holy Spirit does not reveal the things of God to our mind because He knows that our mind is incapable of knowing the things of God. The mind is not an organ for knowing things pertaining to God and man. Although the mind can think and even design many things, it cannot say that it *knows* these things because only the spirit of man can know the things of man.

Here we see how highly God esteems the regenerated spirit of man. If a man is not regenerated, his spirit is still dead; thus, God has no way to reveal to him the things pertaining to God. Although he may be very intelligent, he still cannot comprehend the things of God. God's fellowship with man and man's worship of God require the regenerated spirit as the unique uniting ground. Without a regenerated spirit, there will always be a separation between God and man; He cannot come to our side, neither can we go to His side, because man's intuition, apart from his mind, emotion, and will is still dead and unable to know the intention of the Holy Spirit. Consequently, man is unable to know the revelation of the Holy Spirit. The enlivening of the spirit is the *first step* towards fellowship between God and man.

Man has a free will. He has the full right to decide his own things. Therefore, even after a sinner has been regenerated

and has become a believer, he still has many temptations.
Due to ignorance or prejudice, many believers do not give a
proper place to their spirit or to the intuition of the spirit.
God regards the spirit as the unique place where He can
have fellowship with man and as the only location where man
can worship Him and communicate with Him. However, many
believers only walk according to their mind or emotion. Many
times they almost ignore the voice of their intuition. The
principle of their conduct is to do things according to what
they regard as reasonable, appealing, pleasing, and interest-
ing. Even when they have a heart to carry out God's will,
they mainly take the instant thoughts of their heart or some
logical ideas as God's will and follow those. They do not realize
that they should follow the notion expressed by their intuition
through their spirit, not their own thought. Even when they
are willing to listen to their intuition, they do not maintain
their emotions in a calm position; they fluctuate up and down
according to their emotion and confuse the voice of their
intuition. Consequently, walking according to the spirit
becomes an occasional event in the believers' life and not their
lasting, daily, life-long experience.

Since this is our situation even in the initial step of
knowing the will of God, it is no wonder that we do not have
any deeper revelation. In this condition, we will never be in
our spirit which enables us to know God's plan for this last
age, the reality of spiritual warfare, or the deep and profound
truths in the Bible. Furthermore, in the matter of worshipping God, we will follow either what we deem to be right, or
we will follow the transient outbursts of our emotions. In
these circumstances, fellowship with the Lord in our intuition
becomes nonexistent.

A believer must know that only the Holy Spirit knows the
things of God, and that He knows the things of God through
the intuition, not through the mind. Therefore, only He can
impart this knowledge to men. However, the one who receives
this knowledge must receive it in the same way. This means
that he also must use his intuition to know what the Holy
Spirit knows through His intuition. The union of these two
intuitions will result in man knowing the things of God.

Verse 13 says, "Which things also we speak, not in words taught by human wisdom but in words taught by the Spirit, interpreting spiritual things with spiritual words." Now we come to the way to speak to others about what we know by our intuition in our spirit. The things pertaining to God are already known in our spirit. Our responsibility is to preach these things. The apostle said that he would not use "words taught by human wisdom" to speak about the things he knew in his spirit. Man's wisdom belongs to man's mind; it is the product of man's brain. The apostle said that he would not use words conjured up in his mind to speak about the things of God that he knew in his spirit. The apostle Paul's wisdom was very great. He was well able to come up with novel expressions. He knew how to speak, what illustrations he should use, and how to structure his speech. He could use his natural eloquence very well to make his listeners fully understand his meaning. However, he said that he would not use words taught by man's wisdom. This means that not only is man's mind useless in knowing the things of God, it is also useless in speaking about spiritual wisdom.

He spoke in words "taught by the Spirit." This refers to the instruction of the Holy Spirit which he received in his intuition. Nothing is of any value in the Christian life except being in the spirit. Even when we speak about spiritual knowledge, we must use spiritual utterances. Not only does the intuition know the things revealed to us by the Holy Spirit, it also knows the words that the Holy Spirit has instructed us to use to utter what He has revealed. Many times a believer receives God's revelation, becomes clear about a certain matter, and wants to preach this to others. For him, this matter is very clear, and he understands it. However, his preaching cannot convey his thought fully because he has not received the words in his spirit. Sometimes when a believer is waiting before the Lord, something seems to rise up in his innermost being. It may be just a few words, but those few words when spoken in a meeting fully convey God's revelation. Through this experience, he realizes that God has truly used him to testify for Him.

These experiences show us the importance of receiving

"utterance" from the Holy Spirit. There are two kinds of utterance. The first is our natural utterance, and the other is given to our spirit by the Holy Spirit. The utterance mentioned in Acts 2:4 is indispensable in spiritual works. No matter how good our natural eloquence is, it cannot speak forth the things of God. Even when we feel that we have expressed everything well, we still may not have conveyed the intention of the Holy Spirit. Only spiritual words—those which we receive in our spirit—can relate spiritual knowledge. Sometimes we have the Lord's message in our spirit; it seems to be compelling and burning us, and we feel that there is a spiritual burden pressing on us. Yet we have no way of discharging it. At these times we have to wait for the Holy Spirit to grant us the "utterance," so that we can speak forth the message in our spirit and discharge the burden. If we do not receive the utterance from the Holy Spirit through our intuition, but instead replace it with the words of man's wisdom, all spiritual value will be lost. All these words only make people feel that our ideas are good. Sometimes we have many spiritual experiences, but we do not know how to express them. However, one short remark by another believer often clears away our clouds, enabling us to know the significance of a past experience which was hidden from us because the Lord had not yet instructed us in our spirit with a clear word. But someone can, with the simplest of words, open up our past experiences.

"Spiritual things" must be explained by "spiritual words." We must use spiritual means to achieve spiritual goals. This is what the Lord is diligently teaching us these days. It is not enough for the goal to be spiritual; the means and procedures must also be spiritual. Whatever is fleshly, no matter what it is, cannot fulfill what is spiritual. If we try to use our mind and emotion to fulfill a spiritual goal, it is just like hoping that a bitter fountain will yield sweet water. Everything related to our fellowship with God, whether seeking His will, obeying His charge, or preaching His message, will only be useful if we do it in our intuition and in fellowship with God. If we use our own mind, talent, and methods, it will be dead in the eyes of God.

There is a small note in the Chinese Union Version Bible, recommending that these last two phrases in verse 13 be translated as, "communicating spiritual things to spiritual men." This is very meaningful and relates to the next verse. Let us study this together with the next verse.

SOULISH AND SPIRITUAL

Verse 14 says, "But a *soulish* man does not *receive* the things of the Spirit of God, for they are foolishness to him and he is not able to *know* them because they are discerned spiritually."

Soulish men are those who have not been regenerated and who do not have a new spirit. They do not have an intuition; what they have is only the mind, emotion, and will of the soul. They can reason, judge logically, and express what they like, but they cannot "receive the things of the Spirit of God" because they do not have a regenerated spirit. In man's intuition God reveals His things to man. Even though a soulish man can think and observe, he lacks the capacity of the intuition. As a result he cannot receive what God reveals. Whatever man originally has is useless. Although man has many things in himself, none of them can replace the work of the intuition. God has not intentionally tried to be particular. He has not purposely exalted the spirit and intuition, which He gave to man through regeneration, above everything that man originally possessed. However, because man is dead in his spirit toward God, He cannot communicate Himself and His things to man. There is not a single organ in man which can receive God's things. Among all the things which comprise a soulish man, there is not one which can fellowship with God. Even the mind, intellect, and rationality that is highly esteemed by man is as corrupt as man's lusts; none of them can understand God. Not only is it impossible for unregenerated ones to fellowship with God with their mind, it is even impossible for the regenerated believers to fellowship with God without using their regenerated spirit. It is equally impossible for believers to use their mind and observation to understand the things of God because it does not change in function after regeneration. The mind is still the mind, and the will is still the will; these cannot become the organs for fellowship with God.

Not only is a soulish man incapable of receiving these things; he also thinks that they are foolishness. This again turns us to man's mind. According to man's mind, the things that are known through intuition are foolish because they cannot be rationalized. They are far beyond human feelings and contrary to the worldly mentality. They even contradict man's common sense. Our mind likes what is logical and analytical and what suits its natural psychology. However, none of God's acts are according to human law. Therefore, they are foolishness to him. The foolishness spoken of in this chapter refers to the crucifixion of the Lord Jesus on the cross. The message of the cross not only speaks of a Savior who died for us, but of all the believers who died with Him. Everything that belongs to a believer's self has to pass through the death of the cross. If this is only an idea, the mind may receive it; but if it is something to be put into practice, the mind rejects it.

Since the soulish man cannot receive, he cannot know. Receiving is first, and knowing is second. Whether or not a person can receive is determined by whether he has the Spirit. Whether or not a person can know is conditioned on whether he has an intuition. He must first have the Spirit before he can receive the things of God. If he has the Spirit and has received the things of God, the intuition has a chance to know these things of God. Other than the spirit of man, no one can know the things of man. A soulish man cannot know because he does not have a new spirit. Hence, he does not have the intuition to know.

Later the apostle says that a soulish man "does not receive" because the things of God are "discerned spiritually." Do we see that the Holy Spirit is repeatedly emphasizing that man's spirit is the organ for fellowship with God? The focus of this portion of the Scriptures is to prove, indicate, and clarify that through God's Spirit, man's spirit is the basis for fellowship with God and for knowing the things of God. There is nothing else besides the spirit of man.

Everything has its own function. The function of the spirit

is to discern the things of God. We are not annulling our mind, emotion, and will. They all have their functions and stand in a secondary position. They should be restricted; they should not be in control. The mind should be under the restriction of the spirit; it should act according to the will of God which is known through the intuition. The mind should not suggest a thought by itself and demand that our whole being act according to its thought. The emotion must also obey the command of the spirit. All of its love and hatred should be according to what the spirit wants and not according to what it wants. The will should also follow God's will as expressed in the intuition. The will must not ignore the will of God and have other desires. If the mind, emotion, and will are all being kept in a secondary position, a believer will advance swiftly in his spiritual progress. If this does not happen, the mind, emotion, and will become the masters, and the place of the spirit will be usurped. Spontaneously there will be no spiritual living and spiritual usefulness. The spirit must be given its own proper position. A believer must wait on God's revelation *in the spirit*. If the spirit is not elevated, a man will not be able to discern what is only discernable to the Spirit. The previous verse refers to communicating spiritual things to spiritual men because only those with a keen spirit can know the things in the spirit.

Verse 15 says. "But the spiritual man discerns all things, but he himself is discerned by no one." A spiritual person takes the spirit as his center, and his intuition is very keen. The mind, emotion, and will of his soul do not disturb the quietness in his spirit. His spirit is able to perform its duty.

"The spiritual man discerns all things" because the intuition obtains its knowledge only through the Holy Spirit. "He himself is discerned by no one" because others do not know how the Holy Spirit touches his intuition and what the senses in his intuition are. If a believer can only gain knowledge through his intelligence, only those who are more intelligent will discern all things. If this were true, scholarship and worldly education would become indispensable. These ones would also be discerned by others because whoever is their equal or whoever is more intelligent would understand their thoughts. Spiritual knowledge, however, *has as its base* the intuition of the spirit. If a man is spiritual and has a keen intuition, his knowledge will be unlimited. Even though his mind may be slow, the Holy Spirit can bring him into spiritual reality. His spirit can also enlighten his mind. Revelation by the Holy Spirit is often beyond the expectation of man.

Verse 16 says, "For who has known the mind of the Lord and will instruct Him? But we have the mind of Christ." Here is a question. No one in the world has known the mind of the Lord to instruct Him, because all men are of the soul. The way to know God is solely through the intuition. Then where can we find one, without the spirit, who has known the mind of God? This question confirms the last sentence in the previous verse. A spiritual man is "discerned by no one" because no one has yet known the mind of the Lord. "No one" refers to the soulish man. The spiritual man knows the mind of the Lord because he has a keen intuition. The soulish man cannot know because he does not have the intuition. Hence, he cannot fellowship with God. Since the soulish man cannot know the mind of the Lord, he cannot know the spiritual man who fully submits to the Lord's mind. This is the meaning of this verse.

"But *we*," means that we are different from soulish men. This "we" includes all the saved believers, even though there are many who are fleshly. "But we have the mind of Christ." Those who have been regenerated, whether infants or adults, all have the mind of Christ. We all know the intention of Christ because we all have obtained the resurrected intuition. This is why we can know and already do know what Christ has prepared for us in the future (v. 9). The soulish man does not know, but those who have been regenerated can know. The difference is whether or not one has the spirit (Jude 19).

SPIRITUAL AND FLESHLY

First Corinthians 3:1-2 says, "And I, brothers, was not able to speak to you as to spiritual men, but as to fleshy, as to infants in Christ. I gave you milk to drink, not solid food, for you were not yet able to receive it. But neither yet now are you able." These few sentences are closely connected with the previous section. Furthermore, the teaching here follows the previous section and continues on the subject of the spirit of man. The division of the Bible into chapters and verses was made by men later for the sake of convenience; they are not inspired by the Holy Spirit. Therefore, we should look at these words together with the words in the previous chapter.

Before we cover the proper meaning of these two verses, let us look at the apostle Paul and consider how clear his spiritual perception was. He knew what kind of people would receive his letter, whether they were spiritual or soulish, and whether they were controlled by the spirit or were under the domination of the flesh. Although his speech was concerning the spiritual things, he did not feel that he could simply pour out everything to his listeners regardless of whether or not they could receive it. He only communicated spiritual things to spiritual men. It was not a matter of how much he had but how much his listeners could receive. There is not any sense of boasting in his own knowledge. The apostle received in his spirit the words which he needed to speak. He had the spiritual knowledge, and he also had the spiritual words. He knew how to deal with believers on different levels. Therefore, we ought to know the spiritual words or the words taught by the Holy Spirit. Spiritual words are not necessarily words fully loaded with profound matters of the Holy Spirit of God. Spiritual words are the words revealed by the Holy Spirit in the spirit. They may not be very high or profound. They may be very ordinary words and may not be special at all. The fact that these words are known through our intuition, as taught by the Holy Spirit, is what makes them spiritual words. When these words are spoken, there will be significant spiritual effects.

In the previous passages, the apostle told us that the intuition is the only faculty to know God, to fellowship with God, and to know the things of God. He also told us that in every regenerated spirit there is the mind of Christ; this means that every regenerated spirit understands what Christ will give us in the future. He then proceeded to divide all Christians into two categories—the spiritual and the fleshly.

He also mentioned the difference between the intuitive power of these two kinds of Christians. These two verses are a response to the question, "If the spirit of man knows all the things of man, and if a spiritual man discerns all things, why are there so many Christians who are regenerated in their spirit yet do not feel that they have a spirit and are unable to know the many deep things of God through their spirit?"

In response to this kind of question, the apostle said, "But the spiritual man discerns all things." Even though Christians *have* a regenerated spirit, not all Christians are *spiritual*. There are many who are still fleshly! Although man's intuition has been revived, man must still reserve a place for it and provide a chance for it to work. Otherwise, the intuition will be suppressed and unable to fellowship with God; it will not know what it is able to know. The "spiritual" believer does not do anything according to the mind, emotion, or will. He puts all these on the cross so that they will take a submissive position. In this way the intuition will have the full freedom to receive the revelation of God and direct the mind, emotion and will to carry out the revelation. However, "fleshly" believers are not this way. They are regenerated, and their intuition has become alive to God. They even have a good chance to become spiritual believers; nevertheless, they are bound by the flesh. The lusts of the flesh are still very strong and powerful, pressing them to sin. There are still many unbridled thoughts, reasons, and plans in the fleshly mind; there are still many fleshly interests, likes, and inclinations in the emotion; and there are still many worldly judgments, decisions, and opinions in the will. As a result, these believers walk according to the flesh day and night. They are busy and cannot find the time to listen to the voice of their intuition. The voice of the spirit is always very small. Even if a believer calms everything down and listens very attentively to this voice, he still may not hear it. How much worse will it be when every part of the flesh is stirred up throughout the day? When a believer is very manipulated and in every way affected by the flesh, his spirit becomes numb and unable to receive "solid food."

The Scripture likens a newly regenerated believer to a baby because the life he has obtained in the spirit is as feeble as a physical baby. There is no problem if the believer grows out of babyhood within a short time, because every grown-up begins by being a baby. However, if a believer remains a baby for a long time, and if the stature of his spirit remains the same several years after regeneration, then something is wrong. A man's spirit can grow, and the intuition in the spirit can also grow and become stronger. A newborn baby does not have self-consciousness; his nerves are very feeble, and he is childish in every way. A newly regenerated believer is just the same. His spiritual life is like a spark of fire, and his intuition is feeble and not very functional. However, a baby should grow daily. His knowledge should be broadened daily through use, exercise, and growth until his self-consciousness becomes fully developed, and he can utilize his senses. The same is true with a believer. After he is regenerated, he should gradually learn to use his intuition. The more he uses it, the more experience and knowledge he will gain, and the more he will grow. Just as a person's consciousness is not very keen when he is born, a believer's intuition is not very sensitive when he is first regenerated.

Fleshly believers are those who remain as babies for a long time and do not grow. This does not mean that they do not have the outward suppression of sin or an increase in biblical knowledge during that time. It does not mean that they do not strive to work for the Lord or have not received the gift of the Holy Spirit. The believers in Corinth had all of these. They were "in everything...enriched in Him, in all utterance and all knowledge...[with no] lack in any gift" (1 Cor. 1:5, 7). According to man's view, are these not growth? We would probably say that they were the most spiritual believers because of their growth in utterance, knowledge, and gifts. Even so, the apostle said that they were still babies and fleshly. How could this be? Is growth in utterance, knowledge, and gifts not growth? We can observe a very important fact that the Corinthians grew in secondary issues, but their *spirit* did not grow, and the intuition in their spirit had not become stronger. An increase of eloquence in preaching, an increase in biblical knowledge, and an increase in the gifts of the Holy Spirit are not increases in spiritual life! If a believer's spirit, with which he fellowships with God, has not become stronger and keener in the eyes of God, he has not grown at all! How many Christians are growing in the wrong direction today? How many think that after they are saved, they should pursue higher biblical knowledge, better eloquence in preaching, and more gifts of the Holy Spirit? They forget that they should pursue the growth of the spirit with which they have fellowship with God. Eloquence, knowledge, and gifts are just outward; only the intuition is inward. The most pitiful thing today is that believers allow their spirit to remain as a baby, but they fill their mind, emotion, and will with eloquence, knowledge, and gifts. Even though these things are precious, they cannot be compared with the position of the spirit. God has newly created this spirit in us which can be called our spiritual life. What should grow and become full-grown is this spirit. If we misunderstand and do not pursue the growth of the spiritual life and the intuition, which enable us to know God, the matters of God, and have fellowship with Him, but instead we pursue the increase of riches in the soul, we will not have any progress at all in God's view. In the eyes of God, our spirit is all-inclusive. He is concerned with the growth of this spirit. According to His view, no matter how much our eloquence, knowledge, and gifts increase in our mind, emotion, and will, they are worthless in the spiritual realm if there is no growth in the spirit.

We expect daily to have greater power, broader knowledge, more gifts, and better eloquence. But the Bible says that even if we have all these things, our spiritual life has not necessarily grown. On the contrary, our spiritual life may remain the same, without an inch of growth. The apostle said that the Corinthians "were not yet able to receive it. But *neither yet now* are you able." In what aspect were they not able? They were not able to use the intuition to serve God, to know God deeply, and to receive the revelation of God. The Corinthian believers were not able to do these things. "Were not yet able" means that they were unable when they had just believed in the Lord. "Neither yet now are you able" means that even after they had believed in the Lord for several years, after they were full of eloquence, knowledge, and gifts, they were still not able. Through the word "yet," the apostle indicated that even though they were rich in eloquence, knowledge, and gifts, their spiritual life was the same as when they were without eloquence, knowledge, or gifts. There was no difference. Real growth is measured by the growth of the spirit and intuition. Everything else is fleshly. These words should be deeply engraved in our hearts.

The most pitiful thing today is that Christians appear to have growth in almost everything; but their spirit, which is for fellowshipping with God, has not grown. After believing in the Lord for years, one may still say, "I do not feel that I have a spirit." How different is our thought from God's thought! We are like the Corinthians in that we try to utilize the intelligence in our minds to search for the so-called spiritual knowledge, and we really do acquire a great deal of it. But growth in the mind is not and cannot substitute for the growth of the intuition. In God's view, we have remained the same. Please remember that God wants us to grow not in our knowledge, eloquence, or gifts. He only wants the growth of our spirit, our spiritual life, and the intuition of our spirit. He expects the new life that we received in our regeneration to grow. The old creation should be totally forsaken. Otherwise, even if we are full of eloquence, knowledge, and gifts, He will still say that we are fleshly believers, babies without an inch of growth in the spiritual life!

When a believer is overly influenced by the flesh, he cannot successfully become a spiritual man and take solid food. Only one who has a sharp intuition and unceasingly fellowships with God will really know the deep truths. If one's intuition remains weak, he cannot help but drink milk. It is said that milk comes from the mother after she digests solid food. This means that the fleshly believers are unable to fellowship with God clearly in their intuition. They can only depend on more experienced believers to tell them the things of God. Experienced believers fellowship with God through their intuition, transform what they know into spiritual milk, and give it to fleshly believers. At the very beginning of a young Christian's life, the Lord allows this to happen. However, the Lord does not want His people to be dull all their life and unable to fellowship directly with Him. Drinking milk only means that one cannot fellowship directly with God and needs the transmission through others. A full-grown man is one that has his intuition well exercised; he knows how to discern. If we cannot fellowship with God and know the things of God in our intuition, all of our idealistic thinking is useless. The Corinthian believers had much eloquence and knowledge and many gifts, but their spirit was very inactive. The church in Corinth was of the flesh because they only had what was stored in their minds.

Many Christians today err in the same way as the Corinthian believers. They study theology with their dispassionate mentality to search out the hidden meanings in the Bible in order to arrive at the best explanations. The Lord's words are spirit and life, but they do not receive them as spirit and life. They only want to satisfy their own "lust for knowledge" and want to tell others, either verbally or by writing books, what they have learned. Although their meanings, theories, and outlines are the best, and although they appear very "spiritual," in reality they are dead in God's view. Their knowledge comes from the mind of one person and is transferred into the mind of another without passing through the spirit. Those who listen to them or read their writings may say that they have been helped, but what kind of help have they received? Nothing has happened other than the addition of a thought into their mind. This kind of knowledge has no spiritual effect. Only that which comes from the spirit will enter into man's spirit. Whatever comes from the mind will enter into man's mind. Furthermore, only that which comes from the Holy Spirit will enter into our spirit, and only that which comes out of the Holy Spirit through our spirit will enter into someone else's spirit.

THE SPIRIT OF WISDOM AND REVELATION

In our fellowship with God, a spirit of wisdom and revelation is indispensable. "That…the Father of glory, may give to you a spirit of wisdom and revelation in the full

knowledge of Him" (Eph. 1:17). At the time of our regeneration we received a new spirit; however, many of the functions
of the spirit are not manifested and remain concealed inside
the spirit. Therefore, the apostle prayed that the regenerated
Ephesian believers would receive a spirit of wisdom and
revelation so that they could really know God in their
intuition. Whether this spirit of wisdom and revelation is a
hidden potential within the believers' spirit, which is enlightened by God through prayer, or whether it is some fresh
wisdom and revelation, which comes from the Holy Spirit
being added into the believers' spirit, the fact remains that
a spirit of wisdom and revelation is indispensable in a
believer's fellowship with God. It is also a fact that believers
can receive this spirit through prayer.

Although our intuition can fellowship with God, it needs
wisdom and revelation. We need wisdom to know what comes
from God and what comes from us. We need wisdom to
recognize the counterfeits and attacks of the enemy. We need
wisdom to deal with people. In numerous matters we surely
need God's wisdom in order not to err. How foolish we are!
How hard it is to do everything according to God's will! God
wants to give us wisdom; He does not give it to our mind,
but He gives us a spirit of wisdom so that we can have
wisdom in our spirit. God wants us to have wisdom through
our intuition. He will guide us to the pathway of wisdom
through intuition. Our mind may still be foolish, but there
is much wisdom in our intuition. It often seems that our
wisdom is useless, but inside us there is a gradual feeling
which brings wisdom along with it. Wisdom and revelation
are tightly connected. This is because all God's revelations
are revelations of wisdom. If we live only according to our
nature, we will never be able to fathom anything of God by
our thoughts. When we are in our flesh, whatever we have
is just darkness. God and the things of God can never be
fathomed by our minds. Even when our spirit is alive, we
would still live in darkness if we did not have the revelation
of the Holy Spirit. When our spirit is alive, there is *a
possibility for our spirit to receive the revelation of God.* It

does not mean that *the spirit alone can do anything independently.*

In our fellowship with God, He often gives us revelation, and we should often ask God for revelation. A spirit of revelation means God's revelation in spirit. Therefore, the phrase "spirit of wisdom and revelation" merely indicates where God gives us revelation and wisdom. Sudden thoughts are not a spirit of revelation. A spirit of revelation is God's operation in our spirit to the extent that we know His intention through our intuition. All of the fellowship that we have with God takes place only in our spirit and nowhere else.

Having a spirit of wisdom and revelation gives us "the full knowledge of Him." Only when we receive God's revelation in our spirit can we really know Him. All other words are superficial, imaginary, shallow, and, therefore, false. We often speak of God's virtues, including His holiness, righteousness, kindness, love, etc. It seems that through our thoughts alone, we can speak of these virtues and know these virtues of God. But this knowledge is not like seeing through a window; rather, it is like trying to see through a stone wall. When a believer receives God's revelation of His holiness, he knows that God dwells in the light and is unapproachable by natural and sinful men. He finds out how inferior, dirty, and unclean he is in comparison. There should be many among us who have had this kind of experience. We should make the comparison to see if the holiness of God in our heart which we receive from God's revelation is the same as the holiness of God which is spoken by men without revelation. The words used may be the same. But for those with revelation, it seems that there is so much more significance to the words that they speak. Their whole being is in their speaking. This is the spirit of revelation we have mentioned. Only by receiving revelation in our spirit do we really know God. It is the same with many doctrines in the Bible. Many times we understand teachings in our mind and know that they are important, but God gradually reveals these words to us in our spirit. Then it seems as if we have a different emphasis when we preach the same words again. Only knowledge that comes from revelation is real knowledge; everything else is just the activity of the mind.

If we seek for many things concerning God outwardly and do not acquire these things through revelation, they do not move us and do not move others. Only the revelation that is in our spirit has any spiritual usefulness. Proper fellowship with God is receiving God's revelation in our spirit. It is true that God's revelations are not frequent, but how frequently do we wait and pray for God's revelation? If we are constantly busy, how can we be guided just by revelation? Actually, if we are willing to give God the opportunity, we will have revelation frequently. The apostle's living is a testimony to this fact.

SPIRITUAL UNDERSTANDING

There is soulish wisdom, and there is spiritual wisdom. Soulish wisdom comes from man's mind, but spiritual wisdom is given by God to us in our spirit. If a fleshly man does not have a good understanding or is short of wisdom, this can be remedied by education. Of course, this never changes a person's natural endowment. However, this is not the case with spiritual wisdom. It can be obtained by prayer through faith (James 1:5). We have to remember one thing: in God's redemption, "God is not a respecter of persons" (Acts 10:34). He places all sinners, whether wise or foolish, in the *same* position. They need the *same* salvation in all matters. Wise men are as fully corrupt as foolish ones. In God's sight, the minds of the wise and foolish are equally useless. The wise and foolish need the same spiritual regeneration. Even after regeneration, the wise are not able to understand God's Word more easily than the foolish. Finding the most foolish person in the world and trying to lead him to know God is very difficult. Even so, finding the wisest person in the world and trying to lead him to know God is *equally* difficult. This is because the knowledge of God is discerned clearly in the spirit. Although their minds are different, their spirits are both dead and equally foolish. Man's natural wisdom cannot more easily enable him to know God and His truths. It may be easier for us to make the wise one understand and comprehend than the foolish one, but this would only be in the realm of the mind. However, the degree of ignorance in the intuition is the same in both cases. They both need resurrection in the spirit.

Even after the spirit has been resurrected, we should never think that the wise will progress faster than the foolish because of their better mind. If there is no difference in their faithfulness and obedience, whatever differences they have in the understanding of their minds will not produce a difference in the intuitive knowledge in their spirit. The old creation can never be the source of the new creation. The speed of progress depends on faithfulness and obedience. Natural talents never help one to excel on the spiritual path. According to the flesh, a man has the opportunity of being better than others because of differences in natural talents. But in spiritual experiences, every person has to start from the same place, go through the same procedures, and arrive at the same goal. Therefore, every regenerated believer, even if he is more clever than others, must still acquire a spiritual understanding before he can have proper communication with God. Nothing can replace this.

"Therefore we also, since the day we heard of it, do not cease praying and asking on your behalf that you may be filled with the full knowledge of His will in all spiritual wisdom and understanding, to walk worthily of the Lord to please Him in all things, bearing fruit in every good work and growing by the full knowledge of God" (Col. 1:9-10). This is the apostle's prayer for the Colossian believers. This verse shows us that one must have spiritual understanding before he can *know* God's will. After knowing God's will, one can then (1) walk worthily of the Lord to please Him, (2) bear fruit in every good work, and (3) grow by the full knowledge of God.

No matter how good a man's understanding is, it is not enough for him to know God's will. Knowing God's will and having fellowship with God require spiritual understanding. Only spiritual understanding leads one to the realm of the spirit and enables one to know God's will. Fleshly understanding enables one to know some truths, but these truths will only remain in one's mind and not issue in life. Because spiritual understanding comes from the spirit, it can transform what it has understood into life. Even the word "know" is connected to God; there is no real knowledge that does not come from the spirit. A spirit of revelation and spiritual understanding go side by side with each other. God has given us a spirit of wisdom and revelation; He has also given us spiritual understanding. The wisdom and revelation we receive in our spirit must be realized by the understanding before we can know the real meaning of the revelation. Revelation is what we receive from God; understanding is comprehending the revelation we have received from God. Spiritual understanding tells us the meaning of all the movement within our spirit; it enables us to know God's will. Our fellowship with God relies on our spirit receiving God's revelation, on the intuition of the spirit sensing this revelation, and on the spiritual understanding to interpret the meaning of this revelation. Our own understanding can never resolve anything. When our spirit enlightens our understanding, the latter knows the purpose of God's movement.

According to Colossians 1:9-10, we can see very clearly that if we want to please God and bear fruit, we should know His will in our spirit. The relationship with God in our spirit is the basis of God's pleasure and our fruit-bearing. It is vanity for a believer to try to please God on the one hand, while walking according to the soul on the other hand. God is pleased with His will and nothing else. Nothing else can satisfy His heart. The most painful thing for believers is to not know God's will. Although we can conjecture and search, it seems that we cannot touch God's will. These verses tell us that the way to know God's will is not to have more thoughts, considerations, and judgments according to human sentiment, but by spiritual understanding. Only the human spirit can fathom God's will in the spirit because only the spirit has the intuition to know God's movements. By the understanding of the intuition, believers can know God's will.

When believers continue to know God's will, they will be "growing by the *full knowledge* of God." This means that the believers' real knowledge of God will grow gradually. These verses also speak of the spirit. If in everything we seek God's will in our spirit, we will know God more. The intuition in our spirit will grow without limit. The intuition can grow. The growth of the intuition speaks of the believers' total growth in the spiritual life. Each time we have real fellowship with God, there is a result; it trains us to know how to fellowship with Him more the next time. Since a believer has been regenerated and can fellowship with God in his intuition, he should pursue perfection. He should utilize every opportunity to train his spirit so that he can know God more. We need to really know Him in the deepest part of our whole being. Many times we think that we really know His will, but with the passage of time and events, it is proven that we have made a mistake. Everyone of us needs to *really* know Him and His will. Therefore, we should seek to be filled with the full knowledge of His will in all spiritual understanding.

CHAPTER THREE

CONSCIENCE

Besides the intuition and fellowship, our spirit has another important function which is to correct our wrong doings and reprove us so that we will not have peace when we come short of the glory of God. We are talking about the conscience. Just as God's holiness condemns evil and delights in goodness, the conscience of the believers also rebukes uncleanness and pursues goodness. The conscience of the believers is where God's holiness is expressed. If we wish to walk according to the spirit, we cannot ignore what the conscience speaks to us because it is impossible not to make mistakes or incline toward making mistakes, no matter at what stage we are. The conscience does not just reprove us when we have done something wrong to bring us to repentance; if this were the case, the function of the conscience would not be complete. Additionally, while we are considering our path, and before we do anything, the conscience will rise up to protest along with our intuition if we think about something that does not please the Holy Spirit. This will cause us to lose the sense of peace. If believers are willing to listen to the voice of the conscience speaking through the intuition, they will not fail like they do at the present time.

CONSCIENCE AND SALVATION

When we were unbelievers, our spirit was completely dead. The conscience was also dead and unable to function in a normal way. This does not mean that the conscience was completely devoid of any function. The conscience of a sinner still works, but it is in a deep sleep. Even when it is awakened, it only condemns the sinner; it is powerless to lead men to God. Although the conscience of man is dead towards God, He is pleased that the conscience still remains in man's heart for the purpose of doing a very small work. It seems that in

the deadened spirit of man, the conscience can still do more
than the other parts. The deadness of the intuition and
fellowship is more severe than that of the conscience. There
is a reason for this. When Adam ate of the fruit of the
knowledge of good and evil, his intuition and fellowship
towards God died completely; nevertheless, his power to
differentiate between good and evil (the conscience) increased.
To this day a sinner's intuition towards God and his fellowship
with God is completely dead without a trace, but the
conscience still has a little activity. This is not to say that
man's conscience is living because, according to the meaning
of the Bible, living is related to having the life of God. Being
without the life of God is to be dead. According to the Bible,
the conscience of a sinner is dead because it does not contain
the life of God, but according to the sensation of man, it still
can act. This activity of the conscience only causes a sinner
with a deadened intuition to feel more painful.

Because the conscience can still act in this manner, the
Holy Spirit starts to do the work of salvation by first
awakening the dormant conscience. He uses the thunder and
lightning of Mount Sinai to shake and enlighten this darkened
conscience to realize that it has already transgressed God's
law and cannot meet His righteous requirements. In this way,
it has been condemned and should perish. If the conscience
is willing to confess its transgressions and the sin of unbelief,
it will reproach itself and seek mercy from God. The parable
of the publican who went to the temple to pray illustrates
the working of the Holy Spirit in the conscience. According
to the words spoken by the Lord Jesus, the first step in the
work of the Holy Spirit causes men to reprove themselves
because of sin, righteousness, and judgment. If the conscience
rejects this work, a sinner would not have the possibility of
receiving salvation.

The Holy Spirit shines the light of God's law into the
conscience of a sinner so that he may know his sins. The
Holy Spirit also grants man's conscience the light of the
gospel so that he may be saved. After the sinner knows
about sins and has heard about the gospel of grace, God
will also give him the faith to receive salvation, if he is

willing to accept it. Then he will see how the precious blood
of the Lord Jesus satisfies all the accusations of his
conscience. Even though he has sinned, the blood of the
Lord Jesus has already been shed. The punishment for sin
has already been received. Is there anything left to be
accused of? The blood of the Lord Jesus has washed the
believer of all the sins in his life; therefore, the conscience
does not need to accuse him anymore. Since the conscience of
the worshipper has been purified, it does not sense any
more sin (Heb. 10:2). The precious blood of the Lord Jesus
has been sprinkled on our conscience (9:14) so that we may
stand boldly before God. The certainty of salvation is a fact
because the voice of the conscience has been silenced by the
precious blood. If the heart does not believe in the precious
blood, the conscience still accuses us of how evil we were
before our regeneration.

Both the terrifying light of the law and the loving light
of the gospel shine into the conscience. Therefore, should we
not pay attention to men's conscience when we preach? If our
purpose is only to cause men to understand with their minds,
to be stirred up in their emotions, or to resolve in their will,
and if our message does not reach their conscience, then even
if they understand, are stirred up, and decide in their will,
the Holy Spirit will have no way to do a deeper work. This
is because the deeper work of regeneration is based on the
conscience thoroughly knowing sins and the precious blood.
In our teachings, we must give equal attention to the precious
blood and the conscience. Many people emphasize the conscience and seldom speak of the precious blood; hence, men
strive to repent and do good, hoping that through these things
they might turn away God's anger. Others emphasize the
precious blood without talking about the conscience. As a
result men may understand in their minds, be stirred in their
emotions, and resolve in their will, but their "faith" has no
root because their conscience still has not been moved by the
Holy Spirit of God. Therefore, these two things must be
equally preached. Whoever sees the offenses of his conscience
accepts the significance of the precious blood.

CONSCIENCE AND FELLOWSHIP

The following verse shows us the relationship between the conscience and man's fellowship with God in the intuition. "How much more will the blood of Christ, who through the eternal Spirit offered Himself without blemish to God, purify our conscience from dead works to serve the living God?" (Heb. 9:14). If man wants to fellowship with God and "serve God," his conscience must first be cleansed by the precious blood. Because the conscience of the believer is cleansed by the Lord's blood, he is regenerated. Therefore, according to the Bible, the cleansing by the blood and the regeneration of the spirit happen at the same instant. The conscience must be cleansed by the blood so that a believer can obtain a new life and have his intuition quickened; then he may serve God. The spirit can only serve God in the intuition if the conscience receives the cleansing of the blood first. The relationship between the conscience and the intuition cannot be separated.

Hebrews 10:22 says, "Let us come forward to the Holy of Holies with a true heart in full assurance of faith, having our hearts sprinkled from an evil conscience and having our bodies washed with pure water." When we come forward to God, we do not use our bodies like those in the Old Testament, because our Holy of Holies (v. 19) is in the heavens; neither do we use our thoughts and feelings because these parts of the soul cannot have fellowship with God. Only the regenerated spirit can come forward to God. The believer can only worship God through his revived intuition (we have said this in the past). This verse of the Bible shows that washing away the offenses of the conscience is the foundation for fellowship with God in the intuition; if the conscience is conscious of any offense, there cannot be any fellowship with God in the intuition. If the conscience has any offense, a believer will spontaneously condemn himself. Then the intuition, which is closely knit with the conscience, is immediately affected. The believer therefore dares not, and cannot, draw near to God. Moreover, when the believer is fellowshipping with God, there cannot be a lack of "a true heart in full assurance of faith."

Once the conscience has any offense, the believer will draw near to God with reluctance and not out of a true heart; naturally, he will not be able to believe that God is for him, and that He has nothing against him. This type of self-condemnation and doubting oppresses the intuition so that it cannot freely have fellowship with God. The believer must not have any condemnation from the conscience at all. He should know that he has already been washed of his sins by the blood of the Lord, and that there is nothing to oppose him (Rom. 8:33-34). A tiny offense in the conscience is sufficient to oppress, hinder, and stop the work of fellowship by the intuition. Whenever a believer is conscious of any sin, all of the spirit's power is concentrated on getting rid of this particular sin, and there is no strength to go outward or ascend toward heaven.

THE CONSCIENCE OF THE BELIEVER

After the spirit of the believer has been regenerated, his conscience is made alive. The precious blood of the Lord Jesus has purified the conscience so that the conscience is clean, possessing the sharpest feeling, and able to work according to the will of the Holy Spirit. The sanctifying and renewing work of the Holy Spirit in man and the work of the conscience are mutually related and interconnected. If the believer wants to be filled by the Holy Spirit, wants to be sanctified, wants his life to fit into God's purpose, and wants to walk fully according to the spirit, he cannot ignore the voice of the conscience. If we do not give the conscience the position it deserves, we definitely will fall into the position of walking according to the flesh. Being faithful in dealing with the conscience is the first step in the work of sanctification. Walking according to the conscience is a sign of real spirituality. If a fleshly believer does not allow the conscience to do a thorough job, he has no way of entering into the spiritual realm. Even if a man thinks of himself as being spiritual, his spirituality is without foundation. If sins and the things which are not according to God's purpose and do not befit the saints' proper conduct are not dealt with, according to the voice of the conscience, then a spiritual foundation has not been properly laid. No matter how many spiritual ideals are built upon it, they will eventually collapse.

The work of the conscience is to testify to us whether we are right with God and men, and whether our deeds, thoughts, and words are according to God's will and not in rebellion against Christ. Whenever there is progress in the Christian life, the testimony of the conscience and the testimony of the Holy Spirit are almost identical. When the conscience is completely controlled by the Holy Spirit, the conscience becomes keener day by day until it matches the speaking of the Holy Spirit. Moreover, the Holy Spirit also speaks to the believers through the conscience. This is the meaning of the words of the apostle: "My conscience bearing witness with me in the Holy Spirit" (Rom. 9:1).

If our conscience testifies that we are wrong, then we are wrong. If the conscience condemns us of sins, we must repent immediately. We definitely cannot cover up or bribe the conscience. "If our heart blames us, it is because God is greater than our heart" (1 John 3:20). Will God not condemn us even more? The condemnation of the conscience tells us that we are wrong. Whatever our conscience condemns is definitely condemned by God as well. There is certainly no such thing as the righteousness of God being less than the standard of our conscience. Therefore, if our conscience tells us that we are wrong, we must certainly be wrong.

Since we are wrong, what should we do? If we have not done the thing yet, we should stop; if we have committed it, we must repent, confess our sins, and seek the cleansing of the precious blood. It is a pity that believers do not walk this way today. Once the conscience reproves, they think about bribing and making peace with it so that the conscience will no longer voice its disapproval. In this situation, believers usually have two choices. One choice for believers is to argue with the conscience, trying to use reasons to justify their actions. They think that anything that can be justified by reasonings must be according to God's will. Therefore, they hope that the conscience will also be quiet. Little do they know that the conscience, like the intuition, does not function by reasonings. It knows God's will through the intuition; it condemns whatever is not the will of God. It only speaks on behalf of the will of God and does not care about the reasons. A believer should not walk according to reason nor do whatever is reasonable; rather, he should do the will of God as revealed in the intuition. Whenever the believer rebels against the moving of the intuition, the conscience will speak out to condemn. Although explanations by way of reason may satisfy the mind, they are not sufficient to satisfy the conscience. Once the conscience has condemned a certain matter, it will never accept any reasoning or stop condemning until the matter is removed. Initially, the conscience only testifies of right and wrong; after the believer has grown in the spiritual life, it not only testifies of right and wrong, but also of what is and is not of God. Therefore, even though many things are good in the eyes of man, they are condemned by the conscience unless they are based on God's revelation and not the believer's initiation.

The second choice is that a believer will try to do many other things to comfort the conscience. On the one hand, he is not willing to obey the voice of the conscience and follow its direction to please God. On the other hand, he is afraid of the condemnation of the conscience which troubles him and makes him feel miserable. Therefore, he thinks of doing many good things to cover up. He tries to replace God's will with good deeds. He does not submit himself to God, but he says that his present deeds are as good as God's instructions and perhaps, they are even better, more beautiful, wider in scope, more profitable, more useful, and more influential. He considers his work as the best. Regardless of how much he does and how men appraise his work, there is not any spiritual usefulness in the eyes of God It is not how much fat there is, nor how many burnt offerings there are, but how much obedience there is to God. If God has revealed in the spirit that something should be removed, then no matter how good your intentions are, no matter how fat your cattle are, or how heavy your gold and silver are, they are not sufficient to move God's heart. The voice of the conscience must be obeyed. Otherwise, God is not pleased, no matter how good your work is. Even if the offering is many times more than what is required by God, it will not stop the voice of the conscience. The conscience requires us only to obey; it does not require us to do anything extraordinary to serve God.

Therefore, let us not have any self-deceiving conduct. If we want to walk according to the spirit, we have to obey the guidance of the conscience. Do not try to escape the "inward rebuke!" Moreover, listen carefully. If we want to walk according to the spirit all the time, we must humble ourselves and give heed to the corrections of the conscience. A believer should not make a general confession, thinking that his mistakes are so numerous that they cannot be articulated. A vague confession does not allow the conscience to do a thorough job. The believer must allow the Holy Spirit, through the conscience, to point out his sins one by one. He must humbly, quietly, and submissively allow the conscience to rebuke and condemn him of his sins one by one. He must accept the rebuke of the conscience and be willing, according to the mind of the Holy Spirit, to remove everything that opposes God. Dare you allow the conscience to examine your life? Do you have the boldness to let the conscience tell you the real condition of your whole life? Are you willing to allow the conscience to place your entire living and conduct before you, according to God's mind? Are you willing to allow the conscience to open up all of your sins? If you are unwilling and draw back, afraid in your heart, this indicates that there are still many things in your life that should be condemned and nailed to the cross; yet you do not obey. It also indicates that you do not completely submit to God in many things, nor do you walk according to the spirit. Between you and God there is still not a complete fellowship, and many obstacles still remain. Consequently, you cannot say to God, "There is no separation between You and me."

An unconditional, unlimited acceptance of the rebuke of the conscience and a complete willingness to walk according to its revelation prove whether our consecration to God is complete, whether we genuinely hate sins, and whether we sincerely want to do His will. Many times we are willing to submit completely to the Lord, walk according to the Spirit, and be a man who really pleases God; now is the time to test our intentions, whether they are true or false, whether they are complete or lacking. If we are still involved with sins and not completely cut off from sins, then most of our spirituality may be false. If a believer cannot walk completely according to the conscience, then he cannot walk completely according to the spirit, because the requirement of the conscience has not been fulfilled. Therefore, other than the "imaginary spirit" which leads him, the real spirit is persistently demanding that he listen to the speaking of the conscience. If the believer is stricken in his conscience after self-examination, but does not want to be judged by the light of God, does not repent, and is not thoroughly dealt with, then his spiritual life will surely have no real progress. Whether the believer's consecration and work are true or false depends on his willingness to submit completely to the Lord, obeying His commandment and rebuke.

After the believer has allowed the conscience to work, he should not just remain at this stage. A certain sin may have been dealt with already but other sins also need to be dealt with progressively, until all the sins have been thoroughly dealt with. If the believer is faithful to deal with all his iniquities and walk according to the conscience, then the heavenly light will shine brighter and brighter within him. Then he can discover the sins which were not noticed formerly; he can comprehend more and more each day, reading and knowing the law which the Holy Spirit has written in his heart. In this manner, the believer will know what is holiness, righteousness, purity, and uprightness. The former things that were unclear will be deeply inscribed in his heart. The intuition will be greatly helped, and its keenness in understanding the intention of the Holy Spirit will be increased. Therefore, when the conscience rebukes, the believer should tell God, "I am willing to submit." He should let Christ be the Lord of his life again, and he should be willing to be taught and rely on the teachings of the Holy Spirit. If the believer truly follows the conscience, then the Holy Spirit certainly will come to help.

The conscience is the window of a believer's spirit. The light from heaven shines through it so that the believer's

spirit and whole being are filled with light. The entire being
of the believer and his spirit will see the light of heaven
through it. Every time we think, talk, and do something not
good or not befitting the proper conduct of a believer, the
heavenly light will shine through the conscience to expose
our wrongdoing and condemn our failures. If we allow the
conscience to work, submit to it, and remove everything which
it condemns, the heavenly light will shine even brighter the
next time. If we do not confess our mistakes or remove our
sins, the stain of sins will remain and the conscience will be
defiled (Titus 1:15) because we do not walk according to the
teaching of God's light. Then one sin will come after another,
one mark will be added to another, causing the window to
become darker and darker so that it is difficult for the light
to shine through. Consequently, the believer will sin willfully
without feeling uneasy. The conscience will be stifled and the
intuition will be dulled by sins. The more spiritual a believer
is, the keener his conscience. There is no believer who is so
spiritual that he does not have to confess his sins anymore.
If the conscience is dull and, perhaps, even without feeling,
then he must be spiritually degraded. The greatest knowledge,
diligent toil, fervent emotion, and firmness of will, can never
replace the keenness of the conscience. If a believer does not
take care of the conscience and, instead, seeks after mental
and emotional progress, he will regress in his spiritual walk.

The sensitivity of the conscience can increase and also
decrease. If a believer gives ground for the conscience to work,
his window will become brighter every time. If he ignores
the speaking of the conscience or, as we said before, uses
reasonings or other works to replace the demands of the
conscience, the conscience will speak again and again. But
after about ten times, it will then stop speaking. The voice
will become softer and softer until it vanishes in the end.
Every time a believer does not listen to the voice of his
conscience, his spiritual life is damaged. If he allows his
spiritual life to be continually hurt, eventually the believer
will definitely fall into a fleshly position. He will no longer
hate sins and aspire for victory as he did in the past. If he
does not face the rebuke of the conscience, he cannot know

the importance of listening to the voice of the conscience and walking according to the spirit.

A CONSCIENCE VOID OF OFFENSE

The apostle Paul said, "I have conducted myself in all good conscience before God until this day" (Acts 23:1). This was the secret of his life. The conscience spoken of here is not the conscience of an unregenerated man, but a conscience filled with the Holy Spirit. The apostle was bold in going forward to have full fellowship with God because his regenerated conscience did not reprove him. All of his conduct was according to his conscience. He did not commit, even once, anything that his conscience reproved, nor did he, even once, allow anything that the conscience had condemned to remain in him. Therefore, he was bold towards God and men. Whenever there is any offense in the conscience, we cannot be completely without fear. The apostle said, "I also exercise myself to always have a conscience without offense toward God and men" (Acts 24:16) because "if our heart does not blame us, we have boldness toward God; and whatever we ask we receive from Him because we keep His commandments and do the things that are pleasing in His sight" (1 John 3:21-22).

Many believers do not consider the importance of the conscience. As long as we walk according to the spirit, we think that everything will be fine. But whenever our conscience has an offense, we cannot be completely without fear before God. As soon as we have fear before God, there will immediately be a barrier in our fellowship with Him. The offense of the conscience is the greatest hindrance of the intuition's fellowship with God. If we do not keep His commandments and the things which are pleasing to Him, our hearts will naturally be rebuked. There will be offenses and shrinking back from God. Furthermore, we will not receive the things which we ask of Him. Only a "pure conscience" is capable of serving God (2 Tim. 1:3). A conscience with offense causes the intuition to draw back and fear approaching God.

"For our boasting is this, the testimony of our conscience,

that in singleness and sincerity of God, not in fleshly wisdom but in the grace of God, we have conducted ourselves in the world" (2 Cor. 1:12). This verse talks about the testimony of the conscience. Only a conscience void of offense can testify for the believer. Even though the testimony of man is good, the testimony of one's own conscience is more precious. The apostle said that he boasted in this. In our path of walking according to the spirit, we should often have such a testimony from the conscience. Many times what other people say about us may be wrong because they cannot understand how God is leading us. They may misunderstand us and they may misjudge us, just as the apostles were misunderstood and misjudged by the believers in the past. On the other hand, they may also overly praise and admire us. Because of following the Lord, many people may often disparage us, even though we are actually obeying the Lord. At other times men will extol us because of what they see in us; however, most of this comes from sudden emotions or imaginations. Therefore, outward praise and criticism are not the criteria; only the testimony of our own resurrected conscience counts for anything. We must examine how our conscience testifies concerning us. What kind of person does the conscience testify that we are? Does the conscience condemn us of hypocrisy? Does the conscience say that we cover up our faults and assume an impressive appearance? Or does the conscience testify that we conduct ourselves in this world, according to the singleness and sincerity of God? Does the conscience testify that we have walked according to the light we have received?

What did the conscience testify concerning Paul? The testimony was that "not in fleshly wisdom but in the grace of God, we have conducted ourselves in the world." In fact, this is the only testimony of the conscience. The conscience strives for and insists that the believer live by the grace of God and not according to fleshly wisdom. The wisdom of the flesh is of no use in the work of God and the will of God. Neither is it of any use in the spiritual life of the believer. Man's mind is of absolutely no use in fellowship with God; even in contact between man and physical things, it also occupies a subordinate position. The conduct of the believer in the world is completely dependent upon the grace of God. Grace means that God does everything and man does nothing (Rom. 11:6). Only when the believer lives by fully depending upon God, not allowing himself to initiate anything, not allowing the mind of man to enter and dominate anything, can the conscience testify that we live in the world according to the singleness and sincerity of God. In other words, the conscience works together with the intuition. The conscience only testifies and approves of the conduct of a believer which is according to the intuition. Any conduct that goes against the intuition, even though it may be very much according to the wisdom of man, will be resisted by the conscience. In short, the conscience does not approve anything other than the revelation of the intuition. The intuition leads the believer, and the conscience urges the believer to obey the intuition when he thinks of disobeying it.

A conscience that is void of offense before God testifies that God is pleased with the believer and that there is no separation between God and the believer. Such a testimony of the conscience is indispensable to a life that walks according to the spirit. This should be the goal of the believer; if this has not been attained, the believer should not be satisfied. This is the normal life of a believer; the apostle Paul lived such a life and so must today's believers. Enoch was one who had an undefiled conscience; therefore, he knew that he pleased God. The testimony of God's being pleased with us can help us to progress. But we should be cautious; otherwise, we will exalt the "self," thinking that we can please God in ourselves. All the glory belongs to Him. We should "encourage ourselves" to keep our conscience void of offense. If our conscience is really void of offense, we should guard against the flesh entering in a subtle way.

If our conscience frequently testifies of God's pleasure, then when we unfortunately fail, we will trust more boldly in the blood of the Lord Jesus to wash us again. If we desire to have a conscience void of offense, we should not depart for a moment from the blood that washes us eternally. We should not depart, because we often give opportunities for offenses in the conscience in small matters, even if we have not slipped in great matters. Therefore, confessing sins and trusting in the precious blood should not be avoided. Since our sinful nature and its many hidden works are still within us, we may possibly have to wait for our spiritual life to grow more before we can know them. This is why there are many things which we now consider to be wrong, but which we once felt were not wrong. If it were not for the precious blood covering everything, we would never be at peace. Once the precious blood has been sprinkled upon our conscience, it functions there continually because of the intercession of the Lord Jesus and the eternal life He gave us.

The apostle told us that he entreated that he would have a conscience void of offense before God and man. These two matters, towards God and towards man, are intimately connected together. If we wish to have a conscience void of offense towards man, we must first have a conscience void of offense towards God, because a conscience that has an offense before God naturally has an offense before man. Therefore, all believers who seek after a spiritual living should continually seek after a good conscience before God (1 Pet. 3:21). This does not mean that our condition before man is unimportant. We not only have to seek for a good conscience towards God, we also have to seek for a good conscience towards man. Many things are acceptable before God but are not proper before man. Only a conscience that is clear before men has a good testimony before them. Even if someone misunderstands, you should have a "good conscience, so that in the matter in which you are spoken against, those who revile your good manner of life in Christ may be put to shame" (v. 16). Once the conscience is unclear, then no matter how good your outward conduct is, it is of no use; once your conscience is without offense, it cannot be affected even by men's slandering.

A conscience without offense not only is able to testify for us before man, but it also enables us to receive God's promises. Today's believers often complain that their faith is too small and therefore, that they are unable to have a completely spiritual living. Naturally, there may be many causes, but is not an offense in the conscience one of the most important causes? A conscience without offense and a faith that is strong are inseparable. The moment the conscience has an offense, faith is immediately weakened. Let us see how the Holy Bible links these two matters together: "Love out of a pure heart and out of a good conscience and out of unfeigned faith" (1 Tim. 1:5), and "holding faith and a good conscience" (v. 19). The conscience is the faculty of our faith. God hates sin the most. The zenith of God's glory is His boundless holiness. His holiness cannot tolerate sin even momentarily. If a believer does not follow the guidance of his conscience, but rather prefers whatever is not according to the will of God, he will immediately lose his fellowship with God. It can be said that all the spiritual promises in the Bible given by God to the believers are conditional. None of them are given to the believer to satisfy the intentions of his flesh. If sins and the flesh are not removed, then neither the Holy Spirit, nor fellowship with God, nor answers to prayers will be granted to the believer. If our conscience has already accused us, how can we boldly approach God to seek for His promises? If our conscience is unable to testify that we live on the earth according to the holiness and righteousness of God, how can we be men of prayer who seek for God's unlimited free gifts? If our conscience rebukes us the moment we lift up our hands to God, then what is the use of our prayer? Our sins must be rejected and washed away before we can have the faith to pray.

The conscience must be void of offense. This does not mean that it should be better than in the past or that many evil things have been removed. Being void of offense, having no offense whatever, and being completely without fear before God are the necessary conditions of the conscience. If we are willing to submit to the conscience and let it reprove us, and if we fully consecrate ourselves to the Lord and are willing to do all of His will, our boldness will certainly increase, knowing that a pure conscience can be attained. We would then be able to tell God that we have not held anything back, that there is nothing that is not open to Him, that we have no hidden things, and that there is no more separation between us and Him. In living according to the spirit, a believer should never allow his conscience to be unclear in any small matter. Everything that is condemned by the conscience should be rejected at once and confessions made immediately. The believer should seek for the cleansing of the blood immediately and allow no trace of this matter to remain. Every day he should seek for a conscience that is continually clear, because a conscience that is unclear, for no matter how short a time, will cause the spirit to suffer a great loss. The apostle's example is "to always have a conscience without offense." In this manner, we will see that our fellowship with God is truly unbroken.

CONSCIENCE AND KNOWLEDGE

In walking according to the spirit and listening to the voice of the conscience, we should also remember that the conscience is limited by its knowledge. Our conscience is the organ for distinguishing good and evil. To distinguish means to have the knowledge. The knowledge to differentiate between good and evil is not the same among many Christians. Some have more knowledge and some have less knowledge, because individual circumstances are not the same and, perhaps, the lessons learned are also not similar. Therefore, we cannot act according to someone else's standard, nor can we expect others to live according to the light we have. In the fellowship between the believer and God, an unknown sin will not hinder the fellowship. If the believer walks according to the standard which he already knows: keeping (obeying) everything which he knows to be according to God's will and rejecting everything which he knows to be condemned by God, he is able to have a complete fellowship with God. A young believer always thinks that his knowledge is insufficient and, there-fore, that he cannot please God. On one hand, spiritual knowledge is very high in value, but on the other hand, the lack of knowledge is not an obstruction in the fellowship with God. In God's fellowship with man, He cares about our attitude toward His will, not how much we know concerning His will. If our attitude is to seek after His will sincerely and truly, even desiring to keep it wholeheartedly, the presence of many unknown sins will not cause us to lose our fellowship or even have a limited fellowship with God. If fellowship is determined according to God's holiness, none of the most holy saints from the past until the present time would be qualified to have a complete fellowship with God even for a moment. Furthermore, they would all be driven away from the face of the Lord and from the glory of His might. The sins that we are not aware of have been covered under the precious blood.

On the other hand, if we are aware of and tolerate a little sin that the conscience has condemned, spontaneously we will not have a full fellowship with God. Just as a very tiny speck in the eye can impede our eyesight and give us pain, a sin that we are aware of, no matter how small, can prevent us from seeing the smiling face of God. Once the conscience has an offense, fellowship will also suffer. A particular sin may remain in the believer for many years, but as long as he does not know about it, it will not hinder his fellowship with God. However, the moment light (knowledge) comes, the conscience condemns. Then if it remains for another day, the fellowship of that day will be lost. God fellowships with us according to the level of our conscience. If we think that a particular sin, which has remained for many years without causing any hindrance, can continue to remain and cause no harm, we are the most foolish persons.

The reason for this is that the conscience can only condemn according to the most recent light it receives. It cannot condemn any sin that it does not know to be sin. Since there is advancement in the believer's knowledge, his conscience also advances; the more knowledge the believer has, the more sins the conscience will condemn. The believer does not have to grieve for anything that he does not know, nor does he need to strive to do anything. As long as he absolutely submits to what he knows, it is sufficient. "But if we walk in the light," that is, if we walk in the light which we have already, "as He is in the light, we have fellowship with one another, and the blood of Jesus His Son cleanses us from every sin" (even though many are still unknown) (1 John 1:7). God has limitless light, yet God also walks according to His limitless light. The light which we have is very limited, yet we must walk according to this light. Only then can we have fellowship with God, and only then will the blood of His Son cleanse us from all our sins. We still have sins which have not been removed, but if we do not know about them and the light has not yet shone, we are still able to have full fellowship with God. We must remember that even though the conscience is very crucial, the conscience is not the measurement of our holiness because of knowledge. Christ is the unique standard of our holiness. But in our fellowship with God, God uses the matter of having a conscience void of offense as the condition of His fellowship with us. Therefore, after we completely submit to the guidance of the conscience, we should never think, even for a moment, that we are already "perfect." A good conscience only tells us that according to what we know, we have achieved what we should achieve at the present.

Thus, as our biblical knowledge increases and our spiritual experiences grow, the standard of our conduct will also rise accordingly. In the gradual increase of light, our conduct must become gradually more holy for our conscience to be preserved without offense. Once we have another year of knowledge and experience, our conscience will accuse us if our conduct is the same as the previous year's. In the previous year God did not cut off His fellowship with us, because we were ignorant of our transgressions. But once we have knowledge of the same transgressions, the fellowship with God will be lost if we do not renounce them. The conscience is given by God to the believers to be the present standard of their holiness. If a believer violates the standard, they will be considered as having sinned.

The Lord still has many things to speak to us, but because of the immaturity of our spiritual understanding, He still has to wait. God deals with His children according to their individual condition. Some matters are considered to be extremely evil and sinful by some believers, yet others may not feel the same way. This is due to differences in the knowledge of their conscience. Therefore, let us not criticize one another. Only the Father God knows how to deal with His children. He certainly does not expect to see His "little children" have the strength of the "young men," or His "young men" to have the experiences of the "fathers." However, He expects all of His children to submit to Him according to what they already know. If we know with certainty—this is not easy—that God has already spoken to our brother's conscience concerning a certain matter, and he does not obey, then we can urge him. But we must never force our brother to follow the feeling of our conscience. If the absolutely holy God did not reject us because of past wrongdoings which we were ignorant about, then how can we, according to our present level, judge our brother who only possesses the knowledge which we had last year?

In fact, if we are helping others, we do not have to compel them again and again to obey every minor point. We only have to beseech them to walk fully according to the guidance of their conscience. If they have surrendered to God, then whenever the Holy Spirit enlightens them on any of the things clearly recorded in the Bible, they will obey. If the will has been surrendered, then any time the conscience receives light, a believer will walk according to the will of God. This is the same for us. We do not have to extend ourselves to use the strength of the soul to understand many truths for which the right time has not come. As long as we are willing to hear the present speaking of God, this is good enough. If the Holy Spirit wishes to lead us in our intuition to examine some truths, we should not hesitate to comply; otherwise, we would lower our own standard of holiness and become complacent. In short, if we are willing to move according to our spirit, there will be no problem at all.

THE WEAKNESS OF THE CONSCIENCE

We have clearly said before that Christ is the standard of holiness for our life. Even though the conscience is important, it is not the standard. At the same time, even though the conscience is not the standard of holiness, it is the standard that testifies whether or not we please God in our daily living. In other words, the conscience is the standard of the present level of our holiness. If we can live every day according to the leading of the conscience, we have attained to the level we presently should attain to. If we maintain a good conscience, we will not fall behind in our spiritual journey. Thus in our daily path of walking according to the spirit, the conscience is a very necessary factor. In whatever our conscience guides us, if we disobey it, we will be rebuked, lose our peace, and be temporarily cut off from God in our fellowship. It is indisputable that we should follow the spirit completely through all the guidance of the conscience. But is the leading of the conscience perfect? This question still remains.

We know that the conscience is controlled by its knowledge. It can only guide people according to what it knows. Then if men do not obey, it condemns. It does not condemn something that it does not know. Therefore, if we compare the standard of the conscience with the standard of God's holiness, the standard of the conscience is very inferior. It has at least two shortcomings. One, as we said before, is the limitation of its knowledge; it can only condemn the wrongdoings that it knows. Consequently, since our conscience does not possess certain knowledge, we allow many things that are not according to God's will to remain in our lives. God knows, and believers who are more mature than us also know, that our shortcomings are numerous. But since we have not received the light, these shortcomings remain. Is this not a big defect? This, however, is permissible because God does not condemn what we do not know. Even though we are at fault, God is well pleased, and He fellowships with us because we have acted according to the leading of the conscience.

There is still a second defect which can hinder the fellowship of the believer with God. A little knowledge can not only lead the believer to condemn something that should be condemned, it can also lead him to condemn something which should not be condemned. What should we say then? Has the conscience led wrongly? No, the leading of the conscience cannot be wrong and should be obeyed by the believer. But the measure or degree of knowledge differs. Due to a believer's lack of knowledge, there are many things which he will be permitted to do when he possesses more knowledge, but these things are not allowed at the present time because of the lack of knowledge. If he were to do them, the conscience would condemn, and he would have sinned. This is the immaturity of the believer. This means that many things are fully permissible for the fathers because they have the knowledge, experience, and position. But if the children were to do what the father does, it would definitely not be permitted due to their lack of knowledge, experience, and position. This is not to say that there are two criteria for right and wrong, but that it is impossible for the criteria for right and wrong not to be different according to each one's position. This is true in spiritual things as well as in physical things. Many things, when done by the mature believer, are completely in accordance with the will of God. However, if a young believer were to follow and do the same, to him it would be a sin.

The reason for this is none other than differences in the degree of the knowledge of the conscience. If, according to the conscience of a believer, a certain thing is permitted, and he does it, he is doing the will of God. But if the conscience of another believer does not permit the same thing, he will sin if he does it. As we said before, this does not mean that the highest will of God is different, but that God leads each one according to his respective position. One who has knowledge has a stronger conscience; consequently, he has more liberty. One who is without knowledge is weaker; consequently, he is more restricted.

This matter is clearly taught by the apostle in 1 Corinthians. At that time, the believers in Corinth had many misunderstandings about the matter of eating things offered to idols. Some thought that idols were nothing and that the food could be eaten, whether or not it was offered to idols, since God is one and there is no other God (8:4). Others, before they were believers, had been idol worshippers. Therefore, when they saw that the food they were eating had been offered to idols, they could not help remembering the past. Consequently their conscience was not at peace. When they ate, they were defiled because their conscience was weak (v. 7). The apostle understood that this distinction was caused by the presence or absence of knowledge (v. 7). The former, because of their knowledge, were not rebuked by their conscience; therefore, after eating, they did not sin. The latter, because of their lack of knowledge, were not at peace in their conscience; therefore, their eating became their sin. From this we see that knowledge is very important. More knowledge can sometimes cause the conscience to condemn more, but it can also cause the conscience to have less condemnation.

Therefore, in similar matters of the shadows of the things to come, we should ask the Lord to grant us more knowledge so that we will not be unreasonably bound. However, such knowledge should be kept with a humble heart; otherwise, we will fall into the flesh like the Corinthian believers. If our knowledge is inadequate and the conscience still rebukes, we still have to obey the voice of the conscience no matter how great a price we have to pay. We should not think that because this is not wrong according to the highest standard, that we do not need to care for the conscience and can just do it. We should remember that the conscience is the current standard of God's guidance. We should obey; disobeying is a sin. What is condemned by our conscience is certainly condemned by God.

We have spoken concerning outward things such as food. Concerning more spiritual things, regardless of how much knowledge we possess, there can never be the difference of freedom or bondage to us. What is spoken of here concerns outward things of the flesh. God's dealing with His children is according to their age. Towards young believers, God is very concerned about outward things such as eating, clothing, and so on because God wants to put to death the evil deeds of their bodies. If young believers have the heart to follow the Lord, they will see that the Lord often causes them to subdue these things through the conscience of the spirit. Those who have more experience in the Lord, because they know how to submit to the Lord, seem to have a little more freedom in their conscience.

However, older believers have a big danger in this regard; their conscience may be too strong, and it may become cold and hard. Immature believers who seek the Lord wholeheartedly will submit to the Lord in many things because their conscience and intuition are sensitive, and they are easily moved by the Holy Spirit. Elderly believers may become cold and hard in their conscience because too much knowledge has caused their mind to be overdeveloped; consequently, the sensitivity of the intuition is lost. They do everything according to the knowledge of their mind; the Holy Spirit seemingly cannot move them. This is a fatal wound to the spiritual life. It causes the believer's life to lose its freshness; everything is old. Regardless of how much knowledge we have, we should not follow the knowledge but the intuition of the spirit (conscience). If we do not care for the condemnation of the conscience through the intuition, but use our knowledge as the standard of our conduct, then we will walk according to the flesh. Many times, according to the truth which we know, it is permissible for us to do a certain thing. Yet does not our conscience become unrestful if we go ahead and do it? If the conscience condemns a certain matter, it still does not fit into God's will even if, according to the knowledge of the mind, the matter is good. Often the knowledge which we have gained is acquired through the intelligence of the mind, and it is not the revelation of the intuition. Therefore, the leading of the conscience can be at conflict with the knowledge.

The apostle reckoned that if a believer does not care for the rebuke of the weakened conscience and instead walks according to the knowledge of the mind, his spiritual life will be grievously damaged. "For if anyone sees you who have knowledge reclining at table in an idol temple, will not his conscience, if he is weak, be emboldened to eat the things sacrificed to the idols? For the one who is weak is being destroyed by your knowledge, the brother because of whom Christ died" (1 Cor. 8:10-11). This concerns believers who have knowledge and those who do not. If a believer who does not have knowledge sees one who has knowledge eating food offered to idols, then he will reason that if the other believer can eat, he also can eat. He will not care for the voice of his conscience and will eat. This causes the believer to fall. This is the meaning in these verses. A believer who does not have knowledge can only understand with his mind the knowledge that his brother possesses. If he walks according to this knowledge, ignoring his conscience, he will fall. May we always remember that we should not walk according to the knowledge that we have, even if it is only for a short period of time. All believers, regardless of their knowledge, should walk according to the intuition and the conscience of the spirit. Their knowledge may influence their conscience, but they should directly follow the conscience alone. Concerning the conduct of believers, God cares more for their obedience to His will than for their good conduct. Listening to the voice of the conscience guarantees that our consecration and obedience are true. Through the conscience, God observes whether our priority is submitting to Him or whether we have other motives.

There is another matter which a believer should pay attention to. He should be cautious not to allow his conscience to be surrounded. Many times our conscience loses its normal function because it has been encircled. Our conscience becomes cold because the consciences of those around us are cold and hard, and because their reasonings, talk, teachings, encouragement, examples, and hindrances influence us. We should be wary of teachers whose consciences are cold and hard. We should guard against any man-made conscience; the conscience made by others for us should be rejected. Our conscience should be directly responsible to God in every single matter. We should know the will of God, and we should be responsible to keep it. If we do not care for our own conscience and follow the consciences of others, we will fail.

In short, the conscience of the believer is an important faculty of the spirit. The believer should fully follow its leading. Even though it is influenced by knowledge, all of its speaking represents the highest will of God for us today. As long as we attain to the highest peak that we should attain to today, this is sufficient. We do not need to worry about all the other things. We should always keep our conscience healthy and not allow a single sin to damage its perception. Once we become cold and hard at any time, nothing will be able to move us. Then we should know that we have fallen deeply into the flesh. All of our scriptural knowledge will be kept in the mind of the flesh and not have a living power.

We should always walk according to the intuition of the spirit and be filled with the Holy Spirit so that the perception of the conscience becomes keener day after day. Then even a small matter that is not right with God can be detected and repented of. Do not labor just in the mind and forget about the intuition of the conscience. The growth of our spiritual stature ensures the increase of the sensitivity of our conscience. So many believers do not possess any liveliness today because they did not care for their conscience, but only kept dead knowledge in their mind. We should be watchful every day and not fall into complacency. Do not fear being moved easily. If it is the moving of the conscience, we should fear that it is too little, not that it is too much. The conscience is God's brake. It tells us what parts are in trouble and should be repaired before proceeding. If we are willing to listen, we will avoid a great deal of tearing down work later.

SECTION SIX

WALKING
ACCORDING TO THE SPIRIT

CHAPTER ONE

DANGERS IN THE SPIRITUAL JOURNEY

ACCORDING TO SPIRIT

In the Christian life, nothing is more crucial than to walk daily according to the spirit. This will always keep the believer spiritual, keep him from the power of the flesh, keep him following the will of God, and keep him from Satan's attack. Once we know the function of the spirit, it is very important to walk according to it immediately. This is a minute by minute matter, and we must not be at all slack concerning it. We need to be extra cautious about receiving the teachings of the Holy Spirit but not following His leading. Many believers have failed, and this is the reason for their failure. Just receiving the teaching is not enough; following His leading is a must. We should never be satisfied with spiritual knowledge; we must treasure the matter of walking according to the spirit. We often hear talk about "the way of the cross." What really is the way of the cross? It is none other than walking according to the spirit. This is because in order to walk according to the spirit, all self-will, love, and thoughts must be put to death. To follow the intuition and revelation of the spirit requires us to bear the cross daily.

Perhaps all spiritual believers know something about the functions of the spirit as we mentioned earlier, but what they know does not last. They only *sometimes* have spiritual experiences because they still do not clearly understand all the functions and laws of the spirit. Therefore, they do not know how to follow the spirit in a lasting manner. After hearing this truth, their experience may testify that it is true. Regrettably, however, they cannot experience this continuously. If their intuition had sufficient growth, they could always walk according to the spirit and not be affected by the outside world. (Note: everything outside of the spirit is the outside world.) Many believers, due to their lack in understanding the law of the spirit, consider a life that is according to the spirit to be vacillating, standardless, and hard to practice. Many believers have determined to do the will of God and follow the guidance of the Holy Spirit given in the spirit, yet they lose the boldness to come forward because they are uncertain of the trustworthiness of the intuition's leading. This is because they have not yet learned to apprehend the mind of the intuition. They do not know the intent of all the feelings of the intuition—whether to have them act or stop. Neither do they know the proper condition of the spirit; therefore, they cannot receive continual guidance from the spirit. By not maintaining the spirit in the proper condition, they often cause the spirit to lose its working power. Sometimes they receive a revelation from the intuition, but they do not know why it is given at a particular time. They also do not understand why they fail to receive any revelation when they diligently seek at other times. They do not know the reason for this failure.

They receive the revelation of the spirit because they sometimes unconsciously walk according to the law of the spirit; at other times, they cannot obtain the revelation because their seeking is not according to the law of the spirit. If they could always walk according to the law of the spirit as they did unconsciously, they would always receive the leading of the spirit. But they do not know this. If we wish to obtain revelations in spirit, know the will of God, and do what is pleasing to Him, we cannot afford to be ignorant of the law of the spirit. All the feelings of the spirit are meaningful. We must learn to discover their meaning before we can act according to the spirit's requirements and walk continually according to the spirit. Understanding the law of the spirit is indispensable to walking according to the spirit.

Many believers treat the Holy Spirit's occasional working in their spirit as the most wonderful experiences of their life. They do not expect to have such experiences daily. They consider these as special occasions, possibly occurring only a few times in a lifetime. If they followed the spirit according to the law of the spirit, they would see their life becoming so transcendent. Nevertheless, they regard spiritual experiences as extraordinary and impossible to maintain constantly, not realizing that spiritual experiences should be their *ordinary* daily experience. To depart from this position and live in darkness is what is truly extraordinary.

Sometimes we seemingly receive a certain thought. If we know how to discern, we can tell whether this thought is from our spirit or from our soul. Some thoughts are burning in the spirit, but some are merely anxieties in the soul. Believers must learn to differentiate between them. After examination, a believer can easily discern between spiritual and soulish. Therefore, at all times, a believer must know how each part of his whole being is functioning. When thinking, he ought to know the source of his thought; when feeling, the source of his feeling; and when working, what power to use. Consequently, we can know what is from the spirit and follow it. We can also be kept from working according to feeling, and we can know whether the things that happen to us are of the spirit or the soul.

We know that our soul is our "self-consciousness." Hence, much of our self-examination and self-consciousness are completely of the soul and harmful. Why? This kind of self-examination and self-consciousness causes a believer to constantly consider himself, resulting in the growth of the self-life. Self-exaltation often comes from this self-consciousness. However, one kind of self-analysis provides indispensable knowledge for the spiritual journey, enabling a believer to truly know where he is and how he is walking. Harmful self-consciousness includes those proud or discouraging thoughts derived from considering one's own successes or failures. Beneficial self-analysis concerns itself *only* with those considerations that investigate the *source* of thoughts, feelings, and preferences. God desires that we should get rid of self-consciousness, but He does not mean that we should live in the world brainlessly. Excessive self-consciousness must be eliminated; but at the same time, we should know, through the Holy Spirit, what is going on within our own inner being. Therefore, it is necessary to carefully observe the activities of the self.

Many believers, although regenerated, seem to feel that

they do not have a spirit. Actually, it is not that they do not have a spirit, but only that they do not feel that they do. One can have the sense of the spirit, but not know that these feelings come from the spirit. For every genuine, born-again believer, the real life to live by is the life of his spirit. If he is willing to learn, he will see what the sense of his spirit really is. One thing is certain, the soul can be affected by the outward world, but not the spirit. For example, after seeing beautiful scenery, enjoying peaceful nature, hearing melodious music, or touching many other outward surroundings, the soul can be immediately moved, resulting in a kind of emotion. However, this is not so with the spirit. If the spirit of a believer is filled with the power of the Holy Spirit, it is independent of the soul. Unlike the soul, which depends on outward influences for its activities, the spirit can move on its own. Hence, the spirit can function in any kind of situation. Therefore, if a believer is truly spiritual, he can continue to work, whether his soul has any feeling or his body has any strength, because he lives according to the continually active spirit.

Practically speaking, the feeling of the soul and the intuition of the spirit are markedly different. Yet sometimes, the feeling of the soul is very similar to the intuition of the spirit. Sometimes these two are almost identical, and it is very hard for believers to differentiate. Although these times are rare, they still occur. Between the two it seems that only a hairbreadth of difference exists. At these times, a hasty believer cannot avoid being deceived. However, if he waits patiently, discerning again and again the source of his feeling, the Holy Spirit will reveal the truth to him at the proper time. If we want to walk according to the spirit, we must not act in haste.

All soulish believers, for the most part, have certain inclinations. Generally speaking, they either tend to the emotions or to the mind. When they desire to be spiritual and walk according to the spirit, they often fall into the trap of the *opposite* inclination. This means that an emotional believer will regard his cool rationality as the leading of the spirit. Since he realizes that his zealous life style in the past was soulish, he misjudges his present rationality as being spiritual. An analytical believer will treat his hot emotions as the leading of the spirit. Since he also realizes that his cool life style in the past was soulish, he regards his present emotion as being spiritual. Alas, these two only exchange places and they are not any less soulish. Therefore, we must remember the function of the spirit. In other words, to walk according to the spirit is to walk according to the intuition, because spiritual knowledge, fellowship, and conscience are all obtained from the intuition. The Holy Spirit uses the intuition to guide the believers. Hence, a believer should not imagine what is spiritual. It would suffice if he follows the intuition. If he desires to obey the Holy Spirit, he needs to know His will in the intuition.

Some desperately seek after the gifts of the Holy Spirit. Many times, their seekings are merely a search for happiness; there is an "I" behind it. Furthermore, if they feel the descending of the Holy Spirit, their body being taken over by some external power, or a warm heat flowing from head to toe, they consider that they have obtained the baptism of the Holy Spirit. The Holy Spirit can no doubt cause one to sense Him through his feelings, but seeking Him according to emotion is exceedingly harmful. Not only will this stir up one's own soul-life, but it may bring about the disguise of Satan. What is valuable before God is not our sense of the Lord's presence or our love toward Him through our emotion; rather, it is our following of the Holy Spirit in our intuition and living according to what He reveals to us in spirit. Often we see someone who has had the "baptism of the Holy Spirit" still living according to the natural life and not according to the spirit. Neither does he have a keen intuition to dissect the spiritual world. Only fellowship with the Lord in the intuition, not in the emotion, is valuable.

When we have read about the functions of the spirit recorded in the Bible, we realize that the spirit can be as hot as the emotion and as cool as the reason. But experienced ones in the Lord know the difference between what is from the spirit and what is from the soul. If a believer does not seek to truly know God in the intuition and walk according

to the intuition, but simply postulates in the mind or, even
more commonly, seeks after the stirring of the Holy Spirit
in his feelings, he still is walking according to the flesh and
causing his spiritual life to sink into a lifeless condition.

By observing Paul's conduct, we can better realize the
importance of walking according to the intuition of the spirit.
He said, "But when it pleased God...to reveal His Son in me
that I might announce Him as the gospel among the Gentiles,
immediately I did not confer with flesh and blood, neither
did I go up to Jerusalem to those who were apostles before
me, but I went away to Arabia and again returned to
Damascus" (Gal. 1:15-17). Revelation is a matter of the spirit.
Even when the apostle John was inspired to write the book
of Revelation, he received the revelation in spirit (Rev. 1:10).
The Scriptures testify in unison that revelation is in the
believer's spirit.

The apostle told us that after he received the revelation
in spirit, knew the Lord Jesus, and realized that God was
sending him to the Gentiles, he followed the leading in the
spirit. He did not confer with flesh and blood; he no longer
needed to listen to men's opinions, thoughts, and arguments.
Neither did he go to Jerusalem to see the "spiritual seniors"
to ask for their opinions regarding this matter. He followed
the leading of the spirit all the way. Once he had obtained
the revelations of *God* in his intuition and understood the
will of God, he no longer sought other proofs. According to
him, the revelation in spirit was sufficient to guide him, even
though preaching the Lord Jesus among the Gentiles was an
unprecedented move in those days. According to man's soul,
the more we consider, the better it is, and the more we seek
others' opinions, especially of those experienced in preaching
the gospel, the better. But Paul only followed the spirit and
did not care for the opinions of men, even of the most spiritual
apostles.

Therefore, we should not follow the words of some spiritual
person, but instead, the direct guidance of the Lord Himself
in our spirit. Does this mean that the words of the spiritually
mature are useless? No, they are still of great profit. Their
reminders and teachings are helpful, but we still need to

think carefully and clearly to see whether their speaking is from God, and we still need to receive the Lord's personal instruction. When we are not certain whether our stirring within is really the revelation of the spirit, the teachings of those deeply experienced in the Lord are very helpful. However, if we are *certain* that the revelation is from God, as Paul was in his day, we would not need to check with the apostles even if they still existed today.

If we read the context, we can see that the apostle considered it important that his gospel was by revelation and not taught by other apostles. This is a crucial point. Our gospel must not be obtained from listening to a certain man, from reading a certain book, or from a certain mental exercise. If our gospel is not by God's revelation, it has absolutely no spiritual value. Today young believers stress the matter of learning from an instructor, and spiritually advanced ones stress the need to pass correct beliefs on to the next generation. They do not know that these are spiritually worthless. What we believe, what we preach, and what we have are all a big zero if they are not by revelation. A believer may receive many wonderful thoughts from another person's mind, and yet his spirit may still be poor and empty. Of course, we are not expecting some new gospel, nor do we look down on the speaking of other servants of God, because the Bible clearly states that we should not despise prophesying. Nevertheless, we must know that revelation is absolutely indispensable.

Without revelation, all that has been said is in vain. We must gain the revelation of God's truth in our spirit, then our preaching can have spiritual results. Otherwise, the supply from others will still be useless. For each worker of Christ, revelation in the spirit must have the highest position. This is the foremost qualification of every worker. Only by this way can we do spiritual work and follow the spirit. Today too many workers rely on their intellect and thinking! Even the believers of the purest faith probably receive truth merely in their mind. These are all dead [works]. Let us ask ourselves, is our preaching from God's revelation or from man?

THE ATTACKS OF SATAN

Since our spirit, as the organ for fellowship between the Holy Spirit and the believers, is so crucial, it is no wonder that Satan utterly abhors the believers knowing about the functions of the spirit and walking according to the spirit. His aim is to have the believers live in the soul and "quench the Spirit." He can cause their bodies to be filled with many kinds of strange feelings and their minds with many wandering thoughts. Through these feelings and thoughts, he can confound the spiritual senses of the believers, so that in a state of confusion, the believers cannot distinguish what is really from the spirit and what is from the soul. He knows that "reading" the sense of the spirit is mandatory in order for a believer to be victorious. (How pitiful that many believers are unaware of this!) Therefore, he does his utmost to attack the spirit of the believers.

So let us repeat, in spiritual warfare a believer must never act according to his own feelings or some sudden thoughts. Never consider that a matter can never go wrong once it has been covered in prayer. Many believers believe that all of their thoughts while praying are God-given. This is a mistake. They seem to believe that their prayer can make their work infallible. They reckon that all of the work done through prayer is unerring. Nevertheless, they do not know that seeking the will of God is not the same as *knowing* the will of God. Moreover, the mind is not the place to know the will of God. He instructs us in our spirit.

Satan not only uses feelings and thoughts to cause the believers to live by the soul and not walk by the spirit; he has far worse devices. If he can succeed in causing a believer to live in the outward man through feelings or thoughts, he then takes a further step to disguise himself as the spirit within the believer. This is accomplished through first obtaining a position within the believer and then by fabricating many feelings. If the believer does not reject these feelings, they can gain ground within him. Soon they will overcome the function of the spirit or numb the sense of the spirit. If the believer is unaware of the enemy's tactics, the function of his spirit will be stopped. In following these deceiving feelings, he still considers himself to be following the spirit. Once the sense of the spirit stops and Satan takes this step to deceive, the believer will consider that God is leading him through his renewed mind. Through his failure to *use* his own spirit, Satan's operation will be secretly covered up. Once the spirit stops working, there can be no co-laboring with the Holy Spirit, and everything from God is cut off. Once the believer follows sudden thoughts and the feelings of the false spirit, he walks completely according to the flesh and soul, and there is no longer a genuine spiritual life.

If the believer is still ignorant, Satan will attack him even more fiercely. He may cause the believer to be void of the feeling of God's presence, but tell him that there is no need of feelings since he is living by faith. He may cause the believer to be in anguish without reason, but tell him that this is suffering with Christ in the spirit. In these conditions, Satan will deceive the believer through this counterfeit spirit, so that he actually follows his will. These experiences are common with spiritual (yet unwatchful) believers.

A spiritual believer must possess spiritual knowledge so that all his conduct and actions are according to his (spiritual) rationality. Consequently, he does not act according to impulsive emotion, some stress, or sudden thoughts in the mind. He ought not to be hasty or rushed. All of his doings must be done only after realizing that they are from God, based on observation with the spiritual eyes and apprehension with spiritual intuition. Nothing should be done out of impulse, feelings, or sudden thoughts. Decisions should only come after quiet, cool calculations and deliberations.

The most crucial point in a living of following the spirit is to search and test. In spiritual living, a believer must not pass his days in ignorance; everything that happens to him, whether thoughts or feelings (both happy and sad), must be thoroughly and carefully scrutinized to determine their source: God, Satan, or self. By nature every believer loves to be at ease. Whatever he encounters during the day is treated lightly; many times he even accepts the arrangements of the enemy. He does not investigate, but the Bible commands us

to "prove all things" (1 Thes. 5:21). The power and charac-
teristics of a spiritual believer come from "interpreting
spiritual things with spiritual words" (1 Cor. 2:13). In the
original language *interpret* means "compare," "test," "see
together," and "judge." This power can be attained by all
spiritual believers. The Holy Spirit gives them this power so
that in their living they will not allow the things that are
happening to them to go untested. Otherwise, it is very
difficult not to live a life under deceit from the evil spirit.

THE ACCUSATION OF SATAN

Satan has another way to attack the believer who diligently
follows the guidance of the intuition in spirit; he impersonates
the believer's conscience to accuse him. In order to keep the
conscience blameless, a believer is willing to accept the
accusations of the conscience and remove all the things
condemned by it. The enemy uses the desire of the believer
to accuse him, causing him to mistake this as the condemnation of his own conscience so that he will be without peace,
become weary of dealing with the problems, and lose his
boldness to go on.

Spiritual believers must know that Satan accuses us not
only before God but also within us. An accusation within
disturbs the believers into thinking that they have erred
and deserve some punishment. Satan realizes that believers
must have boldness in order to progress in the spiritual
journey. Therefore, through counterfeiting the conscience to
accuse the believers, he causes them to believe that they
have sinned, and thus they lose their fellowship with God.
The difficulty with the believers lies in not knowing how to
differentiate between the accusation of the evil spirit and
the condemnation of the conscience. Often they are afraid
of mistaking the condemnation of the conscience for the
accusation of the evil spirit and, consequently, disobeying
God. However, if they disregard the inner voice, it becomes
more and more intense and even uncontrollable. Spiritual
believers, therefore, not only must be willing to obey the
rebuking of the conscience, but also must be able to discern
the accusation of the evil spirit.

Sometimes, the accusation of the evil spirit is related to an actual sin of a believer. But sometimes the believer has not sinned, and the evil spirit still causes him to *feel* sinful. If the believer has really sinned, he can always confess immediately before God and ask for the cleansing of the precious blood (1 John 1:9). If the accusation still continues, it must be the voice of the evil spirit.

A believer can tell whether he has really erred and is under the reproach of his conscience or whether he is merely under the accusation of the evil spirit by asking himself whether he sincerely hates his sin. Before deciding whether it is the conscience or the evil spirit, it is very important that he ask himself this question: if I am truly wrong in this matter, am I willing to remove it and confess my sin? If he truly desires to follow the will of God and hates sin, then before submitting to the voice of accusation, he can be bold because he is not deliberately disobeying God. Having determined to do God's will, he must thoroughly investigate whether a matter was definitely done by him. He must clearly know and ascertain that it was his doings, because often the evil spirit accuses us of unrelated matters. If this was his doing, he must examine whether it was truly in error. After fully realizing his failure through the teaching of the Bible and the leading of the intuition, then and only then is he required to confess his sins to God. Otherwise, even though he may not have committed any sin, Satan will cause him to suffer as if he had really sinned.

The evil spirit can give all kinds of feelings to man. He can cause one to feel joyful or sorrowful. He can make one feel as if nothing is wrong or as if there is gross error. Just because a believer feels fine, it does not mean he is really all right. Many times, when he feels all right he is really wrong. Similarly, when he feels that he is wrong, it may not be so. Perhaps he only feels this way and is not really in error. However a believer may feel, he must prove with certainty what is really true so that he can decide whether he has sinned or not. As for all the accusations, a believer should take a neutral attitude. Before he acts, he must determine the source of the accusation. If he is still unclear whether it is the reproach of the Holy Spirit or the accusation of the evil spirit, he should wait patiently for evidence and not be anxious. If it is from the Holy Spirit, and he is sincerely willing to remove it, the present delay is not due to his rebellion but to uncertainty. A believer must absolutely reject the confession of sins compelled by an external power, because the enemy often uses this strategy.

In short, genuine self-condemnation caused by the Holy Spirit sanctifies us; Satan's purpose is merely for accusation. His accusation causes us to frequently accuse ourselves. His aim is none other than inflicting sufferings on us. Not only so, if a spiritual believer accepts his initial accusation, Satan can also give him a false peace so that the believer is not remorseful over his actual failures. This is the greatest damage. Concerning the rebuke of the conscience, everything will be all right after the confession of sin and a request for cleansing by the precious blood. But the accusation of the enemy does not cease even after the removal of the accusing matter. The reprimand of the conscience leads us to the precious blood, but the accusation of the evil spirit causes us to lose heart and consider ourselves to be hopelessly incurable. Satan's purpose, through his accusations, is to cause us to fall by thinking that "since we cannot be perfect, then we might as well let the things run their own course."

Sometimes, Satan's accusation is added to the rebuke of the conscience. Sin is present and not only does the conscience condemn, the evil spirit also accuses. Then after the believer obeys the will of the Holy Spirit, the voice still will not stop. A believer's determination to be completely separated from sin, leaving no ground for the evil spirit to accuse, is very crucial today. In addition, we must learn how to discern the rebuke of the Holy Spirit from the accusation of the evil spirit—knowing when it is just the accusation of the evil spirit, and when both the condemnation of the conscience and the accusation of the evil spirit are present. Actually, no matter what sin there is, if it is truly sin, after rejecting it and asking for the cleansing of the precious blood, the chiding of the Holy Spirit ceases.

FURTHER DANGERS

In the life of walking according to the spirit, spiritual believers should be aware of other dangers besides the disguise of Satan and his various attacks. Many times our own soul, for reasons of its own (without the counterfeiting of the evil spirit), initiates a certain feeling to prompt us to act. A believer must know that his body has feelings, his soul has feelings, and his spirit also has feelings. Not all feelings are from the spirit. Therefore, it is extremely important not to mistake the feelings from the soul or the body for the intuition of the spirit. In his daily experience, a believer must learn what really is his intuition and what is not. It is easy for a believer, after realizing the importance of following the intuition, to forget that other parts of his being besides his spirit have feelings, and thus he falls into error. A genuine spiritual living is not as difficult as some would think; in fact, it is rather simple. However, it is also not as easy as some may consider because it also has complex areas.

Here are two difficulties: first, we mistake other feelings as the intuition of the spirit; second, we misunderstand the meaning of the intuition. Such difficulties are often encountered in our daily life. Therefore, the teachings of the Bible (not verses randomly picked) are crucial. To prove whether the stirring within us and our intended actions are from the Holy Spirit, we need to check if this matter agrees with the teachings of the Bible. It is impossible for the Holy Spirit to inspire the prophets to write the Scriptures in one way, and then move in us in another way today. It is impossible that what the Holy Spirit has forbidden to others would be permissible to us today. The intuition in our spirit must be confirmed by the teachings of the Bible. By simply following the intuition and not the Bible, one will definitely go wrong. The revelation of the Holy Spirit sensed in our spirit perfectly matches the revelation of the Holy Spirit in the Bible.

Our flesh likes to exercise its power everywhere. Therefore, we must be watchful of its incursions even while we are following the teachings of the Bible. We know that the Bible completely reveals the mind of the Holy Spirit.

Therefore, we think that if we absolutely follow the Bible, we surely must be in accordance with the desire of the Holy Spirit. Not so! Many times a believer can use his own natural mental ability to search the doctrines of the Bible and, having understood, can determine to act accordingly. In this situation, there is the danger of comprehending and executing through the fleshly power. Although what was understood and carried out is completely according to the Bible, there was absolutely no reliance on the Holy Spirit. Instead, it was totally in the realm of the flesh. Not only should the intent of the Holy Spirit, as understood in our spirit, be confirmed by the Bible, but even the Scriptures, as understood by us, should be executed through the spirit. We should realize that even in the matter of following the Bible, the flesh desires to be first! The spirit has not only the intuition but also the power. If the doctrines that we understand in our minds are not executed through the power of the spirit, they have no spiritual value at all.

One more matter requires our attention. There is a great danger for us to live excessively by our own spirit or walk excessively according to our own spirit. Although the Bible attaches great importance to the individual spirit of the believer, we may fall into the danger of being extreme. The importance of a believer's spirit is due to its being indwellt by the Holy Spirit. We live and walk according to the spirit because this spirit is indwelt by the Holy Spirit, who makes known His will through our spirit. The guidance and restriction we receive are the guidance and restriction of the Holy Spirit. Since the Holy Spirit moves through our spirit when we pay much attention it, we also pay considerable attention to our spirit, an organ usable by Him. But there is a danger, having understood the work and function of the human spirit, of relying solely on the spirit and forgetting that it is merely a servant of the Holy Spirit. The One that we directly look to for leading us into all truth is not our spirit but the Holy Spirit. We must realize that apart from the Holy Spirit, the human spirit is just as useless as the other parts of our being. We must never reverse the positions of the human spirit and the Holy Spirit. We have spoken in great detail of the human spirit only because believers today hardly know its functions. This does not mean that the position of the Holy Spirit within man is lower than that of the human spirit. We need to understand the human spirit in order that we may better know how to obey and exalt the Holy Spirit.

This is greatly related to receiving guidance. From the beginning, the imparting of the Holy Spirit is meant for the entire Body of Christ. The indwelling of the Holy Spirit in the individual believer is due to His indwelling in the entire Body of Christ, because a believer is a member in the Body. The work of the Holy Spirit is of a corporate nature (1 Cor. 12:12). He guides individuals because He guides the whole Body. The guidance of the individual is for the whole Body. The actions of a member affect the entire Body. The leading of the Holy Spirit in our spirit individually must be related to the other members. All spiritual leadings are the leading of the Body. Therefore, even though we may have the leading individually in our spirit, we still should seek the concurrence, the proof, and the sympathy from the spirit of "two or three" other members. Such actions in the relatedness of the Body must never be neglected in a spiritual work. Much of the failure, fighting, hatred, division, shame, and pain is due to believers (with good intentions), who acted alone according to their own spirit. Hence, all the believers following the spirit ought to judge whether their guidance comes from the Holy Spirit according to the relatedness of the spiritual Body. Our work, actions, faith, and teachings must be by the relatedness of the members.

In his last journey to Jerusalem, the apostle Paul fell into this mistake. God allowed His best apostle to err in order to teach us. In Paul's mistake, God was especially merciful to cover him. Only out of this mistake could he witness at Rome and have time to write so many Epistles. Paul thought that he was "bound in the spirit" (Acts 20:22) to go up, but the Bible says that the disciples at Tyre, who were moved by the Holy Spirit, told him not to go up (Acts 21:4). Although we know that God was especially merciful to cover the apostle in this failure, we should see the principle of God's leading—

not only is it of the individual but also of the corporate body. A spiritual believer should know when to go on alone, without regard to others' advice, and when to listen to his brothers.

In summary, there are many traps along the roadside of the spiritual path. A little carelessness can defeat a believer. We have no shortcuts. Learning a little knowledge cannot safeguard us forever. On the contrary, everything must be personally experienced by us. Those who were before us can only point out the coming dangers to save us from falling. There is no such thing as expecting certain methods to help us bypass considerable travel on the spiritual path. Faithful followers of the Lord will always see fewer unnecessary failures.

Chapter Two

THE LAWS OF THE SPIRIT

A believer must learn to know the sense of the spirit because this is the first condition of walking according to the spirit. If he does not know what is the sense of the spirit and the feeling of the soul, he will not be able to walk according to the spirit. When we are hungry, we know that we must eat. When we are cold, we know that we should put on clothes. Our senses tell us our needs and demands. A man must be able to interpret the senses in his body before he will know how to meet its needs with material things. In the same way, a believer must learn to know the senses in his spirit—what they mean, what their demands are, and how to meet their demands. Only when a believer knows the senses of his spirit can he walk according to the spirit.

There are a few things concerning the laws of the spirit which we must know. Because we do not understand the laws of the spirit and the importance of the senses of the spirit, many times when the spirit expresses its desires, we are still ignorant of them. Since we fail to identify the many things that come from the spirit as being spiritual, the spirit loses its place in our daily life. After we know that the spirit has the function of the intuition, fellowship, and conscience, we must still learn to know its activities and how to walk according to this spirit. After we have been filled with the Holy Spirit, our spirit will surely become very active. If we then ignore it, we will suffer loss. It is very important to have a habit of examining the moving of the spirit. We should know the activities of our spirit more than the activities of our mind.

THE WEIGHT OF THE SPIRIT

The spirit should be kept in a very free condition. It should constantly be light, as though soaring in the air. Only then will life grow and the work go on unhindered. For this reason, a believer must know the meaning of spiritual weight. Many times he feels that his spirit is suppressed and not free; a thousand pounds of weight seem to press upon him. When he searches for a reason for such weight, he may not find any. Furthermore, many times this weight creeps in suddenly upon a believer without his even noticing it. This weight is the enemy's means of suppressing spiritual believers; it takes away their joy and lightness so that they can no longer work with the Holy Spirit, and consequently, they lose their spiritual effectiveness. If believers do not understand the source of this weight and the meaning of the suppression in their spirit, they will not know how to deal with it in order to immediately recover their spirit to a state of normalcy.

Believers may wonder about the cause of such feelings. They may think that this is something natural or accidental. They may heedlessly allow their spirit to be suppressed. Many times believers ignore such weight and continue with their work, only to find that it becomes worse and worse. They do not realize that the enemy is playing tricks on them with the weight. Many times, God wants to use these believers, but they are not able to fulfill God's work because of this weight. Under this suppression, spiritual senses become very dull. This is why Satan and his evil spirits concentrate their efforts on applying weight to the believers' spirit and on taking away their freedom. Unfortunately, many believers do not realize that this weight comes from Satan. Even if they know, they do not reject it; they allow it to remain.

If believers carry this weight around with them, they will fail. If they find themselves with this weight in the morning and do not immediately remove it, they will be defeated the entire day. A free spirit is the basis for victory. We must have a perfectly unbound spirit before we can battle with the enemy and live out God's life. If there is any pressure in a believer's spirit, he will lose his power of discernment and the genuine leading from God. When the spirit is suppressed, the mind is affected, and when the mind fails to work, everything stops or runs into error.

Hence, once you experience pressure or weight in your spirit, it is very important for you to *immediately* deal with it. You must never allow this condition to continue. If you allow it to continue, you will suffer, and the weight will become heavier and heavier. If you do not try to remove it, you will become accustomed to it after a period of time and not try to remove it at all. Subconsciously this weight will become part of your life. You will find that all spiritual things appear burdensome, and you will find it hard to go on in the spiritual journey. If you do not deal with such weight the first time, it will come back more easily the next time. The way to deal with it is to immediately stop what you are doing and take care of the demand of the spiritual senses. You should immediately reject this weight with your will and refuse it through the exercise of your spirit. Sometimes you have to speak a word to oppose this weight. Sometimes you have to reject it in prayer by the exercise of spiritual strength. If you do this, the evil spirits will not be able to weigh down your spirit.

However, another necessary step is to remove the cause of this weight. If the cause is not removed, the weight will remain. Hence, while you are rejecting the work of the enemy, you should, at the same time, reject the cause of the enemy's work. If you do this, you will claim back the ground that you have given to the enemy. If you have the power of discernment, you will see that you have failed because you did not cooperate with God at certain times and in certain matters. When this happens, the enemy gains an opportunity to oppress you with weight. This ground must be reclaimed. You must reject the cause of the enemy's work which comes as a result of your failures. If you do this, the enemy will flee away.

THE BLOCKAGE OF THE SPIRIT

The spirit requires the soul and the body to be the organs for its expression. The spirit is like the lady of the house, and the steward and servant must carry out the lady's wishes. The spirit is also like electricity, and there must be a filament before it can express its light. If the soul and body are attacked by the evil spirits and become abnormal, the spirit will be blocked and have no outlets. The enemy knows the importance of the spirit. He often works in a believer's soul and body, causing them to lose their function so that the spirit no longer has an organ for its expression. By this, the spirit loses its victorious position.

At such times, the mind may come under attack and become confused. The emotion may feel lonely and sad, and the will may feel tired and lifeless, unable to direct the person. The body may feel very weak or somewhat lazy. If the believers' soul and body are attacked, and if they do not oppose it right away, their spirit will be blocked; they will not be able to fight vigorously with the enemy and maintain their victorious ground.

Once a believer's spirit is blocked, he loses his vigor. He will appear shy or withdrawn, and he will not want to do anything in public. He will prefer to retreat to the rear of the battle line, and he will not want to expose himself. He may think that this is an enlightenment for him, but actually this is a blockage of his spirit. When he reads the Bible, he does not seem to have much energy. When he prays, he does not seem to have any words to say. When he considers his spiritual work and experience, they seem meaningless and even, at times, silly. When he preaches, he does not sense any result and feels that he is only going through the motions. If this condition persists, the believer will come under further attack and find himself choked and muffled. This will continue unless God intervenes through other men or through his own prayer. If a believer does not have the proper knowledge, he will become very bewildered. Usually he does not try to search for the reason, but instead allows it to go on. Strictly speaking, every spiritual experience and feeling has a cause to it. We should study it carefully and not allow it to remain in us indefinitely.

Such an experience happens when there is a blockage of the spirit. The soul and body outside the spirit have been locked up, and the spirit has no chance to express itself. Satan has imprisoned the spirit and locked it up in a dark room so that the soul no longer has the leading of the spirit. Once the thing that blocks the spirit is removed, the believer will find the outlets cleared, and he will recover his former lightness.

It is very important for a believer at such times to exercise his will to speak *aloud*. He should speak words of rebuke against the enemy, and he should speak out with a loud voice the victory of the cross and the defeat of the enemy. He should single-mindedly oppose the enemy's work in his soul and body. The will must stand behind a person's words and actively reject all blockages. Prayer is another way. Prayer is often the way to remove the blockages. But at these times, one has to pray *out loud*. The best kind of prayer at such a time is to call on the victorious name of the Lord Jesus and withstand all the attacks of the enemy. One should also exercise his spirit and channel its strength to break open a way to come out.

THE POISONING OF THE SPIRIT

A believer's spirit can become poisoned by evil spirits. This is what the fiery darts of the enemy do. He can shoot his darts directly into a believer's spirit. He can shoot sorrow, sadness, suffering, grief, and heartbreak into a believer's spirit, causing him to have a "sorrowful spirit" (1 Sam. 1:15). "But a wounded spirit who can bear?" (Prov. 18:14). Hence, this greatly affects a person. When a believer feels sorrowful, he thinks he is feeling sorrowful, considering this sorrow to be very natural. He does not try to find out its cause nor does he try to oppose it at all. He accepts everything that comes to him silently and without any objection. We have to remember that this is very dangerous. We can never accept a thought carelessly or allow any feeling to come into us. If we want to walk according to the spirit, we have to be watchful in everything; we must study all our thoughts and feelings and find out where they come from.

Sometimes Satan causes our spirit to become hard, stubborn, narrow, selfish, wild, and disobedient. Consequently, the spirit is not able to cooperate with the Holy Spirit and carry out God's will. We will lose all of our love for men and all of our gentleness, sympathy, and considerations for the weaknesses of others. When this happens, the Holy Spirit cannot use us to any great extent; we will have lost the Lord's broadness and set up a boundary for ourselves.

Sometimes the enemy puts an unforgiving spirit into the believers. This is the most frequent poison that believers take in. This probably accounts for the majority of the cases of failure in spiritual believers. This kind of poison, such as fastidiousness and vengeance, is the most deadly poison to the spiritual life. Even after a believer has suffered from this poison, most of the time he will still not be clear about what happened or realize that this poison came from Satan. Instead, he thinks that *he* hates others and that this cannot be removed.

Sometimes Satan causes believers to become narrow. He will cause believers to set a boundary for themselves and separate themselves from others. If believers do not have the concept of the church being the Body of Christ, instead making their own little group their foremost concern, it is a sign that their spirit has dwindled and become narrow. A spiritual believer considers God's business as his own business and the whole church as the object of his love. If his spirit is open, the river of life will flow everywhere. But if he becomes narrow, he will frustrate God's work and minimize his own usefulness. If our spirit is not big enough to include all of God's children, it means that our spirit has been poisoned.

Sometimes Satan causes the believers' spirit to become proud. In this way they become boastful, self-respecting, and self-esteeming. Satan causes the believers to think that they are not destitute, that they are somewhat important, and that they have some worth in God's work. This kind of spirit is also a great cause for the believers' failures. "Pride goeth before destruction, / and a haughty spirit before a fall" (Prov. 16:18).

The evil spirits inject such things together with other poisons into the believers' spirit. If the believers do not oppose these things immediately, they will quickly turn into things of the flesh. If believers know how to live in the spirit, these things will only be Satan's poison at the beginning; they will not have an opportunity to become a sin of the flesh. However, if believers do not oppose them, subconsciously accepting them instead, they will soon turn into sins of the flesh.

If the spirit is poisoned, and the poison is not quickly dealt with, it will turn into sins in the spirit. Sins in the spirit are more serious than any other sins. "Lord, do You want us to command fire to come down from heaven and consume them? But turning, He rebuked them and said, You do not know of what kind of spirit you are" (Luke 9:54-55). The kind of spirit we have is very important. Many times our spirit is stirred up by Satan, and we do not know it. Once the spirit errs, everything else errs.

When we consider the experience of the two disciples, we can see that a wrong spirit is very easily detected in our words. However, the words probably do not reveal as much as one's tone of voice. Many times the words may be right, but the tone is wrong. If we want to overcome, we have to take care of the tone in our speaking. Once evil spirits touch our spirit, our tone will lose its gentleness. All harsh voices, rash voices, and sharp voices do not come from the Holy Spirit. Rather, they are a sign that the ones with these voices have already been stirred up by Satan's poisons.

How do we ordinarily speak? When we speak about others, can we speak without any sense of condemnation? Perhaps what we say is true, but a spirit of criticism, condemnation, wrath, and jealousy may be lurking behind truthful words. We should speak the truth in love. If our spirit is pure and meek, we can speak the truth. But if a spirit of condemnation is lurking behind our words, we are committing a sin. Sin is not only an act, but also a condition. The spirit behind all of our actions is very important. Many times we can be working for God or man and committing sins at the same time. The work may be done, but a spirit of dishonesty, unwillingness, or grudge is hidden behind it.

We should maintain our spirit in a sweet and tender condition. Our spirit should be clean and pure. Do we consider a wrong spirit a sin? When does the enemy attack our spirit? When is our spirit poisoned? If we know about sins, will we remove them humbly? When we detect a hardening of our tone, we should immediately stop and not go on. We should immediately say to others, "I would rather say the same words with a clean spirit. I would rather oppose the enemy." If we are not willing to tell our brothers that we are wrong, our spirit retains its sins. Believers should learn to guard their spirit from the provocation of the enemy and to guard their spirit in sweetness and gentleness.

Ordinarily a believer should have the shield of faith for the quenching of the flaming darts of the evil one. This means that he should exercise a living faith to oppose the attacks of the enemy and should trust in God's protection. Faith is our shield; it is not our extracting pliers. It is for quenching the fiery darts, not for pulling them out.

If believers are hit by the darts, they should immediately remove the cause of the fiery darts and take up an opposing stand. They should immediately reject everything from the enemy and pray for God's cleansing.

THE DEPRESSION OF THE SPIRIT

Believers become depressed in their spirit mostly when they turn inward to look at themselves. It may also be due to the fact that the soul-life is still functioning and has not yet been replaced. As a result, they consider all the experiences as their own. It may also be caused by the invasion of the power of darkness from the outside, or even by self-centered prayer and worship. If the believers' spirit is turned inward instead of outward, God's power will immediately stop. If they do not deal with this introspection immediately, they will quickly find themselves surrounded by the soul.

Sometimes the spirit will indulge in the soul. This happens when believers are deceived by the evil spirits. The evil spirits give believers bodily feelings and all kinds of strange, happy experiences. If the believers are not alert, they will think that these things are from God, and they will subconsciously live in the world of feelings and drag the spirit into the place of the soul.

Sometimes believers are deceived, and their spirits are depressed because they do not understand the position Christ holds. The Holy Spirit abides in the believers for the purpose of unveiling to them the Christ that is sitting on the throne.

The books of Acts, Ephesians, and Hebrews clearly depict Christ's position *in heaven* today. The believers' spirit is joined to the heavenly Christ, but in their ignorance, they may turn inward to look for Christ. They may try to be joined to the Christ within them. In this way, their spirit cannot be uplifted above the clouds, and they are depressed and fall into the realm of the soul.

In short, these activities keep the believers in a life of feeling rather than a life in the spirit. The believers should realize that before they were spiritual, they did not live practically in the spirit, and there was no need for much counterfeit work from the enemy. But once they have experienced the power of the Holy Spirit infused into their spirit, a new world seems to open up before them. It is a world that they have never known before. The danger lies here. Satan's work is to prevent the believers from living a life in the spirit, because such a life is very damaging to him. His tactic is to entice and deceive the believers with the senses of the soul and the body, causing them to think that these are spiritual experiences to indulge in.

Many believers have entered into a spiritual living. Yet because they do not understand the laws of the spirit, they fail. Satan will give believers all kinds of physical feelings and supernatural experiences. If believers depend on outward, supernatural things or spiritual experiences in their senses, they will suffer many hindrances in the spiritual life within their spirit. When this happens, believers will live in the outward soul or the body which frustrates the innermost spirit from working together with God. Under such circumstances, the soul and the body will surely be uplifted once again; they will gain ascendancy, and the spirit will eventually be completely submerged.

When the spirit is depressed, its senses are suppressed. This is the reason many spiritual believers often feel that their spirit is gone. When the soul and the body occupy too prominent a position, and when the whole person lives by the senses, the soul and the body will have an acute feeling of suppression, suffering, and conflict. When this happens, man's senses will supersede the work of the spirit, and the senses of the spirit will be buried under the strong feelings of the soul and the body. As a result, all spiritual living and work will come to a standstill. If this continues for a long time, the person will become completely fallen and may even become possessed by the evil spirits.

Therefore, we have to reject everything that kills the spirit's senses. We should reject uncontrollable laughter, deep grief, and all of the intense signals from the body. The body should be completely calm. It is even wrong to feel supernatural things and to be overly sensitive towards natural things. These things will only cause the mind to walk according to the body, not according to the spirit. We should not allow anything to stop us from knowing the smallest senses in the spirit.

Once the spirit is depressed, the soul surrounds the spirit and controls the spirit. Hence, a believer must learn to maintain his spirit in a constant outward posture; it should never turn itself inward. A believer should realize that if his spirit is not turned outward in an assault on Satan, Satan will attack his spirit instead and cause his spirit to become depressed. Only when the believers' spirit is flowing outward will the Holy Spirit spread His own life to others through their spirit. If believers turn to themselves and suppress their spirit, the flow of the Holy Spirit is immediately blocked. The *outflow and gushing forth* of the Holy Spirit is carried out through the believers' spirit. If the believers turn inward and suppress their spirit, the life of the Holy Spirit will not be able to flow out.

Hence, believers have to know the reason for any depression in their spirit, and they should know how to recover their spirit to its original position. Once a believer detects any leakage in his spirit, he should realize that his spirit is sick and that he should seek a remedy at once.

THE BURDEN OF THE SPIRIT

There is a difference between the burden of the spirit and the weight of the spirit. The weight of the spirit is from Satan, and its purpose is to cause believers to suffer; Satan uses the weight to suppress them. The burden of the spirit,

however, is from God. Its purpose is to make known His will
and secure the believers' cooperation. The weight of the spirit
has no other purpose except to suppress. As such, it is useless
and fruitless. The burden of the spirit is a burden from God,
and its goal is to cause men to work, intercede, and preach
for God. Such a burden is purposeful, reasonable, and
profitable. Believers must differentiate between the burden
in their spirit and the weight in their spirit.

Satan does not give any burden to the believers; he only
surrounds the believers' spirit and *oppresses* the believers
with the weight. Satan's weight causes the believers' spirit
to be bound and their minds to stop functioning. A person
who bears a burden only has to bear the burden itself; but a
person who is oppressed is bound in his whole being. Once
the power of darkness comes to a believer, he loses his freedom
immediately. However, a burden from God is not like this. No
matter how heavy God's burden is, it will never be so heavy
that a person cannot pray. The *freedom* of prayer will never
be lost under any kind of burden. But the weight imposed
by the enemy takes away the believers' freedom in prayer. In
fact, except for some wrestling and withstanding prayers, this
weight cannot be removed. God's burden is removed once we
pray. But this is not true with the weight from the enemy.
Moreover, the weight of the spirit creeps in secretly, while
the burden in the spirit is the result of the Holy Spirit's work
in our spirit. The weight of the spirit is painful and
suppresses the believers' life; the burden in the spirit is joyful
because it cooperates with God (cf. Matt. 11:30). (Of course,
the flesh does not feel joyful about the spirit's burden.
Furthermore, this burden is also painful if one does not meet
its demands.)

All real work begins first with a burden in the spirit. (Of
course, when we do not have a burden in the spirit, there is
the need to exercise the mind.) When God wants us to do
something, say something, or pray for something, He first
gives us a burden in our spirit. If we know the laws of the
spirit, we will not rashly continue on with the work in our
hands, allowing the burden to become heavier and heavier.
(Perhaps when we allow the matter to go on for a long time,

the sense for the burden may be lost.) We should drop everything and study the *burden*. After we understand the meaning of the burden, we should walk according to what we know. When everything is accomplished, the burden will be gone from us.

Ordinarily, a believer's spirit must be free and unsuppressed before it can receive burdens from God. Only a free spirit can sense the move of the Holy Spirit. A spirit that has been filled with weight is no longer keen in its intuition and cannot be a good vessel anymore. Many times a believer receives a burden from God, yet he cannot carry out the requirements of the burden. As a result his spirit suffers for many days from the burden, and he is not able to receive any fresh burden from God. Hence, it is very important to find out the meaning of a burden in prayer by the Holy Spirit and through the exercise of the mind.

Many times the burden in the spirit is for us to pray (Col. 4:12). Actually, we cannot pray more than our burden. To continue to pray without a burden is surely ineffective, and it comes from the self-will. The burden of *prayer* that comes from the spirit can only be relieved through *prayer*. Actually, all burdens are this way. If God burdens our spirit with a certain burden, we can only relieve the burden in our spirit by fulfilling what God wants us to do, either through prayer or through proclaiming His message. Only when we have a burden in our spirit to pray can we pray in the Holy Spirit, and only then can we pray with groanings which cannot be uttered. When there is a burden in our spirit to pray, nothing can alleviate this burden and nothing can release us except prayer. When the things we pray for are accomplished, the burden is immediately lifted from us.

Many times believers have accumulated too many burdens of prayer in their spirit. When they begin to pray, it seems to be a very painful task. But the more the believers pray, the more their spirit will say amen. We must try our best to thoroughly pray out what is burdening us in our spirit, until the burden is fully removed from us. The more we express our life in our prayers as well as everything we have, the more comfortable we will become. But there is a temptation in this kind of prayer to stop praying before the burden is gone. Most believers think that as soon as they are somewhat relieved in their spirit, their prayers are answered. Actually this is the time when proper spiritual work begins. If we turn away to do other things at this juncture, the spiritual work will suffer.

Believers must not be misled to think that all spiritual works are happy and joyful; nor should they think that once there is some kind of burden, they have lost their spiritual experience. It is very unfortunate that believers do not realize that the burden in the spirit is the source of real spiritual work. Only those who suffer in this way for God and men truly do not live for themselves. All the other ones who seek for joy in their feelings and who are afraid of taking up any burden for the church are living for themselves and are soulish. Hence, when God gives us a burden, we should not think that we have fallen or that we have committed some errors. Satan loves to see us think this way, for this kind of thinking spares him from our attacks. We should not misunderstand ourselves. If we listen to Satan and think that there is something wrong with us, we will come under his accusations even more and suffer.

Genuine spiritual work is an assault on Satan and a travail in birth for the believers. There is indeed no joy to this! This requires one to die to the self in the deepest way. For this reason, no soulish believer can truly participate in spiritual work. Having a happy feeling all day long is not a proof of a believer's spirituality. The right kind of believers advance with God without caring for their own feelings. Many times when believers are burdened in their spirit to fight with the enemy, they prefer to be alone and cut off all fellowship with the world, so that they can concentrate in their warfare with the enemy. At the end of this warfare, it is difficult to find any trace of a smile on their face. Hence, all spiritual believers should welcome the burdens from the Lord.

Believers must know the laws of the spirit and the way to cooperate with God. Otherwise, they will neglect such burdens and consequently suffer. Soon they even lose their burdens and do not participate in the most glorious co-labor with God.

Therefore, every time there is a burden in the spirit, they should immediately find out what the burden is in prayer. If it is a call to fight, they should fight. If it is a call to preach the gospel, they should preach the gospel. If it is a call to prayer, they should pray. They should seek to work together with God. They should move the old burdens out of the way, so that the new burdens can come.

THE EBBING OF THE SPIRIT

This means that God's life and power can ebb away in the believers' spirit like the ebbing away of the tide. When believers are soulish, they consider it as a spiritual peak when they feel God's presence in their *feelings* making them feel happy. If they feel dry and restless, they think that their spiritual life is at its worst. However, this is only what they feel in their feelings; it does not reflect the real condition of their spiritual life.

Of course, there are times when the spiritual life is indeed low. This is different from the times when a person is in the feeling of the soul. After a believer is filled with the Holy Spirit, he will continue to advance for a time. But soon, he will *gradually* have setbacks. It will not happen suddenly. This is the difference between the ebbing away in feeling and a setback in reality. In the former case it happens suddenly; in the latter case it happens gradually. In the latter case, a person feels that the life and power within his spirit, which he once received, have suffered a gradual setback. At such times he loses the joy, peace, and power in the spirit that he once had. Day by day, he becomes weaker and weaker. Soon he feels that he has lost all taste for fellowship with God; he finds it meaningless to read the Bible, and no message or any special Scripture moves his heart. Even if he is touched by something, it is not as intense as before. Prayer becomes dry, tasteless, and meaningless, and he seems to have nothing to pray about. He finds no joy in testifying, and there is no more outflow as before. The life is not as strong as before, nor as exciting, soaring, and joyful. Everything seems to have subsided.

There is indeed ebbing and rising with the tide. But is

there an ebbing and rising in our spirit as well when it only has God's life and power? God's life does not ebb; it is forever flowing. His life is not like the tide of the sea which rises and falls; it is like a river which flows forever with living water (John 7:38). God's life within us is not like the tide which must ebb after a certain time. The source of life within us is God; He never changes, and with Him there is no shadow of turning. Hence, the life in our spirit should flow unceasingly and should continue to overflow and spread.

If a believer feels that his life has ebbed away, he should realize that his life is not ebbing away; it has merely stopped flowing. He should realize that this ebbing is absolutely unnecessary. We should never be deceived by Satan to think that as long as a man lives in his flesh, he can never again be filled with God's life continuously. God's life is a river of living water within us. If there is no hindrance, it flows on forever. It is possible for believers to have a lasting, flowing experience. Any kind of ebbing is unnecessary and abnormal.

Hence, the question is not one of the ebbing away of the spiritual life but of doing something to make it rise again. The present need is not a question of filling the river but one of facilitating the flow. The river of life remains in the believers, but it is blocked. The inlet is still open, but the outlet is stopped. Because there is no flow, the water of life cannot go out. As soon as the outlet is cleared, the water of life will flow out unceasingly. Hence, a believer does not need more life but more outflow of life.

Once a believer feels that his spiritual life appears to be ebbing away, he should find out where it is blocked. Satan will make you feel that your spiritual life has regressed. Others may feel that you have lost your spiritual power. You yourself may even think that you have committed some great sin. This may be true, but it may not necessarily be true. Actually, the real reason is that *many believers* do not know how to cooperate with God and fulfill God's condition for having an unceasing flow. Ignorance is the greatest cause of such a phenomenon. Therefore, a believer should immediately pray, meditate, test, and search. You should wait on God and ask the Spirit to reveal the reason for the "ebbing away." You should be living and find out if you have failed to fulfill some conditions for a continual flow of the spiritual life which lead to such an "ebbing away."

Not only should you acknowledge that you have setbacks—an important step in itself—but you should actively seek the reason for such setbacks. Although the propositions of Satan, other men, and yourself are all unreliable, they are worth some consideration because sometimes they can be true. Once you find the reason, you should immediately repudiate it. Do not imagine that spiritual life flows out spontaneously. If you do not remove the reason for the blockage, the flow will not resume.

Hence, every time there is a spiritual "ebbing away," we should immediately find the reason through prayer and meditation. We should understand the law for God's life to flow and repudiate all the works of the enemy. If we do this, life will flow again, and we will be invigorated once more. The spirit will become more powerful than before and strengthened to storm the strongholds of the enemy.

THE NEGLIGENCE OF RESPONSIBILITY OF THE SPIRIT

The human spirit is like an electric light. When it comes into contact with the Holy Spirit, it becomes full of light. When it is detached from the Spirit, it immediately becomes dark. The spirit of man is the lamp of the Lord (Prov. 20:27). God's goal is to fill it with light. Yet many times a believer's spirit becomes darkened. This is because his spirit has lost contact with the Holy Spirit, and as a result it becomes darkened. If we want to know whether a believer's spirit has been isolated from the Holy Spirit, all we need to see is whether the spirit has lost its light.

We have said that God's Holy Spirit dwells in man's spirit. Man cooperates with the Holy Spirit through his spirit. When the human spirit deviates from its normal condition, it becomes isolated from the Holy Spirit and loses its light. It is very important for a believer to maintain his spirit in a healthy condition, so that it can cooperate with the Holy Spirit. If the spirit is troubled by outward circumstances, it immediately becomes useless; it is not be able to cooperate with the Holy Spirit and becomes darkened.

All of the above situations can cause the spirit to neglect its responsibility and fail to cooperate with the Holy Spirit. Once the spirit has neglected its responsibility, victory becomes impossible. If a believer feels that his spirit is gone when he wakes up in the morning, the enemy may make him think that he has worked too hard the night before and that his body is tired. If believers are not on the alert, they will allow their spirit to neglect its responsibility. They will find that they have no strength to withstand the temptations of the day and to fulfill the work of the day. They should immediately look into the matter, realizing that their body should not affect their spirit; rather, their spirit should be living and strong, controlling their body. After they understand this, they should confess that their spirit has neglected its duty and is under the attack of the enemy. At such times they should immediately attempt to recover their former condition. If they do not do this, they will fail when they go out to meet others. When our spirit neglects its duty in the morning, we must not allow it to continue this way throughout the day, because this is the way of defeat.

After the believers realize that their spirit has neglected its duty, they should immediately reject all the works of Satan and the cause of all his works. If it is an attack from the enemy, their spirit will be free once they repudiate the attack. But if there is some other reason for the attack, meaning that the believers have given the enemy some ground, they should study the reason for the attacks and remove its ground accordingly. This is very much related to the believers' past history. They should consider how the enemy has attacked their spirit and consider their environment, family, relatives, children, and careers. They should pray over these things one by one. If they feel that they should pray for something, and while praying feel somewhat relieved in their spirit, they should realize that they have identified the cause of the attack. They should then remove the cause before God. After they pray, they should be free, and their spirit should resume its functions. Sometimes the spirit's negligence of duty occurs when believers leave their spirit alone and do not exercise control over it or direct it in the right track. "The spirits of prophets are subject to prophets" (1 Cor. 14:32). Those who "follow their own spirit" are "the foolish prophets" (Ezek. 13:3). This is very important. If believers do not exercise their will to control their spirit, to prevent it from being too much or too little, and if they do not maintain a cooperation between their spirit and the Holy Spirit, their spirit has neglected its duty. Believers should realize that the human spirit can become wild. This is why Proverbs says that there is a "haughty spirit" (Prov. 16:18). Man's spirit can act independently of the Holy Spirit. If a believer does not exercise any control over his spirit and make it subject to the Holy Spirit, it can act independently. Hence, a believer must be on the alert all the time and not allow his spirit to deviate from God's track or from a quiet fellowship with God; otherwise, he will no longer be able to cooperate with God.

Sometimes, the negligence of duty in the spirit is caused by a hardening of the believer's spirit. God needs a tender spirit for His will to be expressed. If the spirit is haughty, self-assured, and not humble, the work of the Holy Spirit will be hindered. Only a yielding spirit will fulfill the Holy Spirit's will. A believer must have a willing spirit (Exo. 35:21), and he must be willing to respond to the will of the Holy Spirit within the shortest period of time. A believer's spirit must be very sensitive to be able to sense the small voice of the Holy Spirit and respond immediately. If there is the slightest stubbornness in a believer's spirit, he will not be able to carry out God's will and hear the voice of the Holy Spirit within his spirit. Hence, believers must maintain their spirit in a pliable condition and always follow the tender sense in their spirit. This is what the apostle meant when he said, "Do not quench the Spirit" (1 Thes. 5:19). Believers should be careful to follow all the work, feeling, and sense of the spirit. If they do this, the sense of their spirit will become keener and keener. Moreover, God will make His will known to them.

If believers desire to walk according to the spirit, they should know when their spirit has become negligent in its duty, no longer cooperating with the Holy Spirit. They should also know why it has neglected its duty. They should guard their spirit watchfully and keep it in constant simplicity and calmness. Then they can fellowship with God and oppose all the distractions from the enemy and from themselves which take away its peaceful contact with God.

THE CONDITION OF THE SPIRIT

In summary, a believer must understand all the laws of the spirit before he can walk according to the spirit. If he is not watchful, and does not cooperate with God, he will become fallen. The most important law of the spirit is to examine the condition of the spirit. An examination of the condition of the spirit is the central issue that we have spoken about in the above discussion.

A believer should understand the condition of his own spirit. He should know the normal condition of the spirit and when the spirit has lost its normalcy. The spirit should rule over man's soul and body; it should have the highest preeminence and be the most powerful part. A believer should check to see if this is indeed the condition of his spirit. He should know if his spirit has lost its normalcy and is being agitated through warfare or the environment. There are generally four kinds of conditions with the spirit:

(1) The spirit is oppressed and suffers a setback.

(2) The spirit is calm, steady, and in the proper position.

(3) The spirit is agitated and forced to overreact.

(4) The spirit is defiled and has become sick (2 Cor. 7:1); it has given ground to sin.

A believer must at least know these four conditions of his spirit, and he must know how to deal with them. Many times through his own carelessness or through the attacks of the enemy, a believer's spirit is "pushed aside," and becomes depressed. At such times, he loses his heavenly, bright, and victorious position and becomes cold, crippled, and flattened. The spirit can become depressed through sorrow or a hundred other reasons, losing its soaring joy. When the spirit is oppressed, it falls below the line of normalcy.

Sometimes the spirit can also be agitated and moved beyond its proper position. A believer can be excited in the soul and become ecstatic to the extent that his spirit is agitated and loses its calmness. Sometimes a believer follows the "creaturely vigor" to the extent that he has an "unrestrained spirit." Uncontrollable laughter and many other reasons can cause the spirit to become wild and uncontrollable. Prolonged warfare with the enemy can also result in overactivity of the spirit. Satan can cause a believer's spirit to become overstretched during or after Satan's conflict with him to the extent that he cannot stop his spirit's activity and hold his composure. Satan can give believers a strange kind of happiness or many other things that cause their spirit to act beyond the control of their mind or will. When this happens, believers are no longer able to guard themselves, and they fail.

Sometimes, the spirit is neither too high nor too low, but it is defiled. Sometimes the defilement appears as an attitude in one's spirit like stubbornness and disobedience. Sometimes it appears as sins in the spirit like pride and jealousy. At still other times, it appears as a mixture of soulish activities in the spirit like natural love, feelings, and thoughts. Once the spirit is defiled, it has to be cleansed (2 Cor. 7:1; 1 John 1:9).

If a believer desires to walk according to the spirit, he must understand his spirit's condition. Is his spirit in a calm and proper condition, or is it in a position that is too low, too high, or defiled? He should know how to uplift his suppressed spirit so that it will match the standard of the Holy Spirit. He should know how to exercise his will to stop the hyperactive spirit and turn it back to its normal condition. He should know how to cleanse his defiled spirit so that he can once again work with God.

CHAPTER THREE

THE PRINCIPLE OF THE MIND
ASSISTING THE SPIRIT

If a believer desires to walk according to the spirit, he must know the laws of the spirit. Only those who know the laws of the spirit are able to understand the various senses of the spirit and their meaning and walk according to the demand of the senses in the spirit. All of the demands of the spirit are expressed through its senses. Ignoring the senses of the spirit will cause us to miss the demands of our spirit. Hence, understanding and walking according to the laws of the spirit are very crucial in our spiritual life.

However, in addition to understanding the laws of the spirit, believers who walk according to the spirit have to know another matter: the principle of the mind assisting the spirit. This principle is no less important than the laws of the spirit. In the pathway of walking according to the spirit, this principle has to be constantly applied. Understanding the laws of the spirit without understanding the principle of the mind assisting the spirit will still cause us to fail.

The laws of the spirit only explain to us the various senses of the spirit, their significance, and the way to fulfill their demands. Whenever we have the sense of the spirit, we can walk according to the sense of the spirit. If the condition is normal, we can walk accordingly; if abnormal, we can adjust our way of living. But we may not always have the sense of the spirit. The spirit may not always speak; sometimes it remains silent. In the experiences of many believers, the spirit often does not speak for many days. At this time, it seems that the spirit is inactive and sleeping within us. If the spirit remains inactive for a few days, should we not do anything for a few days and wait until the spirit moves? Should we sit quietly for a few days without praying, reading the Word, and working? Our spiritual common sense will answer, no, we should not waste time. However, if we do anything, are we not doing it outside of the spirit and in the flesh?

This is when we should apply the principle of the mind assisting the spirit. How does the mind support the spirit? When the spirit is sleeping, we should use our mind to work in place of the spirit, and before very long, the spirit will also join in to work. The mind and the spirit are closely related; they are a help to each other. Many times the spirit gives forth a sense which makes the mind understand and makes the person take action. However, sometimes the spirit does not move. Therefore, it is necessary for the believer to activate the spirit by exercising his mind. When the spirit does not move, the mind must activate the spirit. After the spirit moves, the believers are able to move according to the spirit. Activating the spirit by the mind is called the principle of the mind assisting the spirit. There is a principle in the spiritual life: in the *beginning* we should use the sense of the spirit to perceive the knowledge given to us by God; later we should guard and apply this knowledge with our mind. For instance, according to previous knowledge from God, if you see a great need, you should pray and ask God to meet this need. However, when you see a particular need, your spirit may not have a sense to pray. What should you do? You should apply your *mind* to pray; do not wait for the sense of the spirit to pray. All needs are a call to prayer. If in the beginning you ignore the silence of the spirit and keep on praying, before long you will sense something rising up within you—your spirit is now joining in the praying.

When our spirit is oppressed by Satan, or when we are entangled by our natural life, we sometimes do not even sense where our spirit is. The spirit sinks to such a low position that we do not even have any sensation. We can sense our soul and body, but the position of the spirit seems void. What should we do? If we wait for the sense of the spirit to pray, there probably will not be an opportunity for prayer, and the spirit will also not be liberated. Therefore, the way to pray is according to the truth which we know and remember in our mind, standing against the principality of darkness.

Although we do not sense the spirit, we should pray according to what we know in our mind. This activity of the mind will stimulate the spirit to move.

The prayer by understanding (1 Cor. 14:15) will stir up the spirit. Although at the beginning it may seem that we are only praying with empty and rather meaningless words, if we exercise our mind to resist by praying, the spirit will ascend after a while. Then both the spirit and mind will cooperate to work. Since we have learned some truths about the battle and the way to pray, even though we do not sense our spirit, we can still use our mind so that the spirit will join in because of the stirring in our mind. As soon as the spirit comes, we will feel that our prayer is very meaningful and free. The harmonious co-laboring of the spirit and mind is a normal state of the spiritual life.

SPIRITUAL WARFARE

In spiritual warfare, a believer does not always attack the enemy because he forgets the principle of the cooperation of the spirit and the mind. Therefore, he waits for "God's burden." He thinks that he does not have the "sense" to fight and should wait until he has such a sense before attacking the enemy with prayers. If he would merely pray according to his mind for a while, the sense in the spirit will immediately respond. We already know how wicked the evil spirit is and how he damages both the Lord's children and worldly people. We also clearly know that we should oppose him by prayer to speed him to the abyss. Since this is our realization, we should not wait for a sense in the spirit to pray. Even though we have no feelings, we have to pray. We should first use our mind to initiate the prayer, using words which we know curse the evil spirit; then our spirit will move, and the words with which we have cursed him will be backed up by the power of the spirit. In the morning, for example, the Holy Spirit may grant us a considerable anointing in the spirit to curse the evil spirit, but by noontime we may have lost this anointing. What should we do then? We must apply our mind to act in the same way that our spirit acted in the morning.

This is a spiritual principle. What has been obtained in the spirit must be guarded and applied by the mind.

RAPTURE

It is the same with the faith of rapture. In the beginning we acquired "the spirit of rapture," but before long we may feel as if our spirit is empty, as if we do not have any sense concerning the imminence of the Lord's coming and the reality of our rapture. At this time we should remember the principle of the mind cooperating with the spirit. We should pray with the mind in the absence of a sense in the spirit. If we simply expect our spirit to be filled again with the sense of rapture, we will not acquire it. We have to consider and pray according to what we know in our mind, then what we acquired previously will fill our spirit.

PREACHING

This principle must not be forgotten in the spreading of God's truth. We know that the truths we learned in the old days are just stored in our brain. If we impart them to people only from our mind, there will not be any spiritual effect. In the beginning we no doubt knew these truths in the spirit, but now it seems as if the spirit has faded and there is only the memory. What should we do to have our spirit once again filled with these truths in order to spread these truths to others from our spirit? We can do nothing except exercise our mind. We should reconsider these truths and pray again before God, using these truths as the center. Before long, we will be filled again in our spirit as before. The truths were originally acquired in the spirit and preserved in our mind. Now because of our prayer according to the mind, they reenter our spirit. In this way we are able to once again proclaim the truths which we have known in our spirit.

INTERCESSION

We all know that intercession is a very crucial matter. We often have time for intercession but do not have the inspiration of the spirit. We do not know what we should pray for. This does not mean that we do not need to intercede and can vainly spend our time for other purposes. Rather, it means that we should use our mind to intercede, hoping to stimulate the collaboration of the spirit. Hence, at this moment we should exercise our mind to consider whether our friends, family, and co-workers have any need. When we think of a need, we should intercede for it. If the spirit within us still remains cold, we should realize that He does not want us to pray for that matter. It may occur to us that the church in our locality has some deficiencies, that the churches in all the localities are in the midst of some temptation, that the Lord's work in certain areas is hindered, or that God's children have a need of some particular truth. Once we think of a certain item, we should intercede for it. If our spirit still does not respond after a while, and we are still praying with our mind, we should realize that the Lord does not want us to pray for this matter either. If there is the anointing of the Holy Spirit as we are praying for another matter and the sense of our spirit also responds, we should know that we have touched and prayed for the appropriate item. The principle that we should use is of the mind assisting the spirit to locate its inclination. Sometimes we only need to use our mind to consider a little, and the spirit responds; sometimes, however, we have to wait for a while before the spirit agrees with us, because our mind is too narrow, and we may not quickly realize through the spirit what the Holy Spirit delights in. Sometimes God desires to enlarge the scope of our prayers; He desires us to pray for the nation so that all of Satan's work behind the scenes will fail. He may want us to pray for all the sinners in the world or for the whole church. If our mind is only set on the present, it will take some time before these things occur to us and for us to arrive at the prayer in which the Holy Spirit is in one accord with the mind. After we have obtained the cooperation of the sense of the spirit, we should pour out all the burdens of the spirit for this matter. We should pray for the various aspects of this matter in a detailed and adequate way until our spirit is unloaded. Then we can continue to intercede for other items.

This is one of the principles in our spiritual life. Whatever new prayers God gives to us, we obtain them in our spirit. But after a period of time, we cannot expect God to fill our spirit with this new prayer again. We have to continue praying with our mind, regardless of our feelings. Eventually we will obtain this prayer again in our spirit.

KNOWING THE WILL OF GOD

We already know that God's leadings are not always "direct"; rather, some are "indirect." In His direct leading, God's Spirit moves in our spirit so that we may know His will. We only need to pay attention to the motion in our spirit to know the will of God. However, of all that we should do in our lifetime, not everything will be directly told to us from God. There are many needs which we see. What should we do concerning them? For example, we may be invited to a place to work, or something else may suddenly happen to us. This is not initiated directly from the spirit, but it reaches us through others. Our mind may realize the importance of solving this matter, but our spirit may not be responsive. What should we do to obtain God's leading? After something happens, we should ask God to lead us in the spirit; this is called indirect leading.

This is the time for the mind to assist the spirit. When there is no stirring in his spirit, a believer should use his mind. If the spirit continuously uttered its intention, it would not be necessary for the mind to assist the spirit. Since, however, the spirit is sometimes silent, the mind has to fill the position of the spirit.

At such a time, the believer should use his *mind* to consider and ponder his doubts and difficulties before God. Although his prayer, consideration, and pondering all issue from his mind, after a while, the believer will see that his spirit also joins into his prayer, consideration, and pondering. When he senses the spirit, which was previously silent, the Holy Spirit will lead him in the spirit before too long. In this way we can use our mind to assist the spirit. We should not think that something should not be done because the spirit does not move; rather, we should "draw up" our spirit with our mind to make it alive, and let it resolve whether the matter is according to God's will.

THE PRINCIPLE OF THE SPIRIT'S ACTIVITIES

In our spiritual life there are many things that should be done. For this reason, the work of the mind cannot be neglected. Being filled in our spirit is different from the ocean tide coming in and going out at will. To be filled in the spirit, we must fulfill its requirement. This implies that the mind must initiate what the spirit is ready to do but has not yet begun. If we sit and wait for the sense of the spirit, it will never come. Neither should we overemphasize the work of the mind. We should know that only the activities that are done in the spirit have spiritual value; therefore, we should not walk according to the mind. Then why do we use the mind? We use the mind, but it is not the goal. Rather, our purpose is to stir up the *spirit* to do the work. The spirit must be the one who works. Therefore, the spirt is still very crucial. Employing the mind is simply for stirring up the work of the spirit. Therefore, when we apply the mind to draw up the spirit, if there is neither a response nor an experience of the anointing after a period of time, the work of the mind in that regard should cease and turn in another direction. In spiritual warfare as well, if we have a sense of "void" within us for a long period and no sense of the spirit, we should stop; however, we should not stop simply because of the impatience of our flesh. Although sometimes we are weary, we know that we should continue. At other times we know that we should stop. There is no fixed law.

For the mind to assist the spirit in this way is like priming a mechanical pump. Some pumps require a cup of water to be poured in first in order to create some suction power which draws the water up as we are pumping. The relationship of our mind to the spirit is the same as the cup of water to the pump. If we do not use a cup of water as a starter, water cannot be drawn up; similarly, if we do not initiate with our mind, the spirit will not rise up. If we do not use the mind to initiate prayer, it is like a person who does not pour in a cup of water, and after pumping a couple of times, says that there is no water in the well.

Truly there are differences in the work of our spirit. Sometimes it is as strong as a lion, and sometimes it is as indecisive as a babe. When our spirit is weak and cannot help itself, the mind should act as the spirit's nursing mother to look after it. The mind cannot replace the spirit, but it can assist the spirit to enliven it. When the spirit descends from its controlling position, the believer should use the power of the mind to pray and raise it up again. Should the spirit sink because of oppression, the believer should use his mind to examine the condition and then pray strongly until the spirit rises up to be liberated again. A spiritual mind can maintain the tranquil position of the spirit. The mind can restrict excessive activities of the spirit and also uplift an excessively depressed spirit.

Simply speaking, our spirit can only be filled again by the activities of our mind (in the spiritual realm). In principle, *whatever* we have done in the spirit, we should now do with our mind. Then when the Holy Spirit anoints us, it confirms that we are doing it in the spirit. In the beginning of a certain situation, you may not have any sense of the spirit. However, once you acquire the sense of the spirit, this indicates that the spirit wanted to work this way, but it was too weak to do so. Through the assistance of the mind, it is able to express what it previously was unable to express. Whatever we need in the spirit can be obtained by simply considering in our mind and praying. In this way we will be filled in spirit.

Regarding assisting the spirit, another point must be observed: spiritual warfare involves spirit warring with spirit. When our spirit wrestles with the evil spirit, the strength of our entire being is one with the spirit for the battle. The most important part is our mind. The entire strength of the spirit and the mind must be united together for the attack. If the spirit becomes suppressed and loses its strength to resist, the mind should continually fight for the spirit. When the mind fights by praying, resisting, and opposing, the spirit will receive a supply to rise up once again for the battle.

THE CONDITION OF THE MIND

Because the mind can assist the spirit, even though its position is much lower than the spirit, a believer must keep his mind in a normal condition to enable it to search the interpretation of the spirit and assist in any weakness of the spirit. The activities of the spirit are governed by their laws. Likewise, the activities of the mind are governed by their particular laws. When the mind is free to work, the burden is light. Should it become stretched (like one stretches a sling), it cannot work freely. The enemy knows that we need the mind to assist the spirit in order to walk according to the spirit. Therefore, he always presses us, keeping our mind excessively stretched and unable to function normally in order that it will not be able to assist the spirit when it is weak.

Moreover, our mind is not simply an organ to assist the spirit; we also obtain light through it. The Holy Spirit of God gives light to the mind through our spirit. If the mind is exercised excessively, there is no possibility for it to receive light from the Holy Spirit. The evil spirit knows that if our mind is in darkness, our whole being will also be in darkness. Therefore, it endeavors to cause us to think excessively so that we cannot be quieted to work. As a believer walks according to the spirit, he must prohibit his mind from continually turning. Concentrating on one theme, anxiety, sorrow, or overly considering what the will of God is, makes the mind unable to bear the burden and work. Only by maintaining a quiet and peaceful mind can one walk according to the spirit.

Since the mind occupies such an important position, when working with others, a believer must be cautious not to interrupt the thoughts of his brother. Breaking a train of thought can cause the mind to suffer. When the Holy Spirit leads a believer to consider a matter through the spirit, an interruption by others is a very fearful thing. If a thought is interrupted, the mind will be stretched, and consequently, it is harder to work with the spirit. Hence, not only should we keep our mind free, we should also take care of the mind of our brothers. Before speaking to a brother, we should first check the trend of his thought and then speak to him. Otherwise, we will cause him to suffer.

CHAPTER FOUR

THE PROPER CONDITION OF THE SPIRIT

An erring spirit often leads to improper conduct. If a believer desires to walk according to the spirit, he must continuously keep himself in a proper condition. The spirit, like the mind, can become unrestrained and insolent, or it can shrink back. Without the Holy Spirit guarding his spirit, a believer will fail in his outward conduct once his spirit fails. We should realize that behind the many failures in outward conduct, the spirit has failed even before the conduct failed. If the spirit of a believer is strong and powerful, it can control the soul and body, not allowing them to become dissolute, regardless of circumstances. Otherwise, they will suppress the spirit and cause a believer to fall.

God emphasizes our spirit. This is where the new life dwells and the Holy Spirit works. This is where we fellowship with God, understand God's will, and receive the revelation of the Holy Spirit. This is where we are trained and have growth. This is where we resist all the attacks of the enemy and obtain authority to overcome the devil and his army. This is also where we receive power for the work. The spirit has received the resurrection life, only later will we have a body of resurrection. Therefore, the condition of our spirit will also be the condition of our spiritual life. Therefore, it is very important to keep our spirit in a proper condition. The Lord does not care for the outward man, the soul, in a Christian; He pays attention to our inward man, the spirit. If our inward man is not in a proper condition, our entire living will be upside-down, even though our soul-life is still very prosperous.

The Bible is not silent regarding the proper condition of the believer's spirit. Many experienced believers have already passed through the exhortations of the Bible. They are aware that a believer must keep his spirit in the various conditions taught in the Bible if he wants to keep his victorious position

and ability to co-labor with God. We have already seen that
the spirit is controlled by the believer's renewed will. This is
very important because a believer can put his spirit in its
proper position only by his will. Since we have already
mentioned the importance of the spirit being in a proper
condition, we do not need to repeat it.

CONTRITE

"Jehovah...saves those who are contrite in spirit" (Psa.
34:18). "For thus says the high and exalted One, / Who
inhabits eternity, whose name is Holy: / I will dwell in the
high and holy place, / And with the contrite and lowly of
spirit" (Isa. 57:15).

It is a common misunderstanding to think that we need
a contrite spirit only when we repent to believe in the Lord
or when we fall and commit sins. But God wants us to
continually keep our spirit in a state of contriteness. Even
though we may not commit sins daily, God wants us to
constantly repent with contrition because our flesh still exists,
and it can be active anytime. Such a spirit will keep us from
losing our watchfulness. We should never commit sins, but
we should continually be contrite because we are sinful. The
presence of God can be felt in such a spirit.

God does not want us to occasionally repent, thinking that
this is enough; He wants us to continually repent with
contrition in our living. Consequently, as soon as there is any
discord with the Holy Spirit in our living and conduct, we
can immediately sense it and grieve over it. Only by this can
we admit that we are wrong when people tell us that we are
really wrong. Repentance with contrition is very necessary
because a believer, even though joined to the Lord in one
spirit, still can err. The spirit can err (Isa. 29:24); even if
the spirit does not err, the mind can become blurred, not
knowing how to execute the intent of the spirit. A contrite
spirit can cause a believer to immediately admit, without any
cover-up, the small matters that others see in him that are
unlike the Lord. God saves only those with a contrite spirit;
He cannot save any other because He needs a contrite spirit
to reveal His intent. Whoever covers-up and whitewashes his

mistakes definitely does not have a contrite spirit. Even God cannot completely save him. We need a spirit that can receive rebuke from the Holy Spirit as well as from people in the world, and we need to admit that we have not reached the stage where we should be. Then we shall see the salvation of God in our daily living.

BROKEN

"The sacrifices of God are a broken spirit" (Psa. 51:17).

"Broken" in the original text has the meaning of "trembling." Some believers, after committing sins, remain unperturbed in their spirit as if nothing happened. A healthy spirit, after a sin has been committed, invariably would be broken—just like David's. Indeed, a man with a broken spirit can easily be recovered back to God.

TREMBLING

"But to this kind of man will I look, to him who is poor / And of a contrite spirit, and who trembles at My word" (Isa. 66:2).

"Contrite" in the original text has the meaning of "beaten." God is pleased when the spirit of the believer is very careful, as if it is always under rebuke and beating, fearing God and His word. A believer's spirit must reach a stage of constantly fearing God. The presumptuous and self-willed heart must be completely broken, allowing the word of God to be the guide in all things. A believer must have this holy respect, having absolutely no trust in himself. Since his spirit has already been beaten, he dares not lift up his head; instead, he always obeys the command of God. A hardened spirit is always an obstacle in obeying the will of God. Only after the cross has accomplished a thorough work in enabling the believer to clearly know the unreliability of his ideas, feelings, and desires does he dare not become presumptuous. He becomes extremely cautious in all things, knowing that they will doubtlessly fail without the intervening and keeping power of God. We must not become independent of God. Whenever our spirit ceases to tremble, it will have an independent (presumptuous) intent. We rely on God only when we realize that we are in a completely helpless situation. A trembling spirit keeps us from failing and causes us to really know God.

HUMBLE

"To be of an humble spirit with the lowly" (Prov. 16:19).

"Honor shall uphold the humble in spirit" (Prov. 29:23).

"I will dwell...with the contrite and lowly of spirit, / To revive the spirit of the lowly" (Isa. 57:15).

Being humble is not despising oneself; rather, it is not looking at oneself. An attitude of self-conceit in a believer's spirit is the proof of his fall. Humility is not only before God, it is also before man. A humble spirit can be seen in communicating with the lowly. Only a humble spirit will not despise any man created by God. The presence and glory of God are manifested in the man with a humble spirit.

A humble spirit is one which can be taught, one which can be exhorted, and one which can receive explanation. Many believers are too haughty in spirit; therefore, they can only teach others and cannot be taught. Many believers are so immovably stubborn in spirit that it is hard for them to be taught. Even though they realize that they are wrong, they still hold on to their own view. Many believers are too hard in spirit to listen to others' explanation regarding a misunderstanding. Only a humble spirit has the receiving capacity. God needs a humble spirit to manifest His virtues. How can a proud spirit listen to the voice of the Holy Spirit and co-labor with the Holy Spirit? The spirit must be void of any trace of pride and must always be soft, tender, and flexible. A spirit with any amount of hardness is unlike that of the Lord; therefore, it is unable to fellowship with the Lord. The spirit must be humble, always waiting on the Lord, and without any resistance towards the Lord before it can walk with Him.

POOR

"Blessed are the poor in spirit" (Matt. 5:3).

Being poor in spirit is realizing that one has absolutely nothing. The danger for a believer is that there are too many things in his spirit. Only those who realize that they are poor in spirit can be humble. A believer's experience, growth, and progress very often become self-valued treasures in his spirit, causing it to lose its poverty. To meditate on one's gains and pay attention to one's experiences are very subtle dangers. The believer, however, often does not realize this. What is being poor? Being poor is having nothing. If a believer has the deepest experience and constantly remembers the experience, it is like cargo in his spirit and becomes a snare to him. Only an empty spirit will cause a believer to lose himself in God. A rich spirit will cause a believer to become self-centered. Complete salvation frees a believer *out* of self and back to God. If a believer retains something for himself, his spirit will immediately turn inward and be unable to "reach out" to be joined in God.

MEEK

"A spirit of meekness" (Gal. 6:1).

This is a very important condition for the spirit. Meekness is the opposite of hardness and stubbornness. God requires a meek spirit of us. An unyielding spirit will often lose the leading of God. A meek spirit can forsake one's will and obey God in the shortest time. Whoever has a meek spirit can immediately stop, according to the Lord's leading, without any previous notification from God, even when he is in the midst of utter prosperity in his work. Philip was like this when he was called in Samaria to go to the wilderness. A meek spirit turns freely in God's hands as God wills. A meek spirit does not know how to resist God and follow one's own will. God needs such a submissive spirit to accomplish His will.

A meek spirit is not any less important towards man. A meek spirit is a spirit which is like a lamb, a spirit of the cross. "Who being reviled did not revile in return; suffering, He did not threaten" (1 Pet. 2:23); this is a meek spirit. A meek spirit is willing to be wronged. Even though one is protected by the law and able to take revenge, he would by no means use his fleshly arm to redress himself. This spirit, though suffering pain and damage, causes no harm to others. Whoever has such a spirit conducts himself in righteousness

but does not demand righteousness from others. He is filled
with love, grace, and kindness; therefore, he is able to melt
those who are surrounding him.

FERVENT

"Do not be slothful in zeal, but be burning in spirit, serving
the Lord" (Rom. 12:11).

The flesh can become enthusiastic for a moment from
stimulation or emotion, but this is only temporary and does
not last long. Even when the flesh is most zealous, it can
still be very lazy because it will only be zealous for the things
which suit its will. Its zealousness is merely helped by
emotion. It cannot serve the Lord in those things which it
dislikes or when it is emotionally cold. The flesh cannot labor
with the Lord in continually doing things slowly, step by step,
rain or shine. Being "fervent in spirit" is a long-term matter;
only then can we always serve the Lord. We should avoid all
fleshly enthusiasm. We should let the Holy Spirit fill our
spirit and keep our spirit fervent. Then, even when our
emotion is cold, our spirit will not become cold and immovable
in the Lord's work.

The apostle's word in this verse is a commandment.
Therefore, our renewed will can choose this. We should
exercise our will to choose fervency. We should say, "My spirit
desires to be fervent and is unwilling to be cold." When our
emotion is utterly disinterested, we should let our fervent
spirit control everything, not letting our lukewarm feelings
overcome us. Always serving the Lord in singleness is a
demonstration of a fervent spirit.

COOL

"He that is of a cool spirit is a man of understanding"
(Prov. 17:27, ASV).

Our spirit needs to be fervent. It also needs to be cool or
calm. Fervency is related to not being "slothful in zeal...
serving the Lord"; coolness is related to knowledge.

If our spirit is not cool, our actions will often be
uncontrolled. The purpose of the enemy is to cause the saints
to go astray and lose contact with the Holy Spirit. We often

see that when a saint's spirit is not cool, he changes his living from one which is according to principle to one which is according to emotion. The spirit and mind originally were closely linked together. As soon as the spirit is not calm, the mind becomes provoked; as soon as the mind becomes fervent, the believer loses control of his many actions which then become abnormal. Therefore, it is always profitable to maintain a calm spirit. In order to keep our walk always on the path of the Lord, we have to constantly ignore excitement in the emotion, an increase in our desire, and confusion in the mind; instead, we should retreat to ponder every question in our calm spirit. If we act whenever our spirit is provoked, we fear that all the resulting actions will be against the will of God.

Because of our knowledge of the self, God, Satan, and our thorough perception of all things, we should have a calmness in the spirit which soulish believers never have. The Holy Spirit should fill the believer's spirit. The soul should be completely put to death so that the spirit can have an unspeakable calmness. Regardless of any changes in soul, body, or environment, the calmness within the spirit will definitely not be lost. Just like the sea, regardless of how much the waves roar on the surface of the sea, the bottom of the sea is always very quiet and still. Before a believer separates his soul from his spirit, whenever something happens unexpectedly, his whole person immediately becomes confused, bewildered, or at a loss as to what to do or is at least shaken in his purpose. This is because of the lack of spiritual knowledge and the lack of separation between the soul and spirit. Therefore, in order to maintain a separation between the soul and the spirit, he must maintain a coolness in the spirit. The believer will then have an "unshaken" experience. No matter how disturbing the outward circumstances are, they cannot cause him to lose the calmness and peace within. Even if a mountain collapsed in front of him, he would not lose his calmness. This is not gained by man's meditation but by the believer's reliance on the Holy Spirit's revelation of the real condition of all things and by the restriction of the believer's soul. This prevents the soul from controlling his spirit.

The matter we are discussing relates to the control of the will. Our spirit should be subject to the control of our will. Our will desires fervency; it also desires calmness. We should not allow our spiritual condition to go beyond what our will is able to control. It should be fervent in the Lord's work, but it should also maintain a cool attitude when doing the Lord's work.

REJOICING

"And my spirit has exulted in God my Savior" (Luke 1:47).

The spirit of a believer should take the attitude of brokenness towards self (Psa. 51:17), while simultaneously rejoicing in God. The believer rejoices not because of something joyful or because of any personal experience, work, blessing, or environment. He rejoices because God is his center. Actually speaking, apart from God, there is nothing which can make a believer rejoice.

If a believer's spirit is suppressed by worry, grief, or sadness, his spirit immediately becomes derelict. It becomes depressed and loses its proper position, unable to fulfill the Holy Spirit's leading. Once a believer's spirit is suppressed by heavy burdens, it immediately loses its agility, freedom, and brightness, and it falls from the ascended position. If the period of grief is prolonged, the extent of the damage suffered by the spirit is immeasurable. At such a time, nothing else can help except to rejoice in God. Rejoice in the fact that God is God; rejoice in how God has accomplished everything to be our Savior. A believer must not lose his "hallelujah."

NOT COWARDLY

"For God has not given us a spirit of cowardice, but of power and of love and of sobermindedness" (2 Tim. 1:7).

Cowardice is not humbleness. Being humble is absolutely forgetting one's self—one's weaknesses as well as one's strengths. Being a coward is remembering one's weaknesses and one's self. Shrinking back and timidity do not please God. On the one hand, God desires us to be trembling because we are nothing, but on the other hand, He wants us to be bold to step forward because of His power. To be bold is to witness for the Lord, to suffer pain, to bear shame, to lose everything, to rely on the Lord, and to trust in His love, wisdom, power, truthfulness, and promises. This is what the Lord desires of us. Whenever we see ourselves shrinking back in matters like witnessing for the Lord, we should realize that our spirit has left its proper condition. We should keep our spirit in "fearlessness."

We should have a spirit of power, love, and a sober mind. Our spirit needs to be strong and powerful, but it should not be so strong as to become unloving. Being quiet, self-disciplined, and not easily provoked are also important. To resist the enemy, our spirit needs to be strong; to deal with people in the world, our spirit needs to be loving; to conduct ourselves properly, our spirit needs to be sober.

QUIET

"The hidden man of the heart in the incorruptible adornment of a meek and quiet spirit, which is very costly in the sight of God" (1 Pet. 3:4).

Even though this word is spoken to the sisters, spiritually speaking, the brothers also need such a teaching.

"To aspire to be quiet" (1 Thes. 4:11) is the responsibility of every believer. Today there is indeed too much talking among the believers. Sometimes, there are more unspoken words than those that are spoken. Confused thoughts and garrulous speakings are sufficient to cause our spirit to wander outside the control of our will. An "uncontrolled spirit" will often cause man to act according to the flesh. When the spirit of a believer is uncontrolled, it is very difficult for him to keep himself from sinning. An erring spirit often leads to wrong conduct.

Before the mouth will be quiet, the spirit must be quiet, because whatever is in the spirit will come out from the mouth. We should always be careful to keep our spirit quiet so that we can remain quiet when things become confusing. A quiet spirit is indispensable in order for us to walk according to the spirit. Otherwise, we will fall into sin. If our spirit is quiet, we can hear the voice of the Holy Spirit in our spirit. Then we can execute God's will and understand what we cannot understand amid confusion. This quiet spirit is the ornament of a believer. It is what a believer should express outwardly.

NEW

"In newness of spirit" (Rom. 7:6).

This is a very important step in spiritual life and work. A stale spirit cannot touch people. At the most, it can give people some kind of thought. Even so, it is powerless; it cannot make people think earnestly. A stale spirit only generates stale thoughts. A vivacious life can never flow out of a stale spirit. Whatever the stale spirit generates—words, teachings, attitudes, thoughts, living—is stale and old and belongs to the past. Many doctrines only reach the believer's mind, they have no root in the spirit. Behind the teaching there is no spirit to "touch" another's spirit. Maybe a believer has a doctrine which he once experienced, but now the doctrine has become something of the past, a souvenir, a memory in the mind—it has passed from the spirit to the mind. His thought may be quite fresh, newly received in the mind. But since the thought has not been substantiated by life, those who hear him and those who are near him will not feel that there is a fresh spirit touching them.

Many times we have seen a kind of Christian who always obtains something new from the Lord. When we stand in front of such a person, we almost feel as if he has just come from the Lord's presence and has brought us before the Lord. This kind of person seems to continually obtain new strength, just like eagles do. This is the way young people are. They do not give people dry, rotten, and infested manna in the mind but fish and bread on the fire of coals in the spirit. This is newness. Apart from this, everything is stale. No matter how deep and how marvelous some thoughts may seem, they can never touch people the way the new and fresh spirit can.

We must keep our spirit new and fresh. If our spirit has not been in the Lord and blessed by the Lord, it is unfit to meet others. No matter whether it is our life, thought, or experience, if something becomes a memory in the past, it is stale. All we have must continually be new from the Lord. Imitating others, without the experience in life, definitely does not count, but even imitating one's own past experience also has no effect. This should make us realize the importance of "I live because of the Father" (John 6:57). Only when we constantly draw the Father's life to be our life can our spirit be new and fresh all the time. A spirit that is not new and fresh cannot bear fruit in labor, cannot walk according to the Spirit in life, and cannot overcome in battle. A stale spirit cannot see man because it has not yet seen God. For the spirit to remain fresh all the time, it must always be touching God.

HOLY

"Be holy both in body and in spirit" (1 Cor. 7:34).

"Let us cleanse ourselves from all defilement of flesh and of spirit" (2 Cor. 7:1).

If we want to walk according to spirit, we should always keep our spirit holy. An unholy spirit will mislead people. Having improper thoughts in criticizing people or conjecturing about matters, remembering others' sins, lacking love, talking too much, criticizing harshly, and being self-righteous, unreceptive towards exhortation, jealous towards the brothers, conceited, and so forth are all able to defile the spirit. An unholy spirit cannot be new and fresh.

In our pursuit of a spiritual living, we cannot ignore a sin even for a minute. Sins damage us more than anything else. Even though we understand how to be free from sins and how to walk according to spirit, we still need to be careful that we do not unconsciously return to our past sinful situation. When sin comes, it is impossible to walk according to the spirit. We must always be watchful to have the attitude of being dead so that sin will not overcome us or enter into our spirit to poison it. Without holiness, no man can see the Lord.

STRONG

"Became strong in spirit" (Luke 1:80).

Our spirit must gradually grow and become strong. This is indispensable in spiritual living. Many times we feel that our spirit is not strong enough to control our soul and body, especially when our soul is stimulated or when our body is weak. Sometimes when we want to help others, seeing the heavy burden in their spirit, we feel how powerless our own spirit is. We are unable to release them. Sometimes in our battle with the enemy, we see that we are not strong enough in our spiritual strength, finding it difficult to "wrestle" unto victory with the enemy for a long time. Many times we really feel that our spiritual strength is not enough to control everything. There are many areas in our living and work which we can barely manage. How we wish that we had a stronger spirit!

Once the spirit is strong, there is a sharp intuition and discerning power. There is also the ability to refuse everything which does not belong to the spirit. Some believers intend to walk according to the spirit, but they are unable because the power in their spirit is not sufficient to control everything; on the contrary, it is subject to being controlled. We cannot expect the Holy Spirit to replace us in doing all the work; our regenerated spirit needs to co-labor with the Holy Spirit. We must learn how to use our spirit and use it as best we know how. If a believer uses his spirit, it will gradually become strong and have the power to break through all that is hindering the Holy Spirit, regardless of whether it is the stubborn will, the confused mind, or the unrestrained emotion.

The Bible tells us that the spirit can be wounded (Prov. 18:14), meaning that the spirit can feel hurt. A wounded spirit is very weak. If our spirit is strong, we are able to stand the stimulation of the soul and not be shaken. Moses' spirit may be considered as being very strong, but because he did not constantly keep it strong, the Israelites were able to provoke his spirit unto sinning (Psa. 106:33). If our spirit is strong, we will be able to declare victory in the Lord whatever the situation and however great the suffering in the body or sorrow in the emotions.

Only the Holy Spirit can grant us the strength needed by the inner man. The strength in our spirit comes from the power of the Holy Spirit. Yet there is also a need for the spirit itself to be trained. After a believer has learned how to walk according to spirit, he will learn how to use the power of his spirit in his work and not his natural power. In life, he will know how to live by the spiritual life and not rely on the soulish life. In battle, he will learn how to use the strength in the spirit and not his soulish strength to resist, attack, and oppose Satan and his evil spirits. This naturally will improve and needs to improve. As a believer walks according to the spirit, he receives more power from the Holy Spirit. At the same time, his spirit becomes stronger. A believer should always keep his spirit in a strong condition. He should never let it lose its power lest it become unable to deal with any needs when they arise.

ONENESS

"One spirit" (Phil. 1:27).

We have already seen how the living of a spiritual man is joined with other believers. Oneness in the spirit is very important. If God, through the indwelling of the Holy Spirit in a believer's spirit, is completely joined with the believer, the believer's spirit will also be one with the other believers. A spiritual man is not only one with Christ in God; he is also joined to God who dwells in every believer. Therefore, if a believer allows the soulish life to work, he cannot walk according to the spirit. If a believer allows his mind or emotion to control his spirit, then his spirit cannot be one with other believers. Only when the mind and emotion submit to the control of the spirit can the believer disregard or stop the discord in the mind and emotion and be one with the other children of God in spirit. A believer must keep his spirit in a condition of being one with *all* the believers. This is not being joined only with a small group of those with the same opinion, but with the entire Body of Christ. Our spirit must be without hardness, bitterness, or restrictions; instead, it must be completely open and free before our contact with others can be without barrier.

FULL OF GRACE

"The grace of our Lord Jesus Christ be with your spirit" (Gal. 6:18).

We must constantly guard our spirit. Therefore, the grace

of the Lord Jesus Christ is precious. The grace of the Lord in our spirit is our help at any time. This is a word of blessing; this is also the height of what a believer can receive in his spirit. We should always keep our spirit in the grace of the Lord.

THE RAPTURED SPIRIT

Apart from the conditions of the spirit discussed above, we should also keep our spirit in a condition of being out of the world and ascending to the heavens at all times. We call this the raptured spirit. The raptured spirit is deeper than the spirit of ascension. The person who has obtained the raptured spirit not only lives as if he is in the heavens; he also, through the Holy Spirit's leading, believes and expects the second coming of the Lord and his own rapture. When the spirit of the believer and that of Christ are joined as one spirit, he becomes a citizen of the heavens in experience, living in the world as a sojourner. The Holy Spirit will call him to advance step by step so that he can receive the raptured spirit. Formerly his cry was "Forward!" Now it is "Ascend!" This causes his whole being to go heavenward. The raptured spirit enables a believer to have a foretaste of the spirit which has "tasted...the powers of the age to come" (Heb. 6:5).

Everyone who believes in the doctrine of the second coming does not necessarily have this raptured spirit. Believing in the Lord's second coming, preaching about it, or even praying for it does not mean very much. We can have all of these but still be without the raptured spirit. Not every mature believer has this spirit. It is a gift of grace from God. Sometimes it is given according to His pleasure; sometimes it is given in response to supplication in faith. With this raptured spirit, the believer's spirit is always in a position of being raptured, believing not only in the Lord's return but also in his own rapture. This is not believing a doctrine but knowing a fact. Just as Simeon, by the revelation of the Holy Spirit, knew that he would see the Christ of God before his death, a believer should also believe with assurance in his spirit that he will be raptured to the Lord before he dies. This faith is the faith of Enoch. Naturally, we are not stubbornly believing a superstition. If we are in the period of the rapture, we cannot help but be filled with the faith of being raptured. This kind of faith will enable us to better understand the work of God in this age. Thus, we will receive the heavenly power to help us in our work.

If a believer receives this raptured spirit, or in other words, if his spirit is in the condition of being raptured, we will see that he is more heavenly. His path to the heavens is not like that in the past when he assumed that he must pass through death.

When a believer is doing a spiritual work, he often has many expectations and plans. He is filled with the Holy Spirit, wisdom, and power. He believes in and expects that God will greatly use him, as if the effect of his work will shortly result in much fruit. But in this prosperous situation, God's brake presses down as if to ask him to terminate all the work and prepare for another path. This comes as a surprise. "Why? Is my strength not for the work? Is the wonderful knowledge I obtained not for helping others? Why is everything closed and cold?" Yet under this kind of leading, the believer knows that God's purpose is to call him to take another path. Before it was to go forward; now it is to ascend. This is not to say that there is no more work but that the work can be terminated at any time.

At other times, God also uses the environment—persecution, opposition, plundering, etc.—so that the believers will know that God wants them to have the raptured spirit and not think that the work in the world will gradually progress. The Lord wants to change the path of His children now. Many of God's children do not know that besides the best possible work that progresses, there is something even better—to ascend.

This raptured spirit is not fruitless. Before the believer receives such a spirit, his experiences were frequently changing. If the believer has the witness of being raptured in his spirit, if he has firm faith regarding his rapture, and if his conduct also matches the raptured spirit in life and work, then this spirit will cause the believer to prepare for the coming of the Lord. This preparation does not merely relate to outward corrections; it also causes the believer to be fully prepared in spirit, soul, and body to welcome the Lord.

Therefore, a believer should pray to the Holy Spirit to show him the way to receive and keep this raptured spirit. Believers should pray, hope, believe, and be willing to remove all obstacles in order to obtain this raptured spirit. Our life and work should always be checked against the raptured spirit so that we will know where we have failed. In case this spirit is lost, we should know when we lost it and how it can be recovered. We should pray in order to know how matters in the world relate to our spirit; in this way we know how to overcome. Once we receive this raptured spirit, it is very easy to lose, because we do not know the special prayer and work we should have at this stage in our life in order to maintain our position in the heavenlies and have the clearest sight. Therefore, we should pray that the Holy Spirit would teach us how to constantly be kept in this kind of a spirit. The result of such prayers is that we will be led to have our mind set on the things that are above (Col. 3:2). This is a prerequisite of being kept.

Since we are standing at the gate of the heavens and there is a possibility of being raptured at any moment, we should choose the heavenly white garment and work because we might be called to ascend the very next minute. This kind of hope totally separates us from earthly things and connects us with those above.

Even though God wants us to expect ascension with a single heart, we should not just care about being raptured. We should not ignore the needs of others and forget about the final work on the earth, as God has distributed to us. This only means that God does not want us to allow the work which He has given to hinder us from being raptured. In our living and work we should always see that the "gravity of the heavens" is much stronger than the "gravity of the earth." We should learn to live not only for the Lord's work but also for the rapture by the Lord. May our spirit be lifted up daily to hope for the next coming of the Lord. May the worldly things be so powerless that we not only dislike being "of the world," we also dislike being "in the world." May our spirit ascend heavenward daily and long to be with the Lord soon. May we be so single in minding the things which are above that even the best works in the world cannot distract us. From now on, may we earnestly pray in spirit and with understanding the prayer, "Come, Lord Jesus."

THE ANALYSIS OF THE SOUL
(1)
THE EMOTION

CHAPTER ONE

THE BELIEVER AND THE EMOTION

When a believer has not experienced the sure work of the cross, which is brought about by the Holy Spirit, he may have experienced deliverance from sin yet still be soulish and unable to overcome his own natural life. In the foregoing chapters we have spoken concerning the believer's soulish life and work. If we carefully study the soulish conduct and action of a believer, we see that both issue from his emotion. Although the soul includes three primary parts—the mind, emotion, and will—most soulish believers live by their emotion. We can almost say that they are controlled by their emotion in their soulish life. This is because the emotion appears to occupy a greater part than the mind and the will in human life; its work also appears to assume a greater role in daily human living than the other parts of the soul. Therefore, we can see that nearly all the actions of soulish believers originate from their emotion.

THE FUNCTION OF EMOTION

Our human feelings—joy, happiness, cheerfulness, excitement, sighing, irritation, stimulation, despondency, sadness, grief, depression, misery, sorrow, agitation, confusion, anxiety, enthusiasm, coldness, affection, fondness, covetousness, compassion, kindheartedness, preference, likes, interest, desire, expectation, pride, fear, remorse, hate, etc.—all come out of our emotion. All work related to our thinking issues out of the mind, our thinking organ. All work related to our decision-making originates from the will, our decision-making organ. Aside from our thoughts, decisions, and their related works, all other functions issue from the emotion. Our multitude of diverse feelings are the function of the emotion. Since emotion comprises such a vast area, nearly all soulish believers are emotional believers.

Human emotion is very complicated because it comprises a vast area. In order to help believers understand, we will subdivide emotion briefly into three major parts: (1) affection, (2) desire, and (3) feeling. These three parts cover three aspects of the emotion's function. If a believer can overcome these three aspects, he will soon enter into a pure spiritual life.

In short, our human emotion comprises what we commonly call the "seven passions," which are nothing less than the different feelings we have in our hearts. Whether it is a feeling of love, hate, joy, grief, excitement, despondency, interest, or indifference, all of these comprise the different feelings in our hearts. Therefore, they all belong to the emotion.

If we pay attention to the diverse feelings in our emotions, we will see that our emotion changes easily. In the world there are probably very few things that are as changeable as emotion. We can feel one way one minute and feel another way the next. Emotion changes according to feelings, and the latter changes very rapidly. Therefore, if one lives by emotion, his life is without principle.

Man's emotion always has a reactionary function. This means that when man's feeling is active in one direction for a while, an opposite reaction is bound to follow. For example, extreme happiness is followed by sorrow, high excitement by great depression, and burning fervor by a feeling of deep withdrawal. Even in the matter of affection, although it may begin in love, after a period of time certain influences may change one's feelings, when the intensity of hatred can far exceed the earlier love.

THE BELIEVER'S EMOTIONAL LIFE

The more we consider the function of our emotional life, the more we know its fluctuation and undependability. If believers do not live according to the spirit but according to their emotion, is it any wonder that their living undulates like the waves? Many believers feel sad about their living because their experiences are so unstable. Sometimes they seem to be in the third heavens transcending everything of the human life; at other times they seem to descend and share in the lot of ordinary men. Their life is a series of ups and downs. It does not require something outwardly heavy and big to change them; as long as a little thing is contrary to their wish, they are unable to withstand it. Subsequently, they fall.

This phenomenon relates to the fact that a believer is controlled by emotion and not by the spirit. Since his emotion is still the major element of his life and has not been taken to the cross, the spirit cannot be strengthened by the Holy Spirit. Therefore, the believer's spirit is still weak; he cannot control his whole being, nor can he overcome his emotion so that it becomes secondary, completely under the control of the spirit. If a believer can hand over his emotion to the cross through the Holy Spirit and accept the Holy Spirit as the Lord over all things, he surely can avoid this kind of undulating life.

Emotion may be considered as the greatest enemy to the life of a spiritual believer. A believer should walk according to the spirit. To do this, he must heed every leading of the spirit within him. The sense of the spirit is gentle, fine, and keen. Unless the believer attentively waits to receive and discern the revelation of his spiritual intuition, he can never obtain the guidance of his spirit. Hence, the total silence of the emotion is a prerequisite to walking according to the spirit. The small and delicate sense of the spirit is often confused and ignored by the believer because his feelings are roaring like billows. We cannot ultimately attribute any fault to the softness of our spirit's voice. Actually we can adequately feel the sense of the spirit, but when other feelings are mixed with it, we cannot possibly have discernment. Whoever keeps his emotion calm will see that it is easy to detect the voice of the intuition.

The rising and falling of the emotion not only hinders the believer from walking according to the spirit, but also directly causes him to walk according to the flesh. Since he cannot walk according to the spirit, he naturally walks according to the flesh. If he cannot secure guidance in his spirit, he naturally walks according to the impulse of his emotion. Whenever the spirit ceases to guide, the emotion starts to guide. At that moment a believer will spontaneously take the emotion as his inspiration and the impulses of the soul as the moving of the spirit. An emotional believer can be likened to a pond full of mud and sand. As long as no one comes to disturb the water, it looks clear; but once it is disturbed, it becomes muddy.

INSPIRATION AND EMOTION

Many believers do not know how to differentiate inspiration from emotion. Actually this is not difficult. Emotion always enters from outside of man, whereas inspiration is given by the Holy Spirit within man's spirit. For example, when a believer beholds the beauty of nature, a feeling within him spontaneously wells up. He feels the beauty of the scenery and his own joy. This is emotion. Perhaps, when he sees a loved one, some kind of inconceivable feeling rises up within him as though a certain power is drawing him. This is also emotion. Both the beautiful scenery and the loved one are outside the man; hence, the feelings which they produce simply belong to emotion.

However, inspiration is not the same. It is influenced only by the Holy Spirit within man. Only the Holy Spirit can inspire the spirit. Since the Holy Spirit lives within the spirit, inspiration must come from within. It does not need to be stimulated by the beautiful scenery or a dear one; it can take place in the calmest environment. The emotion, on the contrary, becomes instantly dispirited when the outside stimulus is gone. Hence, an emotional believer lives solely according to his environment. He must be stirred up and encouraged in order to go on; otherwise, he stops. Inspiration does not require outside help. In fact, when the emotion is influenced by the external environment, it is confused, resulting in a believer being unable to know which of the two he should follow.

A believer should be careful not to consider calmness and absence of stimulation as spirituality. This is far from the truth. We should know that emotion can cause people not only to be excited but also to be depressed. When the emotion urges us, we feel quite excited; when it impedes us, we feel very depressed. In the same way that emotion excites, it also calms down. Just as excitement belongs to emotion, so does calmness. A believer often commits many errors because he is under the influence of his emotion; but when he is awakened from the state he is in, he will suppress his feelings and consider this as being spiritual. He does not realize, however, that the stirring of his emotion at this point has produced a reaction opposite to excitement which spontaneously calms him down. This calmness or quietness causes the believer to lose interest in much of God's work; he does not have much affection for many of God's children. Gradually the believer's outer man is reluctant to work. The spirit, therefore, is imprisoned, and the life of the spirit cannot flow out. Since he is no longer enthusiastic and has become extremely calm, he may think that he is walking according to spirit. What he does not know is that he is still walking according to his emotion, only this time it is according to another aspect of the emotion.

In reality, the believers who turn to this kind of emotional calmness are few. The majority of them continue to be excited by their emotion. Because of their stimulation, they do many things which are beyond the bounds of the ordinary. As they quiet down and recall their actions under the influence of this function of the emotion, they cannot help but laugh at themselves and consider themselves to have acted nonsensically. This is usually true of the things done according to the emotion. In retrospect a believer often feels embarrassed and regrets his rudeness. It is very pitiful when a believer is influenced by his emotion; his spirit is powerless to subject his emotion to death and deny its control.

There are two reasons believers walk according to their emotion. First, many believers never understand what walking according to the spirit is, nor have they sought to do so; therefore, they walk according to the influence of their emotion. In these circumstances, they do not have much experience and do not know how to reject the impulse of their emotion when it is activated. They are simply driven by their emotion, and they do the things which they should not do. This is not to say that their spiritual sense does not raise any intuitive objection. However, because of their weakness, they listen to their emotion and ignore their intuition. Then their emotion becomes all the more intense until they lose control of themselves and walk according to their emotion. After having done the things which they should not, they once again repent. Second, there are believers who already know the difference between the spirit and soul experientially. When they are influenced by emotion, they know that this is from their soul, and they instantly resist it. Nevertheless, even this kind of believer sometimes walks according to the emotion. This is a successful counterfeit. If the believer is not spiritual, as in the first case mentioned above, he is overcome by the intense feeling of his emotion. If a believer is already spiritual, his emotion often counterfeits his spiritual sense. Outwardly the emotion and the spiritual sense appear identical; therefore, the believer finds it difficult to differentiate between them. Due to his ignorance, the believer is deceived and has many soulish actions.

The believer should realize that if he walks according to the spirit, all of his actions must be according to certain principles. This is because the spirit has laws, tracks, and principles. To walk according to the spirit is to walk according to the laws of the spirit. In spiritual principles, all the "rights" and "wrongs" have a clearly defined standard. If it is "yes," it is "yes," whether the sky is cloudy or clear; if it is "no," it is "no," whether one is excited or despondent. The Christian life follows a definite principle. If a believer does not completely put his emotion to death, his life will be without a fixed criterion. He will live by unstable feelings without a definite principle.

A life of principle differs completely from a life in the emotions. A believer who walks according to his emotion does not take care of principles or ordinary reasonings in considering whether or not to do something; he only takes care of his own feelings. If there is something that he likes, that makes him happy, or that he loves, he will be tempted by them even if he knows quite well that to do so is normally unreasonable and against the principles. If he feels cold, melancholy, and despondent, he will not fulfill his duty because his feelings do not go along with it. If the children of God paid a little attention to their emotion, they would realize how changeable it is and how dangerous it is to walk according to it. When the Word of God—the spiritual principle—agrees with their feeling, they do it; otherwise, they reject it and do not pay any attention to it. This kind of living is altogether at enmity with the spiritual life. Whoever wishes to have a spiritual life must walk according to God's principle moment by moment.

One distinct characteristic of a spiritual believer in his dealings with his circumstances is the fact that he is most calm. No matter what happens outwardly or if he suffers any provocation, he is always calm and peaceful, maintaining a kind of unchangeable characteristic. This is because his emotion, which is subject to stimulation, has been dealt with by the cross. Furthermore, his will and spirit are full of the power of the Holy Spirit so he can regulate all his feelings. Therefore, outward stimulation cannot move him. But if he does not allow the cross to deal with his emotion, he will be very susceptible to outward influence, regulation, movement, and stimulation. Since emotion easily changes, those who are regulated by emotion are also changeable. Whenever there is a slight threat from outside or a slight increase in work, they panic and are at a loss as to what to do. If they want to arrive at perfection, they must allow the cross to do a deeper work in their emotion.

If a believer could only remember that God does not lead in the midst of confusion, everything would be fine. This would guard him from many errors. He should never decide to do anything or begin to do anything when his heart is in an upheaval and his emotion is in an uproar. This is the time when the emotional impulse is the strongest, and he will commit errors if he walks according to it. Our mind also becomes unreliable when our feeling is in a confused state, because the mind is very easily affected by emotion. Once the mind is weakened, we cannot distinguish right from wrong. At the same time, the conscience is also undependable. When the emotion is agitated and the mind is deceived, the conscience loses its standard for accurately discerning right from wrong. In such a condition, whatever the believer decides to do is bound to be improper and will cause many regrets afterwards. He must exercise his will to reject, stop, and overcome his feelings. Only when his feelings are no longer stirring and are perfectly calm can he make a proper decision.

Likewise, a believer should not do anything which might stir up his emotion. Sometimes our emotion is peaceful and calm, but because we act according to our own will, we stir up the emotion. This kind of experience happens frequently, and it greatly damages our spiritual life. Whatever disturbs the tranquility of our soul (emotion) must be rejected. Not only should we refrain from doing things when our emotion is in turmoil, we should also learn not to do anything which may cause such turmoil. However, we should not think that our actions will be correct just because our emotion is in an undisturbed state. If we are led by the "calm emotion" rather than the spirit, we will stir up our emotions. Those in our midst who have the experience can recall that in meeting someone or in writing a letter, the emotion can become greatly stirred up. These things are then outside of God's will.

EMOTION AND WORK

Elsewhere we have emphasized that only the spirit can do spiritual work; all other works are without spiritual value. Because this point is so important, we will now go into more detail.

Today men pay much attention to human psychology. Some who work for the Lord diligently study psychology. They think that if their words, teachings, presentations, attitudes, and interpretations can appeal to man's psychology, they will win many people to the Lord. This psychology is the working of man's emotion. Although it may prove useful at times, dependence on emotion alone has no spiritual significance at all.

We already know that man's lack is regeneration—the regeneration of the spirit. A work is absolutely useless if it cannot cause man's deadened spirit to be enlivened, cause man to receive God's uncreated life, and cause man to have the Holy Spirit indwell his regenerated spirit. If the purpose of the believer's work is not to impart life to others, the result of his preaching is no different than if he exhorted people to worship the devil. Neither our psychology nor other's psychology can help them receive life. Unless the Holy Spirit Himself does the work, everything is in vain.

A believer must realize that his emotion is altogether natural; it is not the source of God's life. May he truly acknowledge the fact that his emotion is void of God's life! Therefore, he must not consider using the power of his emotion through tears, a sad countenance, weeping, or other emotional expressions to save people. None of the functions of his emotion can influence man's darkened spirit in any way. Unless the Holy Spirit gives life to man, no one can receive life. If we do not depend on the Holy Spirit, but depend on the emotion instead, we will see that all of our work's efforts are futile and bear no real fruit.

Emotion can never give life to man. Those who work for the Lord must clearly see that if they depend on themselves, nothing in them can generate God's life. We can exhaust every psychological method to excite man's emotion to arouse his interest toward religion; we can make him feel repentant, sorrowful, and shameful for his past history and fearful of the coming judgment; we can cause him to admire Christ, desire to contact other Christians, and be merciful to the poor; we can even make him feel happy while doing all of these things, yet we still cannot cause him to be regenerated. Whether we cause interest, regret, sorrow, shame, fear, admiration, desire, mercy, joy, etc., all of these are just the various functions of the emotion. Man can have them all and still be spiritually dead, because he has not apprehended God intuitively. From our human viewpoint, is not someone who possesses these qualities a first-class Christian? Nevertheless, these are only the impulses of the emotion and cannot sufficiently prove one's regeneration. The manifestation of regeneration is apprehension of God in the intuition of the regenerated one, i.e., his spirit is quickened. Therefore, when we work, we must not think that it is sufficient for men to change their attitude toward us, have a good feeling about us, and display all the previously mentioned emotions. This is not regeneration!

If the workers of the Lord would remember that our aim is to help people receive the life of Christ, they would never use their emotion to make people approve of Christ's teaching and express a good feeling toward Christianity. When we clearly acknowledge that man lacks God's life—the quickening of the spirit—we will realize that all the work which has been done by relying on ourselves is vain. No matter how a man changes, he can only change within the boundary of his "self." He can never step outside this boundary and change his own life into the life of God. Therefore, may we truly see the reality that "a spiritual aim needs spiritual means." Our spiritual aim is to cause people to be regenerated. Therefore, when we work we must only resort to spiritual means; emotion is of no use.

The apostle Paul said that every woman who prays or prophesies must have her head covered. Concerning this matter, there are many diverse explanations and opinions. Although we will not decide here which interpretation is right, one thing is clear: the apostle's intention was to prevent the functioning of emotion. He intended to cover up all that arouses the emotion. It is particularly easy for a woman who preaches and prays to arouse people's emotion. From a physical standpoint, only the head is seemingly covered, but from a spiritual standpoint, the purpose of the covering is to put to death all the things that belong to emotion. Although in the Bible, brothers are not physically allowed to have their heads covered, in a spiritual sense, brothers must have their heads covered just like the sisters!

From this we can see that emotion may easily be expressed in the Lord's work; otherwise, the apostle would not have needed to give this kind of prohibition. In spiritual work today nearly the greatest problem is whether or not there is a power of attraction. It seems that those who have a natural attraction have the upper hand, and that the result of their work is superior to others. Those who have no natural attraction are seemingly defeated, and the achievement of their work is inferior to others. The apostle's intention was to cover up everything belonging to the soul, regardless of whether it was naturally attractive. All that is natural must be covered. Therefore, all the Lord's servants must learn this lesson from the sisters. Our natural attraction cannot help our spiritual work, neither can our lack of natural attraction hinder it. Let us refrain from all such thoughts. If we consider our power of attraction, we will lose our heart of dependence. Similarly, if we consider our lack of attraction, we will not walk according to the spirit. Unless the workers of the Lord walk according to the spirit, all the results of their work will be vain.

What are the workers of the Lord seeking today? Many seek for spiritual power. But real spiritual power comes from paying a price. As long as we are dead toward our emotions, we will have spiritual strength. We lose spiritual strength because we use too much of our emotion and have so much desire, affection, and feeling. If we do not walk according to the feelings of our emotions, and in everything deliver to death our own desires and actions which cause us to be happy, we would see strength and power in our human lives. The deeper death of the cross can fill us with spiritual power; other than this, there is no way. When the cross deals with our desires and enables us to live for God, spiritual power spontaneously will be manifested from us.

Furthermore, if a believer does not overcome his emotion in spiritual work, the emotion will hinder him in many ways from going on. As long as the influence of the emotion is present, the believer's spiritual strength is not sufficient to regulate his emotion. Hence, he cannot fulfill the highest will of God. The emotion will use all kinds of things to hinder the work from going on. Let us see the example of our physical weariness. We need to distinguish whether our need for rest is due to (1) bodily fatigue, (2) emotional weariness, or (3) both bodily fatigue and emotional weariness. God does not want us to overwork our spirit, our soul, or our body. God desires us to rest when we are tired. But we need to know whether our need for rest is related to bodily fatigue or emotional weariness, or whether our emotional weariness is using some fatigue in the body as an excuse to demand rest.

Many times our desire for rest is really laziness. Our body needs to rest and so does our mind and spirit, but we should not rest because of a laziness which comes from the evil nature of our emotions. Laziness and weariness use physical fatigue as an alibi. In short, our emotion is pleasure-seeking and self-entertaining. The believer should guard against it creeping in during their proper rest.

THE PROPER USE OF EMOTION

If a believer allows the cross to do a deeper work in his emotion, he would soon learn that the emotion would not obstruct the spirit, but would even cooperate with the spirit. The cross would deal with all the natural life of the emotion, renew it, and make it an instrument of the spirit. We have previously mentioned that a spiritual man is not a spirit, nor is he a man without emotion. On the contrary, he uses his emotion to express the divine life within him. Before being dealt with by God, the emotion cannot be an instrument of the spirit. Rather, it acts according to its own desire. After being cleansed, the emotion can be an organ to express the spirit. The spirit likewise expresses its life through the emotion. The spirit needs the emotion to express its love and feelings towards man's suffering; it also needs the emotion to cause man to sense the operation of intuition. The sense of the spirit is made known to man through the feeling of his quiet emotion. If the emotion obeys the spirit, it causes the spirit to love what God loves and hate what He hates.

After understanding the truth concerning not living according to the emotion, some believers mistakenly think that a spiritual life is a life void of emotion. They think we need to abolish emotion so that we can be without emotion, like wood or stone. If a believer does not understand the meaning of the death of the cross, he cannot know the meaning of delivering the emotion to death and living entirely according to the spirit. We are not saying that the believer should become exceedingly hard, like iron or rock; nor should he be without affection in order to be considered a spiritual man, as if the term "spiritual man" denotes a man without affection. On the contrary, the most tender, sympathetic, merciful, and loving person is a spiritual man. Being entirely spiritual and delivering the emotion to the cross do not mean that a believer will lose his emotion and become emotionless. When we see how a spiritual believer's love is greater than that of others, we will know that a spiritual man is not without emotion; rather, his emotion differs from that of an ordinary man.

In delivering our soul to the cross, we must remember that the *life* of the soul is lost, not the *function* of the soul. To nail the function of the soul on the cross would mean that we no longer think, decide, or feel. We must always remember this fact: losing the soul is to solely and continuously live by the life of God, not living by the natural life. It is being willing to not live according to self or walk according to the pleasure of the self, but to submit to God's will. Moreover, the cross and resurrection are two inseparable facts. "For if we have grown together with Him in the likeness of His death, indeed we will also be in the likeness of His resurrection" (Rom. 6:5). The death of the cross does not mean annihilation; the emotion, mind, and will of the soul-life are not exterminated by passing through the cross. They only lose their natural life in the death of the Lord; they are resurrected in His life. Death and resurrection cause the functioning organs of the soul to lose their life and then cause them to be renewed and used by the Lord. Consequently, a spiritual man is not without emotion; rather, his emotion is the most perfect and noble; it is as if it were newly created by God's hand. If anyone has difficulty here, the problem lies in his theory because no problem exists in his spiritual experience.

Emotion must pass through the work of the cross (Matt. 10:38-39) in order to get rid of its fiery nature, fanaticism, and confusion and to be totally subject to the spirit. The goal of the work of the cross is for the spirit to have the authority to regulate the function of the emotion.

CHAPTER TWO

LOVE

GOD'S REQUIREMENT

In the experience of a believer, perhaps the most difficult thing is to submit to the Lord in the matter of love. But the Lord pays attention to the believer's love more than anything else. The Lord requires him to fully hand over his love to Him that He may be Lord over it. The Lord wants to have the first place in his love. We often hear people talk about consecration. We know that consecration is the first step of a believer's spiritual living. It is not the destination of spirituality; rather, it is the beginning. It leads the believer to the position of being sanctified. If there is no consecration, there certainly cannot be a spiritual living. However, nothing is more important in a believer's consecration than his love. Whether his consecration is true or false depends upon whether or not there is a consecration of love. Love is the touchstone of consecration. It is easy to present our time, money, ability, and many other things to the Lord, but it is difficult to offer our love to Him. This is not to say that we do not love Christ. Perhaps we love the Lord very much; nevertheless, we may give the first place to someone else and give the Lord the second place; we may love someone else besides the Lord, or we may direct our own love. Loving the Lord in these ways should not be considered as consecration, because we have not yet consecrated our love. Every spiritual believer knows that love should be offered first. Unless love is offered, nothing is offered.

In the matter of a believer's love, God requires him to love Him fully. The Lord is not willing to share the heart of the believer with anyone or anything. Even if His share is the major portion, He still is not pleased. The Lord demands absoluteness. This is a deathblow to the believer's soul-life, which is totally for the self. The Lord wants us to part with what we love and not have a divided heart. He wants us to love Him fully and to love according to Him. "You shall love the Lord your God with all your heart and with all your soul and with all your mind" (Matt. 22:37). The word "all" means that every part of our being is for the Lord. The Lord does not want us to withhold any of our love so that we can love according to our wish. He wants absoluteness. He is a "jealous God" (Exo. 20:5) who will not allow anyone else to gain the love of His children.

But we have many loves other than God! Perhaps some are those who are most intimate to us, like an Isaac, a Jonathan, or a Rachel. God demands that we put those whom we love upon the altar. He cannot tolerate us withholding someone who would compete with Him. All that we have should be offered up. This is the way for a believer to obtain spiritual power. When the sacrifice, even the last sacrifice, is put upon the altar, fire will descend from heaven. Without the altar, there is no heavenly fire. Without bearing the cross and offering to the Lord all that we love, how can we have the power of the Holy Spirit? The altar should not be kept empty because fire will consume the sacrifice upon it. What will the fire burn if there are no sacrifices? O brothers, we cannot obtain the power of the Holy Spirit by understanding the cross in our mentality or by discussing the cross; rather, we can obtain it by offering up everything completely. If we have any secret ties that are not yet cut off, if in our hearts we still spare some sheep, oxen, or Agag for God, we will not be able to see the power of the Holy Spirit manifested through us.

Because believers do not allow the Lord to be Lord over their love, God's work is hindered. How many parents love their children so much that they hold back their children and cause God's kingdom to suffer loss! Many couples are so attached to each other that there is a shortage of labor for the plenteous harvest! Many believers are reluctant to part with their friends, so they remain behind while their brother fights alone at the front. It is very pitiful that some believers think they can love their loved ones and the Lord at the same time. They do not realize that if they love their loved ones, they cannot love the Lord; and if they love the Lord, they cannot love their loved ones. If we cannot say with Asaph, "Whom do I have in heaven but You? / And besides You there is nothing I desire on earth," then we are still living in our soul (Psa. 73:25).

We cannot neglect the importance of the believer loving the Lord with all his heart. Nothing satisfies the Lord's heart as much as our love. The Lord does not look at how much we work for Him or how active we are for Him. It pleases Him when He sees us loving Him. The church in Ephesus labored for the Lord; nevertheless, they left their first love toward Him (Rev. 2). Therefore, the Lord was not pleased. The Lord is pleased only if we work out of our love for Him. If we have no heart for Christ, if we are not affectionate toward Him and do not love Him, even though we may accomplish a great deal for Him outwardly, what use is it? We should know that it is possible for us to labor for the Lord and not love Him. This was the case of the Ephesians. May we ask God to shine His light that we may see the reason for our activities and the intensity of our love towards Him. What is the use if we keep saying, "Lord," and labor for Him all day, yet do not love Him in our heart? Oh, may we have an absolute heart for our beloved Lord!

God's children do not realize what a hindrance their loved ones can be to the growth of their spiritual life. When a believer has other loves besides God, he will find out that God gradually becomes less important to him. Although his loved ones may also love God, he will perhaps love God for the sake of his loved ones more than for the sake of God Himself. His relationship with God is lowered from being spiritual to being fleshly. We surely cannot love God for the sake of some persons, matters, or things. We can only love God for His sake. If a believer loves God for the sake of his loved ones, his heart is directed by those whom he loves. God can gain his love only as a beneficiary of his loved ones. If his loved ones can influence him to love God today, they can also influence him to lose his love for God in the future.

Moreover, when we incline our heart toward a certain person, it is very difficult for us to keep our heart calm.

Rather, we are under the influence of our emotions, trying ardently to please this person. At this time, we probably have less of an interest in drawing near to God than we do of drawing near to the loved one. Our interest in spiritual things, things relating to the intuition, will be greatly reduced. Perhaps there is no outward change, but our heart lingers beside the one we love. In this kind of condition, our interest in spiritual things, if not completely gone, is greatly diminished. Then we will not be able to keep our heart from loving the vanities of the world because we can please our loved ones with them. Worldly things, beauty, glory, and many other things unworthy of mention will gradually become the object of our seeking so that we might please our loved ones. God and His requirements will then be forgotten and ignored. We should realize that we can love only one person and serve one master. If we love man, we cannot love God. Therefore, any secret relationship that we may have with a person must be severed.

Only God can satisfy a believer's heart. Human beings cannot satisfy the believer's heart. Many believers fail simply because they seek in man that which can only be found in God. Human love is nothing but vanity; only God's love can satisfy the desires of a believer. If he seeks affection outside of God, his spiritual condition will immediately deteriorate. He can only live by God's love.

In view of this, do we not need to love anyone? If we look at the Bible's repeated charge to love our brothers and our enemies, we know it is not God's intention that we not love others; rather, He wants to direct our love. He wants us to love others not for ourselves, but for Him and also in Him. Our natural goodness and wickedness have no place here. Natural affection also loses its power. God wants us to be directed by Him because we love Him. When He wants us to love a certain person, we can obey; when He wants us to terminate our relationship with a certain person, we can also obey.

This is the life of the cross. Only when we have the Holy Spirit deeply applying the work of the cross in us and causing us to experience the putting to death of the soul-life can we lose the self in our affections. When we have really passed through death, we will not be attached to anyone; we will be guided only by God's commands. When our soul-life goes through this step, it loses its power as if it has died in the matter of affection. Then God can instruct us on how to begin anew to love others in Him. God wants us to have new relationships in Him with those whom we loved in the past. Every natural relationship should be terminated. We should pass through death so that we may begin the relationships anew in the realm of resurrection.

What a difficult life this seems to be to the believer! Only those who really live this way know what a blessing this is! God often "strips" the believer of his loved ones because of the believer's consecration or for the benefit of the believer. God will either work to make our heart submissive, or He will strip us of what we love. When He uses the latter method, He causes our loved ones to change in their love toward us, or He causes the environment to hinder us from loving them. Perhaps our loved one has gone on a far journey, perhaps he has deceased, or perhaps there are other circumstances. If our consecrated heart is honest before God, God will strip us of everything until we have only Him left. If the believer wants to obtain a real spiritual living, he must willingly abandon all that is dear to him. God requires anything that conflicts with a heart that loves Him to be abandoned. The spiritual life does not allow our affection to be scattered and wandering. In God's eyes, our love, whether wrong in its motive, excessiveness, or goal, is just as wrong as our hatred. In the sight of God, the love that comes out of our self is just as dirty as hatred.

When a believer goes through such a time, he will see how pure his heart is in loving others. There is nothing of the self mixed in it. All of his heart is for God and also in God. Although he loved others in the past, he loved himself even more, considering himself more important than others. Now he can share in other's happiness and sorrow, bearing their burdens and serving them with love. He will not love what he loves but what God wants him to love. He will not love himself more than others but others as himself. Since he loves himself in God and for God, he also loves others in God and for God. Therefore, he can love others as himself.

Believers should know that letting God direct their affection is an essential prerequisite to their spiritual growth. How uncontrollable our affection is! If it is not subdued under God's purpose, there is a possibility of endangering our spiritual life at any time. It is easy to correct wrong thinking, but it is hard to handle wrong affection. We should love the Lord with all our heart, allowing Him to direct our love.

LOVING THE LORD SOULISHLY

However, let us issue a warning here. Do not think that we can love the Lord by our self. The Lord rejects all that comes out of our self. Even our love for Him is useless. On the one hand, if a believer does not have a deep love for the Lord, He is grieved; on the other hand, even those who love the Lord can grieve Him because they love Him in their souls. If a believer exercises his soulish power to love the Lord, this love is not pleasing to the Lord. The believer's love, even for the purpose of loving the Lord, should be completely under the control of the spirit. Today there are too many who love the Lord with a worldly love; it is rare to see a love that is of God. What does this actually mean?

Believers primarily receive the things of God with their human hearts. They speak about their Father God; they call the Lord their "dear Lord"; and they remember the sufferings of the Lord. When they do this, their hearts are filled with joy and the sensation of love for the Lord. They think that this feeling is from God. Perhaps when they think of the cross of the Lord, they cannot help but shed some tears, as if they have an unspeakable, burning love toward the Lord Jesus. But these things pass through their life like a ship that sails through the sea without leaving any trace. Such is the love of many believers. But what kind of love is this? This is the kind of love which only causes one's self to feel happy. This is not loving God but loving the feeling of happiness. The outward appearance of the Lord's sufferings moves their heart, but the truth contained therein does not influence their lives.

How powerless have the sufferings of the Lord Jesus become in the hearts of today's believers! When they think about these things, they become proud of how they love the Lord and of how others cannot compare with them! When they talk about these things, they are like heavenly people. But, actually, they have not yet left their pitiful self one bit. When you listen to their talk, you think that they love the Lord very much. You praise and admire them. But actually they love themselves completely. The reason they remember the Lord, talk about the Lord, and long for the Lord is just because this makes them feel happy. When they do this, they feel happy. They do these things because their goal is to obtain happiness. It is not for the Lord. Such remembrance causes their "spirituality" to feel comfortable. Therefore, they continue to remember the Lord in this way. This is soulish and earthly. It is not from God. Therefore, it is not spiritual.

What is the difference between spiritual love and soulish love? It is very difficult to tell the difference outwardly. However, every believer can distinguish the source of his own love. The soul is our self. Therefore, all that is soulish cannot be separated from the self. A soulish love towards the Lord is one that is from the self. Loving God for the sake of obtaining a happy feeling for the self is loving God soulishly. If the love for God is spiritual, then there is nothing for the self mixed in with it. This is loving God for His sake, for the sake of loving Him. Any love for God that is for self-happiness or any other reason, totally or partially, is from the soul. Moreover, if we look at the fruit of this love, we can also tell its source. If it is soulish, this kind of love does not have the power to help a believer to be permanently delivered from the world. He has to labor and struggle to stay away from the attractiveness of the world. However, if the love is spiritual, worldly things and matters are naturally abandoned because of this love. The believer looks down upon them and reckons them as something to be hated. He no longer has his eyes on the world because the glorious light of God has blinded his fleshly eyes. After having this experience of loving God, he does not esteem himself highly because of it; rather, he humbles himself, as if he has diminished before men.

The nature of God's love is forever changeless. Our love is very changeable. If we love God with our own love, our love toward God grows cold when we feel unhappy. After a long period of trial, it surely fails because the believer loves God with his own love; he loves God for his own sake, for his own happiness, etc. Therefore, when he cannot obtain the expected happiness, he shrinks back. If it is the love of God, no matter what situation or position he is in, he still loves God without any change. "Love is strong as death; / jealousy is cruel as the grave / ...Many waters cannot quench love, / neither can the floods drown it" (S.S. 8:6-7). If a believer truly loves God, regardless of his circumstances and feelings, he still loves God. Soulish love ceases when the effect of the emotion ceases; spiritual love is strong, cruel, and does not let go.

The Lord often causes a believer to experience what he considers to be painful in order that the believer would not love God for himself. When the believer loves the Lord with his own love for himself, he has to sense the Lord's love in order to love Him. But when the believer loves God with God's love and for God, God does not let him sense His love. Instead, God wants the believer to believe in His love. In the beginning of one's Christian life, the Lord always attracts the believer to feel His love in many ways. After the believer experiences this, He leads him to take a much deeper journey. God does not let him feel His love, but He causes him to *believe* in His love. We should pay attention to the fact that deeply tasting the Lord's love is a step which *must be* experienced by every believer who desires to go on in a deeper way. Only by the attraction of the Lord's love can the believer leave all for the Lord and come forward to the Lord. In the initial stage of the believer's spiritual life, it is necessary and helpful to have the sense of the Lord's love. This is something the believer should pursue. After the experience of feeling the Lord's love and after a suitable period of time, the believer should not "hold on" to this kind of feeling. Otherwise, his spiritual life will suffer damage. There are different kinds of experiences for different stations on the journey of the spiritual life. It is appropriate and profitable to have a certain kind of experience at a certain station. But if a believer desires to maintain the experiences of the previous stations up to the last station, he would have to go backwards or remain at a certain place. After the believer feels the Lord's love, the Lord wants him to believe in His love; therefore, shortly, but not immediately, after he experiences the feeling of His love, God no longer causes him to sense His love. Then He wants him to believe that His love is still unchanging. If, after an experience of feeling the Lord's love, a believer suddenly does not have the same feeling, he should realize that this is the time for him to believe. He should not be alarmed.

BEWARE OF ONE THING

If we want to walk according to the spirit, we should keep our love calm; otherwise, we cannot hear the voice of the intuition directly. If our affection is not entirely subject to God's purpose, our heart is often disturbed. This hinders the leading of the spirit. The believer should *continually* pay attention in the spirit to the people and things that stimulate his affection. If Satan cannot win in other matters, he will surely tempt you in this area. I do not know how many believers have failed because of this. Therefore, we should be cautious.

Friends can stir our love more than anything else. Among friends, the opposite sex stirs us the most because males and females need to be adjusted not only physiologically but also psychologically. Since there are many differences in their natural make-up, they have the power to attract each other. This is soulish and natural and, therefore, should be rejected by the believer.

It is a fact that the opposite sex can very easily arouse love. The stimulation one receives from the same sex is much less compared to that from the opposite sex. Since there is a mutual psychological demand, this leads one to believe that people of the opposite sex are more approachable than those of the same sex. This kind of inclination is common, natural, and inherent. Therefore, love toward the opposite sex is easily kindled by just a little stirring.

All these matters refer to the natural side. Factually, this is the case. Therefore, if a believer wants to walk according to the spirit, he must pay attention to this. In our dealings with other people, especially in the matter of love, if we treat the same sex in one way and the opposite sex in another way, we should realize that we are under the working of the soul. If we treat people differently for no other reason than that they are of the opposite sex, then our affection is still natural. If the believer feels some kind of mysterious strength attracting him to someone of the opposite sex just because that person is of the opposite sex, he should know that his natural affection has been activated. Sometimes this kind of stimulation is mixed in with a purpose that is very proper. However, if there is a fraction of thought about the opposite sex mixed in with his other thoughts, the believer should realize that the relationship is not entirely spiritual.

In his work and while working, a worker should be cautious that his work is not penetrated by any thought about the opposite sex. Every desire to obtain glory among those of the opposite sex must be absolutely rejected. All the speaking and attitudes that are influenced by the opposite sex are enough to nullify true spiritual power. Everything should be done quietly and with a pure motive. Remember that not only are sins filthy, but everything of the soul is also filthy.

If so, should believers not have friends of the opposite sex? This is not the teaching of the Bible. While the Lord was on earth, He associated with Martha, Mary, and other women. The important point is whether the affection is entirely under God's governing or whether it has the effect of the soul in it. It is normal for brothers and sisters to associate with each other. But there should not be any working of the soul or of sin. Before a believer experiences the thorough working of the cross, it is best not to have friends of the opposite sex. However, no matter what stage of growth that a believer reaches, if he seeks or longs for friends of the opposite sex, he is surely being controlled by the soul. In everything, we should submit to God's arrangement.

In short, the believer's love must be completely consecrated to God. Any time we feel that it is difficult for us to give up someone, we should realize that our soul-life is in control. If our love cannot submit to God's purpose in any area, then there must be a great many unspiritual things mixed in with that area. Soulish love only leads us to the world and sins. If our affection is not of the Lord, sooner or later it will become lust. From the past to the present, Samson is not the only one who failed in this matter. Delilah continues to shave people's hair everywhere!

We have previously said that it is very difficult for believers to consecrate in the matter of love. Therefore, the consecration of this one thing is a sign of true spirituality. The extent to which a believer dies to his affections and his seeking for love is the extent to which he is spiritual. This is the biggest test. Without dying to the affections of the world, we are not yet dead to anything. Being dead to affection is being dead to the world. Desiring friendship and a lover's love indicates that we are not dead to the self-life. Real death to the soul-life can be seen in the giving up of our love, except the love for God. How transcendent is the spiritual man, walking above the love of man!

Chapter Three

DESIRES

Desires comprise the greatest part of our soul-life. These desires join together with our will and cause us to either rebel against or dislike the will of God. Because we have too many desires, our feelings become confused and we are unable to quietly walk according to the spirit. Our desires arouse our feeling, causing us to have many restless experiences. Before a believer is set free from sins, his desire is united with sin, and he loves sin. Hence, the new man is put in captivity, losing his freedom. Even after he has been delivered from outward, apparent sins, his desire still pursues many things for himself, independent of God. When he is emotional, he is governed by his desire. Unless the cross works deeply and the desire is judged by the enlightening of the cross, the believer will never live completely in the spirit for God.

When a believer is soulish, he is under the strong direction of his desires. The natural and soulish desires of man are *all* related to the *self*-life. They are either for self, by self, or according to self. When the believer is soulish, his will has not yet submitted to the Lord, and he still has many ideas of his own. To desire is to cooperate with one's own ideas, to delight in all the ideas of one's will, and to desire one's ideas to be accomplished. All self-pleasure, self-glory, self-exaltation, self-love, self-pity, and self-respect come from the desire of man. Man's desire makes self the center of everything. Let us consider: is there anything which man desires and likes that does not correspond to any of the "selfs" noted above? If we would check our desires under the light of the Lord, we would see that no matter what we desire or how we desire, we cannot escape from the word "self." All of our desires are for the self! They either make the self happy or bring glory to the self. When believers are in this situation, there is no possibility for them to live in the spirit.

THE NATURAL DESIRES OF THE BELIEVERS

Pride comes from desires. The desire of man causes him to seek a position for himself so that he can be glorified before men. Any hidden tendency to boast of one's position, family traditions, health, disposition, ability, appearance, and power comes from man's emotion (desire). To consider how one's dwelling, clothing, and eating are different from others and, consequently, feel self-fulfilled is also the effect of the emotion. Even considering that a gift one has received from God is superior to that of others is a thought urged by the emotion.

Oh, how the emotional believer loves to show off! He loves both to see and to be seen. He cannot tolerate restraints from God. He uses every means to push himself from the back to the front. He cannot be hidden according to God's will nor can he deny his self in secret. He loves people's attention. His desire of self-love is hurt whenever men do not honor him, but he is full of joy when he is esteemed by someone. He loves to hear people praising him and considers such praises to be well-spoken. Even in the work, he tries to exalt himself in many ways. There is always a secret motive stirring him whether he is giving a message or writing a book. In short, his heart of vainglory is still alive; he still seeks after what he loves and what inflates his self.

This natural desire causes a believer to become ambitious. Ambition is inspired by the natural desire. The ambition to spread self-fame, to become one who is above all men, or to be honored by people are all from the soul-life. The desire to be successful, fruitful, and spiritually powerful and useful in spiritual work is often derived solely from the desire to glorify oneself. In our spiritual life, the pursuit of growth, depth, and nobler experiences is often for our happiness and others' appreciation. If we traced the life and work of the believer to their source, we would find a strange fact: a great part is actually for self! The believer's desire for self is the source of everything in his life and work.

A believer must know that if his life and work are motivated by his ambition, even though everything he does may appear to be good, well-spoken of, and outwardly effective, it is just wood, hay, and stubble in God's eyes. This kind of walk and labor does not have any spiritual value. Any thought for the self is enough to corrupt any activity, and God is not pleased with such thoughts. God views the believer's lust for spiritual fame equally as filthy as his lust for sins. If the believer walks according to his natural desire, then he will regard his self highly in all things. However, God loathes this "self"!

Natural desire is equally active in other aspects of a believer's living. The soulish life causes him to hunger after worldly conversations and communications. It impels him to watch what he should not watch and read what he should not read. This is not to say that he does these things all the time. Rather, occasionally he does what he knows he should not do because of a strong urge from within. The soulish life can even be seen in his attitude. Many believers have such an experience to a certain extent. The function of his soul can also be seen in the way the believer walks and is even more evident in the way he talks and does things. Everyone who walks faithfully by the spirit knows these are small things. Yet if the believer is urged by his emotional desire in these things, it is impossible for him to walk by the spirit. The believer must know that in spiritual matters, nothing is too small to hinder his progress.

A believer is inquisitive when he is urged by his natural desire. The more spiritual a believer becomes, the more ordinary he is, because he is united with God in His arrangements. Only emotional believers have a kind of chivalrous nature and take risky actions to satisfy their own hearts and create a great sensation. When urged by such inquisitiveness, many aspects of their behavior are very immature. They would not care for their maturity but pretend to be clever instead. When they look back, they regret; but at the time, they feel glorious. This inquisitive emotion urges man, and if the believers follow it, they lose their normalcy and go beyond what is proper.

Fondness for pleasure is also a great expression of emotional believers. The emotion cannot bear allowing believers to live completely for God; it absolutely opposes the life that is constantly for God. Though believers may accept the demand of the Lord's cross and put to death the emotion so that they may live for the Lord, the emotion still asks that a small area be reserved for its activities. This is why many believers cannot live for the Lord completely. There is no need to speak of much, just a day's living; no need to mention other things, just the warfare of prayers. How many believers can engage in warfare by prayer that is completely for the Lord for one whole day, without saving some time for their own pleasure? To have pleasure is to reserve some ground for our own emotion. How difficult it is for us to live in the spirit through the day! We always keep some time for ourselves to talk with others because this is soothing to our emotions. When we are shut in by God, seeing neither men nor sky, and are required to live in the spirit to work for Him before the throne, we know whether our emotion has been completely put to death or not. We also know how much our emotion demands from us and how much we live by the emotion.

Emotional believers also like to be hasty. Emotion does not know the meaning of waiting for God, waiting for God's revelation, or following the leading of the Holy Spirit. Emotion is always hasty. Emotion always causes the believer to become excited and to be impelled into action. Whenever this excitement comes with its impelling power, it urges the believer to act hastily. The emotion is very upset and unwilling if the believer waits for the Lord, understands the will of God, and takes one step at a time, not walking by his own desire. If a believer has not put his emotion to the cross, he cannot walk according to the spirit. He must realize that of a hundred things done out of impulse, not even one is according to God's will.

We need time to pray, prepare, wait, and be refilled with the strength of the Holy Spirit. How else can there be no mistakes in our hasty acts? God clearly knows that the emotion of our flesh is impatient; therefore, He always uses our co-workers, brothers, family, environment, and material things to hinder us and slow us down. He wants our hastiness to die completely so that He can work. Since God never does things in a hurry, He never grants power to those who act hurriedly. Hence, the hasty doer can only do things by his own strength. This is clearly the work of the flesh. God does not want the believer to walk by the flesh, so the believer must be willing to put his hurried emotion to death. Whenever the emotion operates hastily, let us pray, "O Lord, the emotion is impatient once again. May Your cross operate." A person who walks by the spirit must not be hasty.

God does not want us to do anything by ourselves; He wants us to wait for Him and His command. His command must be in all our doings. Only the things that are commissioned in our spirit are of God. How can this be accomplished by a believer who walks after his own desire? Such a one is hasty even when he wants to follow the will of God. He does not know that God not only has a will but also a time. Although we may be in one accord with His will, He still wants us to wait for His time. The flesh cannot tolerate this. Once a believer presses on in the spirit, he will see that God's time and God's will are equally important. If we are hasty to give birth to Ishmael, later he will be the greatest enemy of Isaac. All those who cannot wait for God's time cannot keep His will.

An emotional believer will not wait for God because his desires are for himself. He likes to do everything on his own. He cannot trust God and allow God to work for him. He cannot commit the whole matter into God's hands and refrain from using his own strength. He is not able to trust because this requires the denial of his self. Unless his desires are banished, his self will always stay active. He loves to help God, as if God were too slow and needed his help. This is the working of the soul, the activity of the self under the instigation of emotional desires. If the believer acts in a hasty manner, he will see that God causes his work to be ineffective; then he has no choice but to deny himself.

Self-vindication is a very common behavior among emotional believers. Being misunderstood and misjudged are matters that are encountered regularly by the believers. Although sometimes the Lord wants His children to clarify certain things, unless they are clear that this is the Lord's command, at most it is being done by the soul-life. More often than not, the Lord desires that His people commit all things into His hand and not vindicate themselves. Oh, how the believer loves to plead for himself! How upsetting it is to be misunderstood, because this reduces his glory and lowers his dignity. The self will not be silent under the false accusations of others. He cannot accept what God has given to him nor wait for God to vindicate, because that is too slow; rather, he wants God to immediately clear him of any charge so that men would know his righteousness. This all comes from the soulish desire. If a believer would submit to God's powerful hand during a misunderstanding, he would see, through the misunderstanding, that God is causing him to deny his self in a deeper way and deny his soulish desire more thoroughly. This is his practical cross. Every time the believer receives a cross, he goes through its crucifixion once more. However, if he vindicates himself according to the desire of the self, he will learn that the power of self is harder to subdue the next time.

If the natural desire of a believer has not been dealt with by the cross, he will seek someone to whom he can pour out his heart when he is cast down in afflictions and worries. His emotion motivates him to long to speak forth his troubles to others so that the sorrow within his heart can be released and his burden lightened. His natural desire is to make known his sorrows to others so that he may feel more comfortable. By making known his problems to others, he also hopes to gain sympathy and comfort from them. He lusts for sympathy and comfort because they make him happy. Because he has not lost his natural desire or the desire for self, he is not satisfied that God alone knows. He cannot commit his burden to the Lord, nor can he silently let God bring him into a deeper death through these matters. He prefers the consolation of men, apart from God. His life lusts after what others can give him and despises God's arrangement. The believer should know that the most effective way for him to really lose his soul-life is to not seek men's sympathy and comfort. The sympathy and comfort of worldly people are foods that feed our soul-life. The life of the spirit is to fellowship with

God so that it is satisfied with God. The power that can endure loneliness is the power of the spirit. Whenever we seek for any of man's ways to lighten our burden, we are walking according to our soul. God wants us to remain silent to enable the cross which He has arranged for us to accomplish its work. Whenever a believer shuts his mouth in his affliction, he sees the cross working. Being silent is the cross! Whoever remains silent tastes the bitterness of the cross! His spiritual life is also nourished by the cross!

THE PURPOSE OF GOD

God's purpose is that the believer would live in the spirit and also be willing to completely put his soul-life to death. Therefore, God has no choice but to banish the natural desire of the believer. He wants to destroy all the natural desire of the believer. Many times the things and matters are not bad or wrong; in fact they are even good and proper. Yet God does not allow the believer to do or possess these things simply because they are the result of an emotional impulse and the believer desires them. If the believer walks by his own likes—even though these things may initially be very good— he is bound to rebel against God. God's purpose is to absolutely destroy the believer's desires which are *apart from Him*. God does not care for the nature of the things; He only asks what directs him—his own desire or the will of God? Even the best work and behavior, as long as it comes out of the believer's own desire and is not according to intuitive revelation, is absolutely and spiritually worthless before God. God may want to lead a believer to do many works, but because the motive is of the believer's own desire, God will immediately oppose this work. Only when the believer fully submits to Him, will He lead him to proceed to work again. God wants only His will (known in our intuition) to be the standard rule in our walk. Though our desires may coincide with His will, He will not let us follow them. We need to follow God's will alone; whatever is of our desire must be denied. This is God's wisdom. Although sometimes our desire may agree with the will of God, God will not let us walk according to it because it is still *our* desire. If we still follow our good and righteous desire, does not our "self" still have its position?

Even though some of our own desires may be the same as God's will, God does not like them because they came out of our self. He wants us to completely cut off anything that we love that is *apart from Him*. Though the things we desire may be excellent, He does not allow us any ground for our independent desire. We must depend on Him in everything. He does not want anything that is not dependent on Him. In this way, He presses on, step by step, to deny the believer's soul-life.

If the believer wants to gain a real spiritual life, he must cooperate with God to put his own desire to death. All of our interest, inclination, and love must be put to death. We must joyfully accept man's opposition, spite, rudeness, misunderstanding, and harsh criticism and allow all the things which are against our natural desire to deal with our soul-life. We should learn to accept all the sufferings, afflictions, and lowly positions given to us by God in His arrangement. No matter how much these cause our natural life to suffer, or how much our natural feelings become displeased, hurt, or uneasy, we have to experience these things in an enduring manner. If we practically bear the cross in this way, we will see that the practical cross we bear will crucify our self-life shortly. Bearing the cross is being crucified. Every time we silently accept something that falls upon us which is against our natural desire, we are adding another nail to firmly nail down our soul-life. All vainglory must be crucified. Our desire to be seen, honored, worshipped, exalted, and proclaimed should be crucified. Our desire to display our self needs to be crucified. All outward adornment to win people's praise needs to be crucified. All self-exaltation and self-boasting need to be crucified. We need to forsake our desire wherever it is expressed. Anything that is initiated by ourselves is filthy in God's eyes.

The practical cross which God gives is contrary to our desires. The purpose of the cross has always been to crucify our desires. No other part in our whole being suffers the pain of the cross more than the emotion. The cross must cut deeply into all that belongs to ourselves. How can our emotion not feel sorrow over our defeated desires? God's redemption requires completely getting rid of man's old creation. God's will and our soulish desires cannot co-exist. If the believer wants to follow the Lord, he must go against his own desires.

Since the purpose of God is such, God allows a believer to pass through many fiery trials under His sovereign arrangement so that all desire, like dross, will be fully burned by the fire of suffering. A believer longs for high position, but the Lord will not allow him to be exalted. He has many hopes, yet the Lord will not allow him to be successful in anything; rather, He causes all his hopes to be crushed. The believer may have many delights, but the Lord will cause him to lose all of his delights and have no way to gain them back. The believer covets glory, but the Lord causes him to suffer shame. Almost nothing in the Lord's arrangements agrees with the thoughts of the believer; everything is like a beating rod. Though the believer still struggles with great effort, he will soon see the Lord—yet not know that it is the Lord—leading him to meet death face to face. It is as if everything were dead; everything wants him to die, and everything wants him to lose the hope of life. At that moment, he realizes that he cannot escape death and that he owes this death to God; hence, he submits himself to God and dies willingly. This death causes him to lose his soul-life in order that he may fully live in God. It is for this death that God has done much work. A believer may resist for a long time, but once he passes through death, everything is fine, and God accomplishes His purpose in him. From then on, the believer can advance quickly on his spiritual way.

Once the believer has lost his heart for self, he can fully submit himself to God. He is willing to become whatever God desires of him; his desire is no longer contrary to God, and he no longer seeks anything other than God. His living is very simple. He expects nothing, he demands nothing, and he covets nothing; he just willingly submits to God's will. A life that submits to God's will is the simplest life on earth because this life does not seek anything for the self but rather silently follows God.

When a believer is willing to forsake all his own desires, he gains a life of real rest. In the past he had many desires, exhausting all of his wits, strength, schemes, devices, and methods to gain them. Therefore, his heart was often confused. When he pursued his desires, he was anxious and troubled. When he failed, he was worried and irritable. How can he have rest? Believers who have not forsaken their own desires and completely submitted to God feel sad about changing human relationships, the unpredictable condition of their environments, the adversities in their life, their loneliness, and many other outward things. This kind of sorrowful feeling is commonly found in believers who are strong in their emotion. Desire can also arouse wrath. Therefore, the believer becomes vexed, anxious, and angry because many outward things are not agreeable or in accordance with his desire. To him they are unfair and unjust. These different expressions of the emotion are caused by people's treatment of him. Pleasant feelings can easily be disturbed, provoked, and hurt by others. The natural desire of a believer yearns for man's love, respect, sympathy, and intimacy. When he cannot obtain these, he murmurs and complains. But who can avoid sorrowful things? Is there anyone living in this bitter world who can fully realize his desires? Therefore, an emotional believer does not have a life of rest. Only when a believer completely walks by the spirit, not seeking the pleasure of his desire and being content with what God has granted, can he have rest.

The Lord Jesus said to His disciples, "Take My yoke upon you and learn from Me, for I am meek and lowly in heart, and you will find rest for your souls" (Matt. 11:29). The word "souls" especially refers to the emotion. The Lord Jesus knows the trials His people pass through. Just as the Father dealt with the Lord, He knows how the heavenly Father will cause the believers to be lonely, misunderstood, and neglected by man (v. 27). He knows that the heavenly Father will allow many unpleasant things to fall upon the believers so that they may be weaned from the world. He also knows how the souls of the believers feel in the fire of the furnace. Therefore, He said that we should learn from Him so that our emotion may find rest. He was meek; He did not care how people treated Him but joyfully endured contradictions from sinners. He was lowly; He humbled Himself willingly and had no ambition. Ambitious ones are troubled, angered, and restless when they cannot attain what they desire. The Lord lived in this world meekly and humbly so His emotion never boiled. He said that we need to learn from Him, and that we should be as meek and lowly as He. He said that we need to take His yoke upon us. This is the restriction borne by the believers. The Lord also took His yoke. He took the yoke of God. He was satisfied with God's will alone. As long as God knew Him, it did not matter if others were against Him. He was willing to accept the restrictions given by God. He said we need to take His yoke, accept His restraint, and walk according to His will alone, not seeking after the freedom of the flesh. Then our emotion will not be bothered and troubled by anything. This is the cross. If the believer is willing to receive the cross of the Lord and fully submit to Him, he will see that the emotion will not be disturbed.

This is nothing less than a *satisfied* life. The believer desires nothing else because he has obtained the will of God. He is fully satisfied with the will of God. God Himself has filled his desire. He considers all that God has given him, arranged for him, required of him, and commanded him is good. He is satisfied if he can follow God's will and does not seek after his own desire. He had many wild desires before, but he has learned how to die to his own desire and be satisfied with God's will alone. Hence, he does not seek after what he likes, not because he forces himself, but because the will of God has filled him. He is satisfied and has no other seeking. This kind of living can only be expressed fully by the word *satisfied*. The characteristic of spiritual living is satisfaction. It is not self-satisfaction or self-sufficiency, nor is it to consider oneself to be in abundance. The meaning of satisfaction is that the believer has obtained all that he needs in God (that is, in God's will), and he considers God's will as the best. Hence, he is satisfied and desires no more. Emotional believers have many desires because they do not consider that God has arranged the best. Therefore, they desire to gain more, become higher, bigger, and happier, have more glory, and be more prominent. Once the Holy Spirit has worked deeply through the cross, a believer no longer loves anything according to himself. His desires are filled by God; hence, he desires nothing.

At this stage, the believer's desire is fully renewed. This does not mean that he never fails after this. His desire has been united with God's desire. At this moment, not only does the believer not resist the Lord negatively, but he delights in what the Lord delights in positively. He does not compel himself to suppress his own desires; rather, he delights in what God requires of him. He delights in God's delights. If God wants him to suffer, he asks God to make him suffer. He feels this kind of suffering is sweet. If it pleases God for him to be wounded, he joyously uses his hands to inflict wounds on himself. He delights in the affliction more than in healing. If God wants him to be lowly, he is happy to cooperate with God and humble himself. He only likes what God likes. He does not seek anything apart from God. Unless God exalts him, he does not wish to be exalted. He does not resist God; he welcomes all of God's doings whether they are bitter or sweet.

The cross produces fruit. All crucifixions will gain the fruit of God's life. All those who are willing to accept the practical cross that God has given them will find themselves living a spiritual life without mixture. We have to practice taking the cross every day according to God's desire for us. Every cross has its particular mission to fulfill as part of God's work in us. May we not allow any cross to come upon us in vain.

CHAPTER FOUR

A LIFE OF FEELING

THE BELIEVER'S EXPERIENCE

When believers have a love relationship with the Lord and are fully satisfied with Him, they usually enter into the experience of a life of feeling. Such an experience is very precious to them. It normally comes after the experience of being freed from sin and before entering into the experience of an absolute spiritual life. Because many believers lack spiritual knowledge, they often regard this experience, which comes after their freedom from sin and gives them much happiness, as the most spiritual and heavenly experience. Since the happiness which proceeds from a life of feeling is so satisfying, they find it difficult to part with this experience.

A believer with a life of feeling senses that the Lord is so near, as though he can touch Him. He feels that the Lord's love is so sweet; he also feels that he loves the Lord very much. A fire seems to burn in his heart, and he enjoys a kind of unspeakable happiness that makes him feel as though he were already in heaven. Something seems to stir in his heart, and it yields an unspeakably comfortable feeling as though he had seized the most valuable treasure. This kind of feeling remains with him wherever he goes and in whatever he does. When a believer goes through such an experience, he has no idea of where he is; it seems as though he has soared out of this world to be with the angels.

At such times, reading the Bible is very enjoyable. The more he reads, the more the feeling of happiness increases. Praying also becomes very easy. He finds it gratifying to express his feelings to the Lord. It seems that the more he prays, the brighter the heavenly light shines. He is also able to make many resolutions to the Lord as an indication of his love for Him. He loves to be quiet, alone, and face to face with God. If he could, he would forever shut the door behind him to fellowship with the Lord because he experiences a happiness which no tongue or pen can describe. Previously, he enjoyed living among the crowd, finding something there that could fill his need. Now, however, he prefers to be alone since the happiness which he obtains before the Lord cannot be compared to that which is derived from the crowd. When a believer feels this way, he desires to be all the more quiet, for fear of losing his happiness among the crowd.

During this time, working for the Lord becomes very easy. Formerly he did not have much to say to others. Now it seems very enjoyable to tell others about the Lord because of the fire of love burning in his heart. The more he speaks, the better he feels. He is also very willing to suffer for the Lord because he feels the Lord is so close. He even rejoices at the thought of dying for the Lord. All burdens become light and all difficulties become easy in this kind of feeling.

When a believer feels this way, his behavior also changes. Perhaps he was talkative. Now he can be quiet with the help of his feeling. When he sees others chattering, he secretly condemns it. Perhaps he was frivolous. Now he can be very solemn. When other believers lack godliness in certain aspects, he senses it most acutely and condemns it. When a believer goes through such an experience, he definitely becomes more sober in his conduct. Furthermore, he seems to have developed a keener sense of judgment which enables him to see the shortcomings of others even more.

Such a believer tends to secretly feel sorry for others because he thinks they do not have his kind of experience. He considers his own happiness as an excellent thing and pities his brothers and sisters for not being able to comprehend it! When he sees them calmly serving the Lord, he invariably concludes that their lives are boring. Only a life like his, full of God's happiness, can truly be the highest life. It seems that the other believers are merely walking in the valley, while he alone soars on the mountain top.

However, does this kind of experience last? Can a believer feel this way every day and be happy all his life? Many believers do not have this experience for long. What grieves the believer the most is that in less than a month or two (generally speaking), the happiness which he most desires suddenly vanishes. One morning when he wakes up as usual to read the Bible, the former taste is gone. He may pray, but after uttering a few phrases he runs out of words. He feels that something is missing. In the past it seemed that other believers were lagging behind him spiritually; now he feels just like one of them. His heart seems to have cooled off considerably. The feeling of a warm fire burning within has disappeared, and he has no idea where it has gone. He does not feel the Lord's presence or His nearness; the Lord seems very far from him. He does not even seem to know where the Lord is. When he suffers, he feels the suffering, not the happiness. When he preaches, it is no longer enjoyable. He utters a few sentences and finds himself with no desire to carry on. In short, everything seems dark, dry, cold, and dead. It appears as though the believer has been left by the Lord in the tomb with nothing to comfort his heart. The lasting joy which he hoped to retain is now lost.

During such a period, the believer will think that he has sinned, and that God has forsaken him. If he has not sinned, why is the Lord no longer with Him? He may search his recent conduct to determine where he offended the Lord, hoping that upon confessing, the Lord will come back, fill him anew, and restore the intimacy and happiness. However, when he examines himself, he cannot find any particular sin; everything is generally the same as it was before. It seems that if his present condition caused the Lord to forsake him, why did his past condition not cause the Lord to forsake him? If he has not sinned, why did the Lord depart from him? He does not have the answer. He simply assumes that he has offended the Lord in some way and that the Lord has forsaken him. Satan also accuses him, making him believe that he has sinned. Hence, he cries for forgiveness before the Lord, hoping to recover what he has lost.

This kind of prayer, however, is ineffective. Not only is he unable to recover what he thinks is lost, but day by day he feels drier and colder. Whatever he does is not enjoyable. Sometimes his actions are even void of any taste. Even his prayers are forced. Previously, he could continuously pray for several hours; now he can pray only for a few minutes, and even they are a strain. As far as his feelings are concerned, his prayers are not even prayers at all. His Bible reading is just as dry. Previously, the more he read the more enjoyable it was; now the Holy Book seems like a field of stones that yields nothing. He finds no pleasure in any of his dealings either with men or matters. Although he obligingly does what is expected of him because he is a Christian, everything is dry and a strain.

Consequently, many Christians fall back. They often know that this is God's will, but they have fallen into such a grievous state that they do not care. They often neglect their duties because they have grown cold. Their conduct, which changed when they were living in their feelings, reverts back to its former state. Previously they felt sorry for those who did not behave as they did; now they are no different from them. They are just as talkative, frivolous, full of jest, and fun-loving as before. Although they experienced a change once, it is gone.

When the believer loses the feeling of happiness, he thinks that everything is lost. If the Lord's presence cannot be felt, he thinks that the Lord must not be with him. If the Lord's warmth cannot be felt, he thinks that the Lord must not be pleased with him. After a while, he does not even seem to know where God is. If he is not disheartened at this point, he will intently seek to recover what he has lost. Even though he loves his Lord and desires to be near Him very much, he does not have any feeling of the Lord's love. How can he bear this?

If the believer does not fall back out of discouragement, he will press on to seek God. However, in spite of his strenuous struggles, he is unable to free himself from the feeling of dryness. Good behavior at this time is a strain. In his heart he secretly rebukes himself for being hypocritical and for putting on a good front despite his inward condition. This pretentious effort does not succeed; it always leads to failure. These failures only serve to increase the believer's suffering. If someone praises him, he feels quite shameful because others do not realize the great darkness he feels in his heart. If someone rebukes him, he feels that it is justified because he knows his own weakness. When he sees how other believers are growing and how they have sweet fellowship with the Lord, he is very desirous. He feels that all the people around him are somewhat virtuous. He has nothing, and everyone else seems stronger.

Will this condition of dryness persist? Or will the believer regain his previous experience? He will, after a while. In a few weeks, the feeling which he lost may suddenly come back. This may happen after he has heard someone preach the word, or after he has fervently prayed; it may happen while he is reading the Bible early in the morning or while he is awake and thinking about the Lord in the middle of the night. The time varies, but the happiness does come back.

At this time, the condition that was lost is altogether restored. The Lord's presence is just as sweet, the love in his heart is just as burning, praying and reading the Bible are just as enjoyable, and the Lord Himself is just as desirable, approachable, and touchable. It is not a burden to draw near to the Lord; rather, it once again becomes the desire of his heart. Everything has changed. There is no more darkness, suffering, and dryness, but light, happiness, and refreshment. The believer, thinking that the Lord forsook him because of his unfaithfulness, after regaining the Lord, thinks that he must diligently keep what he has, so that he will not lose the experience of the life of feeling again. More than ever before, he becomes cautious of his conduct. Daily he serves the Lord with the best of his ability in hope of maintaining his happiness and never failing again.

Even though he is so faithful and diligent, the Lord surprisingly leaves him again after a while. His feeling of happiness disappears again, and he sinks back into a state of suffering, darkness, and dryness once more.

If we examine the history of a believer, we will realize that after a person has been freed from sin and is in touch with the person of God, he frequently has this experience. In the beginning the Lord causes him to feel His love, presence, and happiness, but this feeling disappears after a while. When it comes back, the believer recovers his joy once more, but then it goes away again. Generally, the believer will experience this several times in his lifetime. This kind of experience may not happen to a believer who is still fleshly and has not yet learned to love the Lord. Only when a believer has made some progress and has learned to love the Lord will he experience this.

THE SIGNIFICANCE OF THIS EXPERIENCE

The believer who goes through such an experience thinks that his spirituality is at its highest when he has this experience and at its lowest when he loses it. A believer often speaks of his own life as constantly being up and down. He means that his spirituality is at its highest when he feels happy, when he feels that he loves the Lord, and when he feels the Lord's presence; his spirituality is at its lowest when he feels dark, dry, and bitter. In other words, he is spiritual when he can sense warmth in his heart and soulish when he feels cold. A believer usually thinks in this way, but is it true? These thoughts are based entirely on a misconception. If we are not clear concerning this misconception, we will utterly fail.

The believer must know that "feeling" is forever a part of the soul-life. When he lives by his feeling, no matter how he feels, he is soulish. When he feels happy, when he feels he loves the Lord, and when he feels the Lord's presence, he is just living by his feeling. When he feels dry, sorrowful, and dark, he is still living by his feeling. He is just as soulish when he feels dry, sorrowful, and dark as he is when he feels nourished, happy, and bright. The spiritual life is never regulated by the feeling, nor is it ever in the feeling. The spiritual life should regulate the feeling; the feeling should not regulate the spiritual life. Today the experience of feeling is most commonly, but erroneously, regarded by believers as a spiritual experience. Many Christians have never entered into a spiritual life. Therefore, the sensation of being filled with happiness is interpreted as a spiritual experience. They do not know that it is simply soulish. Spiritual experience is the experience of the intuition; the rest is soulish.

Herein lies the believer's greatest mistake. The effect of the emotion causes him to feel that he has ascended into the heavens. Hence, he thinks that he is in possession of the ascended life, without realizing that this is just something which he feels. When he feels the Lord's presence, he thinks he possesses the Lord; when he does not feel His presence, he thinks that the Lord has forsaken him. He does not realize that this is simply what he feels. He thinks that he really loves the Lord when he senses a warm fire burning in his heart and feels that he loves the Lord very much. When he feels a coldness instead of a burning within, he thinks he has truly lost his love for the Lord. He does not realize that this is only his feeling. Facts do not necessarily correspond with our feelings because our feelings are very unreliable. Actually, a believer is *the same* with or without a feeling. He may feel he is progressing when he is not; or he may feel he is regressing when he is not. These are just his feelings. He thinks that he has progressed whenever he is full of feeling. He does not realize that because he is still soulish, he is merely advancing in a spurt of emotional excitement. When this feeling subsides, he remains the way he used to be. The effect of the emotion helps a soulish person go on; the power of the Holy Spirit helps a spiritual man go on. Of the two, only the power of the Holy Spirit can truly cause a person to go on.

GOD'S PURPOSES

Why then does God give the believer such a feeling and withdraw it again? He has a few purposes for doing this. It is a pity that the believer does not understand God.

God gives the believer happiness for the purpose of drawing him even nearer to God. He draws men to Himself through His gifts. He hopes His children would realize how gracious He is and how much He loves them so that they would believe in His love under any kind of circumstance. Yet believers only love Him in the presence of feeling and forget Him in its absence.

Moreover, God deals with a believer in this manner so that he will know himself. The most difficult lesson for a believer to learn in life is that of knowing himself—knowing his own corruption, vanity, sinfulness, even knowing that he has no goodness at all. This is a life-long lesson. The more he learns, the deeper the lesson becomes and the more he realizes how filthy his life and nature are in the sight of God. However, there is not the willingness in him to learn, nor is his nature able to learn. Therefore, God employs many ways of instructing the believer so that he may be brought to the place where he can know himself. Among God's many ways, one of the most important is by granting the believer a happy feeling and later withdrawing it. Through such a dealing, the believer will come to realize his own corruption. In the midst of dryness, he will recall how he misused God's gift, how he highly estimated himself, despising others, and how he did many things that were not of the spirit as a result of being manipulated by the emotion. This realization humbles the believer. If he understands the experience, it causes him to know himself and no longer wholeheartedly pursue it as though it were the noblest of all experiences. God wants the believer to know that he does not glorify God's name any more when he is full of happiness than he does when he is suffering. He is not making any more progress in the light than he does in the dark. In either case, his life is just as corrupt.

God's intention is for the believer to overcome his environment. The believer should not allow a change in the environment to affect his life. Whoever changes his living according to his environment lacks depth in the Lord. We know that the environment can only change our emotion. Our emotion is affected by the environment which, in turn, causes a change in our living. Therefore, to overcome our environment, we must overcome our emotion—our feeling. This is crucial. Whoever wants to overcome the environment must overcome the fluctuating feeling. If we have no way of overcoming our constantly changing feelings, we have no way to overcome our environment, because our feelings cause us to sense the changes in our environment. As soon as the environment changes, our feeling senses it and changes accordingly. If we cannot overcome our feelings, our living will vary according to how we feel. Therefore, to overcome our environment, we must first overcome our feelings.

The Lord causes the believer to have different feelings so that he may learn how to overcome them and, thereby, overcome his environment. If he can overcome strong and contradicting feelings, he can surely overcome any kind of changing environment. In this way, a believer will stand on sure ground, and his living will be stabilized. Otherwise, he will be carried away by the waves. God wants a believer to behave the same way, whether he is full of feeling or has no feeling. He wants the believer to just as faithfully serve Him, fellowship with Him, work, pray, and read the Bible, whether he is full of feeling or has no feeling. God does not want His children to vary their way of living according to the brightness or darkness of their feeling. If faithfulness, work, or supplication is called for, they should do it with the same fervency in happiness as well as in sorrow. They should not be a certain way when they feel refreshed and cease to be so when they feel dry. If the believer cannot overcome different feelings in his life, he will not be able to overcome different environments.

Another purpose of God for this kind of dealing is to train the will of the believer. A genuine spiritual life is not a life of feeling but a life of the will. The will of a spiritual man has been renewed by the Holy Spirit; it waits for the spirit's revelation and proposal and then orders his whole being to follow the revelation from the spirit. However, most believers have a will that is so weak it cannot follow through with what they want. It may also unexpectedly come under the influence of the emotion and reject what God wants. Therefore, it is very important to train the will to be strong.

A believer advances very easily when he is excited because he is assisted by the effect of the emotion. When he is frustrated, he finds it difficult to advance because he is not being assisted by the emotion, and he has to rely instead on his will for all the decisions. God's intention is for the will to be strong, not for the feeling to be excited. Hence, He often causes the believer to feel dry, dull, and barren so that he can exercise his will through the strength of the spirit to do just what he has done during periods of excitement. When he is excited, the emotion is in effect. But now God wants his will to function in place of his emotion. Without help from the feeling, the will can be gradually strengthened through exercise. Many erroneously believe that their spiritual life is at its peak when they have feeling, and at its lowest level when they are void of feeling. They do not realize that the genuine living is lived *by the spirit through the will.* When a believer has no feeling, the extent to which he can live by his will is the extent of the *reality* in his living. How he lives during dry periods constitutes his *real* living.

Furthermore, God has another purpose in so dealing with the believer. He wants to lead him into the highest life. If we look closely at the experiences of a believer, we can see that each time the Lord leads one to a higher level in his spiritual journey, He first allows him to live in such a feeling. We may say that after each period of living by the feeling, he reaches a further station in his spiritual journey. God grants the believer to first have a taste in his feeling of what He desires him to obtain eventually. He then withdraws this feeling so that the believer will keep, by his spirit and through his will, what he previously obtained through his feeling. If his spirit is able to press on through the will, regardless of how he feels, he will observe real progress in his life. This is confirmed by our experience. As we go through the "now-up, now-down" life, we often conclude that we have made no advancement since the progression and regression cancel each other out. Although we feel that we have been merely going forward and backward during the last few years or months, if we compare our present spiritual condition with our former condition, when we first started to have this kind of an experience, we will see that we have *indeed made* some real progress. Unknowingly, we have advanced.

Many believers make a great many mistakes through ignorance of this teaching. When one consecrates himself wholly to the Lord and seeks after new spiritual experience (such as sanctification, victory, etc.), he evidently enters into a kind of new life where he feels that he has progressed. He is full of joy, light, and lightness, and he thinks he has possession of the perfect life he desired and sought after. But shortly thereafter, his new experience suddenly becomes obscure; the happiness and excitement he once felt disappear.

Therefore, many believers become discouraged. They think that they can never be wholly sanctified or have a more abundant life like others because they are not able to retain the experience which they have desired for a long time. They do not realize that this is a spiritual law. *Whatever is obtained through the feeling must be kept by the will; and only what is kept by the will becomes truly a part of the believer's life.* God only withdraws the feeling. In the absence of feelings, He wants the believer to use his will to do the same thing he did when he had the feeling. When the believer does this, he will eventually discover that what he lost in feeling has subconsciously become a part of his life. This is a spiritual law. If a believer remembers this all the time, he will not be discouraged.

Therefore, the problem is altogether related to our will. Does our will remain surrendered to the Lord? Is it willing to be led by the spirit? If this is so, *it does not matter* how our feelings change. We must be concerned with whether or not our will is obedient to the spirit and ignore our feelings. For example, after a believer has just been born again, he is usually full of happiness. However, after a while (over a year for some) this kind of happy feeling disappears. Can we say that he has perished? Of course not. There is life in his spirit; how he feels makes no difference.

THE DANGER OF THIS KIND OF LIVING

If we understand the significance of this experience which God gives us and walk according to His will, there is no danger at all. However, when the believer fails to understand God's goal and lives by this kind of feeling—intently pursuing in the presence of feeling while refusing to move in its absence—there is inevitably a spiritual danger. He is exposed to many dangers because he makes feeling his principle of life.

If a believer lives by this happy feeling, his will remains weak and is of no use to the spirit. The sense of the spirit also has no way of developing, since intuition in the spirit is being replaced by feeling. The person walks according to his emotion. As a result, the intuition in the spirit is suppressed by the emotion on the one hand, and on the other hand, his idled and unused intuition is hardly able to grow. We can know the intuition only when the emotion is quiet. The intuition is strengthened only when it is constantly in use. When a believer continues to live by his emotion, the will never has the ability to make decisions, and the intuition never gives a clear voice. Because the will is paralyzed, the believer *needs feelings all the more* to push the will into action. Consequently, the will turns according to feeling, proceeding when a feeling is present and halting when it is not. It is not able to function without the feeling. It constantly requires the feeling's encouragement. Hence, the believer's spiritual life declines day after day. In fact, from then on, it seems that there can be no spiritual life without the effect of the emotion. The emotion carries the same effect as a shot of morphine to the believer. What a pity that he remains unaware and still considers it as the peak of spiritual life and something that should be pursued!

Many believers are erratic because when this feeling comes, they not only feel the Lord's love but also feel their own fervent love toward the Lord. Must we deny even the feeling which generates a love for the Lord in us? Can the feeling which causes us to fervently love the Lord be harmful? These types of questions only indicate the believer's foolishness.

Let us ask some more questions. When the believer is filled with happiness, does he truly love the Lord or does he *love the feeling of happiness?* No doubt this kind of happiness is given to us by God, but is it not also God who withdraws it? If we genuinely love God, we will still fervently love Him no matter what circumstance He puts us in. If we only love when the feeling is present but not when it is absent, perhaps we only love our feeling, not God.

The believer, however, interprets such a feeling as being God Himself. He does not realize that God and God's joy are not the same. The Holy Spirit must instruct a believer before he realizes that he has been desperately seeking God's happiness and not God Himself when he feels dry. He does not love God; he loves the feeling which causes him to be happy. Although this feeling brings him the sense of God's love and presence, he does not love God directly. This feeling, which causes him to sense God's love and presence, refreshes him, enlightens him, and uplifts him. When he loses these sensations, he will pursue this feeling again. His heart's delight is God's happiness, not God. If he genuinely loves God, he should still love Him even when he is suffering through "many waters and floods."

This is a very difficult lesson. We must have happiness, and the Lord delights in giving us His happiness. If we enjoy His happiness according to His will (i.e., we do not seek it for ourselves but are thankful when God causes us to feel happy and just as thankful when He causes us to feel dry, not forcing the issue), this enjoyment will be profitable rather than harmful. However, if we find so much pleasure in this experience that after enjoying God's happiness, we seek it every day, we have departed from God in pursuit of the *happiness* which He gives. God's happiness cannot be separated from God Himself. If we enjoy the happiness which He gives apart from Him, our spiritual life is in danger. This means that our joy is not God but instead the happiness He gives, and we will not advance spiritually. How often we love God not for His sake but for our own sakes! As we love Him, our heart feels happy, and so we continue to love Him. This clearly shows that we do not truly love God; we love happiness, even though the happiness is of God.

This is esteeming God's gift higher than God, the Giver of the gift. This shows that we are still living by the soul and do not understand what a true spiritual life is. We make the feeling of happiness our god and erroneously take pleasure in it. Because of our mistake, God withdraws this happiness according to His will. He changes it to suffering to make us realize that He Himself is desirable, not His happiness. When a believer joys in *God,* he still exalts Him and loves Him even in suffering. Otherwise, he will sink into darkness. God withdraws this happiness not to destroy the believer's spiritual life but to destroy all the idols he is worshipping in place of God Himself. He destroys everything that is harmful to our spiritual life. He wants us to live in Him, not in His feeling.

When a believer lives by feeling and not by the spirit through the will, there is another danger that he will be deceived by Satan. We have briefly mentioned this earlier, but let us explain again.

We must know one thing. Satan can give the believer feelings which are counterfeits of those that are from God. When the believer seeks to walk completely according to the spirit, Satan confuses him with different kinds of feeling. How much more opportunity does he have to apply his tricks to the believer who walks according to his feeling! If the believer persistently goes after feeling, he will fall right into Satan's scheme. Satan will give him different kinds of feeling, leading him to believe that they are from God.

Evil spirits can excite people or depress them. Once the believer is deceived into accepting Satan's feeling, Satan gains ground in the soul. Thereafter, he can further deceive the believer until he fully takes over his feeling. Occasionally, he gives the believer supernatural sensations that cause his whole being to shake, be touched, feel hot or cold, sense a kind of leading, be filled, feel a lightness as though floating in the air, feel as if one is burned by fire from head to toe, or feel that one is dealt with and cleansed in his whole being. When a believer is cheated by the evil spirits to such an extent, he continues to exist by these feelings. His will becomes totally numb, and his intuition is fully surrounded. He lives altogether in the outer man, and his inner man is bound. At this point, his every move is according to Satan's will. When the enemy wants him to do something, he only has to give him a certain feeling. The believer, however, is not aware of this. On the contrary, he thinks that he has been granted some marvelous experiences which definitely make him more spiritual than others.

Supernatural experiences are the most damaging things to a believer's spiritual life today. Countless numbers of God's best children have fallen into the snare of thinking that these miraculous experiences must be from the Holy Spirit because they make their body feel the activity of the Spirit's power. They make them feel sad, happy, hot, or cold; they make them laugh or cry; and they offer them visions, dreams, voices, flames, and indescribable, wonderful sensations. To them, this must be the highest point to which believers can attain. They have never realized that these are works of the evil spirits. It never occurs to them that, apart from the Spirit, evil spirits can move the same way. They are ignorant of the fact that the work of the Holy Spirit is always within man's spirit. What one feels in his *body* is mostly from evil spirits. Why have so many believers fallen into this condition? They are in this condition because they do not live in the spirit, preferring instead to live in their feeling! Therefore, they afford evil spirits the opportunity to exercise their tricks. Hence, a believer must reject a life of feeling; otherwise, he leaves ground for evil spirits to deceive him.

We must seriously warn all of God's children to take note of their *physical* sensations. We should never allow any spirit to produce any feeling in our body against our will. We must reject all the feelings of the *body*. Do not believe in any *physical* feeling or act according to it. Rather, we should forbid it because this is the beginning of Satan's deception. We must follow our intuition which is in the *depths* of our being.

After we have carefully considered a believer's life of feeling, we can find an underlying principle in this kind of experience. The principle is none other than "for the self." Why are we after the feeling of happiness? It is for the self. Why do we dread dryness? It is because of the self. Why do we seek different kinds of physical sensations? It is for the self. Why do we want supernatural experiences? It is for the self. Oh, may the Holy Spirit open our eyes to see that there is still so much selfishness in what we consider as a very spiritual life—a life of feeling! May the Lord show us that when we are full of feelings of happiness, our life is still centered on the self and still craves amusement for the self. We can test whether or not our spirituality is genuine by the way we treat the self.

CHAPTER FIVE

A LIFE OF FAITH

The Bible discloses the proper course of a believer's life in the following verses: "But the righteous shall have life and live by *faith*" (Rom. 1:17); "the life which I now live in the flesh I live in faith, the faith in the Son of God" (Gal. 2:20); and "we walk by *faith,* not by appearance" (2 Cor. 5:7). After reading these verses, we know that a believer lives by faith. Although we may be quick to understand this in our mind, we cannot easily experience it in our life.

A life of faith is entirely different from a life of feeling; in fact, the two are opposites. One who lives by feeling does God's will and sets his mind on the things in heaven only when he feels excited. As soon as the pleasant feeling ceases, everything else ceases with it. A life of faith is not this way. Having a life of faith is living by faith. Faith considers the One in whom it believes to be the mastermind, not the believer himself. Faith does not look at the situation it encounters, but at the One in whom it believes. Although everything around faith may change, if the One in whom it believes has not changed, faith continues on. Faith maintains a relationship with God. It does not depend on feeling; it depends on the God in whom it believes. Faith moves according to the One it believes, while feeling moves according to how it feels. Faith looks at God, but feeling looks at itself. God never changes; He is the same whether the day is cloudy or sunny. Hence, one who lives by faith is as unchanging as God. His living is the same in darkness or in light. The feeling of a believer constantly changes. Therefore, one who lives by his feeling inevitably leads a life of ups and downs.

God requires that His children not regard enjoyment or pleasure as their objective. He wants them to live only by faith in Him. Just as they run the spiritual course when they feel good, they should keep going when they feel miserable.

Their attitude towards God should not vary according to how they feel. Although they sense dryness, tastelessness, and darkness, if they know that a certain matter is according to God's will, they should persist onward, trusting God. Often it seems that there is a rebellion in them. They feel sad, depressed, and discouraged to the point that they want to cease all the activities of their spiritual journey. However, knowing that the work in this spiritual journey must go on, they should ignore all contradictory feelings and continue to press onward. This is a life of faith, a life that does not care for feeling but for God's will. If one believes that a certain thing is God's will, even though he has no interest in it, he does it. A person who lives by feeling does things only according to his interest; a person who lives by faith does all of God's will whether or not it is enjoyable.

A life of feeling draws a person to live apart from God Himself by causing him to be satisfied after obtaining a certain amount of happiness. A life of faith causes a person to live by God and to be satisfied after obtaining God. Since he has already gained God, he is not made any happier because he feels happy, nor is he made bitter because he feels bitter. A life of feeling causes a believer to live for himself. A life of faith causes a person to live for God without leaving any room for the self-life. If the self is given a reason to be happy in one area, there is no living by faith in that area, only a living by feeling. Only pleasant feelings keep the self happy. A believer lives by his feeling because he has not committed his self-life to the cross. Therefore, he reserves a place for the self. He hopes that in his spiritual journey there will always be something to make the self happy.

The Christian life is a life of faith from beginning to end. We received a new life by faith. Therefore, we must *continue* by faith to live according to this new life. Faith is the principle for the believer's life. The Christian life is nothing other than living by faith. While many believers acknowledge this principle, they seem to forget to apply it in their experience. They forget that living, acting, and hoping by their emotion and by their feeling of happiness is walking by sight and not by faith. What is a life of faith? A life of faith is a life that disregards feeling. In fact, a life of faith is completely contrary to a life of feeling. Therefore, if a believer wants to live by faith, he should not change his normal behavior and weep bitterly, thinking that he has lost his spiritual life, whenever he feels cold, dry, empty, and painful. We live by faith and not by happiness.

THE DEEPER WORK OF THE CROSS

We may think that the cross's most complete work is accomplished when we forsake outward, physical happiness and worldly pleasures. Little do we know that in God's work of eliminating our old creation, there remains an even deeper work of the cross for us. He wants us to die to His joy and live to His will. While we may feel happy because of Him and His closeness, rather than any fleshly or worldly matter, God's goal is not for us to enjoy His joy but to obey His will. The cross must work until only the will of God remains. If a believer desires the joy which God gives him but dislikes the suffering He gives, he has not gone through the deeper work of the cross.

There is a big difference between God's will and God's joy. God's will is present any time and any place because we see it in all of His arrangements. However, God's joy is not always present. It is experienced occasionally in certain situations. If a believer seeks after God's joy, he merely desires that part of God's will which makes him happy; he does not desire the entire will of God. When God makes him happy, he obeys His will; when God causes him to suffer, he resists His will. If the believer takes God's will as his life, he obeys no matter how God causes him to feel because he recognizes God's arrangement both in happiness and in sorrow.

During the initial stage of a believer's spiritual life, God allows him to enjoy His joy. However, God withdraws the sensation of joy as the believer advances in life because this is profitable to him. He knows that if the believer continues to seek and enjoy this kind of joy for a considerable length of time, he will not live by every word that proceeds out of God's mouth. Rather, he will live by the words which make him happy. He lives in the comfort of God and not in the

God of comfort. Therefore, God must withdraw all the joyous sensations so that he will live wholly by Him.

At the start of a spiritual journey, when a believer suffers for the Lord, the Lord will comfort him and cause him to sense His presence, see His smiling face, feel His love, and perceive His care in the hope that the believer will not become weary or be discouraged. At this time, if the believer knows the will of God and does it, God will fill his heart with joy as he is doing His will. In spite of the price he has paid for the Lord, God will make him feel that the joy he has received is ten thousand times better than what he has lost. Therefore, he is pleased to do God's will. However, God also sees a danger in this. A believer, who has received comfort and joy after suffering for the Lord and doing His will in the past, may strive for just comfort and joy when he has to suffer again for Him or do His will. As soon as he begins to once again suffer for the Lord or do His will, he may expect the Lord's comfort and joy to help him. Hence, the believer may suffer for the Lord and do the will of God merely for the sake of obtaining a reward—comfort and joy—rather than for the sake of God Himself. Then if he does not have comfort and joy as a crutch, he will not be able to go on. If this is the case, God's will becomes inferior to the joy which He gives for obeying His will.

God knows that when He comforts a believer, he is very willing to suffer for Him; when God grants him happiness, he delights to do His will. However, God wants to know his motive. Is he suffering for the sake of the Lord or for the sake of receiving the comfort which comes with the suffering? Is he doing God's will because it is His will or because by doing it, he is made happy? Therefore, when he has advanced somewhat in his spiritual journey, God will withdraw all such comfort and happiness. Thus the believer no longer feels God's comfort when he is suffering for Him. Without the comfort, it is a suffering not only outwardly, but inwardly as well. When he is doing God's will, he has not the slightest interest. He feels dry and pleasureless. Now God will know why the believer suffers for Him and does His will. God is asking him, "If you do not receive any of My comfort, can you bear it simply because you are bearing it for *My* sake? Are you willing to do something because it is *My* will even though it does not interest you at all? When you feel pained, tasteless, and dry, can you work for Me because this is *My* work? When I send you physical suffering, unaccompanied by any soothing feeling, will you gladly accept it because it is given by *Me?*"

This is a practical cross. Through this the Lord reveals to us whether we are living for Him by faith or whether we are living for ourselves by feeling. Often we hear people say, "I live for Christ." What does this mean? Many believers think that living for the Lord is just working for Him or loving Him. Far from it. Living for the Lord is living for His will, for His interest, and for His kingdom. In this kind of life there is nothing for the self. There is no room reserved for our own comfort, joy, and glory. We are not allowed to do God's will if we are merely after comfort and happiness. We are not allowed to retreat, cease obeying, or delay our obeying just because we feel pained, uninterested, and discouraged. It does not mean that whenever the body is suffering for the Lord, the suffering is for His sake. Many times, even though the body is suffering, the heart is still full of joy. If we live for the Lord, we continue to press onward, not only when we suffer bodily, but even when our heart suffers pain and is absolutely unwilling. The believer must know that living for the Lord means not leaving any place for the self but willingly delivering the self fully to death. One who can ignore himself and gladly receive all things from the Lord, even when things are dark, dry, tasteless, or in disarray, is one who lives for the Lord.

If we live by our emotion, we do God's will only when we feel happy. If we live by faith, we see that we obey the Lord in all matters. Many times, we are clear that a particular matter is according to God's will. However, we do not have the slightest interest in it and even as we do it, we feel dry. We do not feel the Lord's pleasure, blessing, or strengthening. On the contrary, we feel as though we are walking through the valley of the shadow of death because of our fight with the enemy. Under this circumstance, unless we press on by faith, we will surely flee to Tarshish. Alas, not even mentioning the believers who do not do the will of God today, many who do His will do only that which interests them! How many believers do only that part of God's will which suits the desire of their emotion!

Let us ask again, "What is a life of faith?" A life of faith is a life that lives by faith in God *under all* circumstances. Job said, "Though he slay me, yet will I trust in him!" (Job 13:15). This is faith. Since we once believed in God, loved God, and trusted God, no matter where He puts us or how He ill-treats us, and even if He causes us to go through the refining fire so that we would suffer both physically and emotionally, yet we will believe in Him, love Him, and trust Him! Most of the believers today only expect to suffer pain in their bodies, while having peace in their hearts. But who would refuse even the comfort to their hearts because they believe in God? This is the highest life. Who can still delight in God's will without being discouraged and still commit himself to God when he *feels* that God has rejected him and even feels that God hates him and wants to slay him? We should know that God does not treat us this way. However, many believers who have advanced in their spiritual journey have the experience of seemingly being rejected by God. When we feel this way, does our faith in God remain unchanged? When the people were going to hang John Bunyan, the author of *Pilgrim's Progress,* he said, "If God does not intervene, I shall leap into eternity in blindness, come heaven, come hell." This was a hero of faith! When we *feel* discouraged, are we able to say, "O God, even if You should forsake me, I will still trust in You"? Emotion begins to doubt when it senses darkness, but faith clings to God even in death.

How few of the believers have arrived at this stage! How our flesh is opposed to a life that gives no room to self but only to God! Since by nature we dislike taking the cross, many believers remain at a standstill in their spiritual journey. They always want to reserve some happiness for their own enjoyment. To lose their all in the Lord, including that which causes the self to be happy, is truly a death too deep and a cross too heavy! They can be wholly consecrated to the Lord, suffer for Him, or even pay a price to do His will, but they find it difficult to abandon that little feeling which gives pleasure to the self. They treasure a small amount of comfort and allow the spiritual life to rest in such a petty feeling. If they have the courage to willingly deliver themselves into God's fiery furnace, without the slightest feeling of self-pity or self-love, they will advance in their spiritual journey by leaps and bounds! However, believers are still regulated by their natural life because they think that what they see and feel is reliable. They do not have the courage, faith, and aggressiveness to explore those areas which they neither feel nor see in order to discover the paths that have not been trodden by those who were before them. They have reached the place where the boundary has been drawn. A little loss or a little gain becomes the cause of their sorrow or joy, and they no longer aim to go any higher or deeper. They are limited by their petty self.

If a believer realizes that God wants him to live by faith, he would not often utter sounds of murmurings and sighings, nor breed thoughts of discontent. If he is willing to accept the feeling of dryness which God has given him and regard everything from God as good, how quickly his natural life will be dealt with by the cross! Ignorance and unwillingness, however, hinder the believer. Otherwise, these experiences of dryness would become the very cross to practically deal with his soul-life, enabling him to truly live in the spirit. What a pity that many believers accomplish nothing in their lifetimes except the pursuit of a little feeling of happiness. But faithful believers—those who have been brought by God into a real life of spirituality—lead a life that is so much of God! When they recall their experiences, they realize that God's arrangement has, indeed, been right, because without their experiences, it would have been difficult to lose their soul-life. The need today is for believers to fully commit themselves into the hand of God without caring about how they feel.

However, this does not mean that henceforth we will become persons without joy. "Joy in the Holy Spirit" is the greatest blessing in God's kingdom. Moreover, the fruit of the Spirit is joy. What does this mean? It means that although we have lost the feeling of happiness, the joy which we receive out of a pure faith will not be quenched. This is deeper than feeling. By becoming spiritual, we lose our former desire to focus on pleasing the self, and we no longer pursue happiness with zeal as we once did; but peace and joy in the spirit, which come out of faith, are always present.

ACCORDING TO THE SPIRIT

If a believer wants to walk according to the spirit, he must renounce a life of feeling. One who walks according to the spirit must walk by faith. To walk according to the spirit is to renounce the pleasant feeling which the flesh holds on to, demands, and desires, which the believer regards as crutches and security in all his activity. When a believer walks according to the spirit, he does not fear the absence of any supportive feeling or the presence of any opposing feeling. Once his faith weakens, however, and he does not walk according to the spirit, he will seek things which he can see, feel, and touch to support him. Whenever the spiritual life is weak, feeling will replace intuition in taking the lead. A believer who lives by his feeling will come to realize that he was after a pleasant feeling in the beginning. Eventually, he will seek the help of the world. If you cannot reject the pleasant effect of feeling, it will lead you to rely on the world. Feeling must have the world as its resting place. Therefore, emotional believers often resort to their own ways, seeking help from men. To be led by the spirit more than anything else requires faith because the intuition's leading is often contrary to one's feeling. Those without faith cannot go on. Soulish believers simply cease to serve God the moment they feel discouraged. However, believers who live according to faith do not wait until they are excited to work; rather, they ask God to increase the strength of their spirit so that they can overcome the sense of discouragement.

A LIFE OF THE WILL

This life of faith may be called a life of the will. Faith is not mindful of emotion. Therefore, during periods of dryness it comes forth through the decision of the will and wants to walk according to the will of God. Although the believer may not *feel* that he should obey God, nevertheless, he wants to obey Him. Here we see two kinds of Christians: one who lives by feeling and the other who lives by the will (referring to the *renewed* will). The believer who lives by feeling obeys God only when he gets help from feeling, that is, when he feels happy. On the other hand, the believer who lives by the will obeys God whatever the environment and feeling. Our will expresses the opinion of our true self, whereas our feeling is just a reaction to an outward stimulus. Hence, a believer who does the will of God only when he feels happy is not of much value to God, because he is stirred by God's joy to do God's will and not by his sincerity. If he is willing and resolves to do God's will even when he does not feel any amount of happiness or pleasant sensation to help him go on, God considers this truly valuable because it comes out of the believer's sincerity. It is an indication that he respects and surrenders to God, not caring or living for himself. This is the difference between a spiritual believer and a soulish one. A soulish believer obeys God only when what he feels is sufficient to satisfy his desire. This gives the self primary consideration. A spiritual believer is fully in union with God in his renewed will. He obeys God's arrangement; even though he does not receive any external help, he remains steadfast.

What is there to boast of if we obey God to the end while we feel physically and emotionally comfortable? What is there to boast of if we obey the Lord while we are receiving God's comfort in our suffering? It is valuable to God when we suffer and do not feel His comfort, love, help, presence, and joy and yet still decide to obey Him and do His will.

Many believers do not know that living by the spirit is living by the will that is in union with God. (A will that is not in union with God is unreliable and does not last. Only a will that has fully surrendered to God's will wants what the Spirit wants.) They have heard other believers telling them what a joy it is to obey the Lord and suffer for Him. Because they desire this kind of life, they also consecrate themselves fully to the Lord with the hope of obtaining this "higher" life. Truly, after their consecration, they have many experiences of the Lord's nearness and love. Therefore, they think they have obtained what they wanted. But shortly afterwards, all these pleasant experiences become history.

Believers suffer endless pains thinking that they have lost their spiritual life because they do not know that the manifestation of a true spiritual life does not depend on the feeling but on the will. However, now that they really do not feel anything, they must determine if their heart of consecration has changed. Has their desire to do God's will changed? Has their willingness to suffer for the Lord at any cost changed? Has their sincere willingness to do any work and go any place for God changed? If these have not changed, their spiritual life has not regressed at all. If these have changed, their spiritual life has truly regressed.

If a believer has indeed gone backwards, it is not because he has lost his happiness, but because his will is not as willing to obey God as before. And if he has indeed progressed, it is not because he now has many wonderful feelings which he never had before, but because his will is in deeper union with God; he is more willing to do His will and more sympathetic to His will. The standard of a true spiritual life lies in how much our will is in union with God's will. It is not determined by our good or bad feelings. Even when we feel good, without a heart which unconditionally obeys God, our spiritual life is at its lowest level. Even when we feel dry, if there is the willingness to obey God unto death, our spiritual life is at its highest level. The spiritual life is measured by the will because the will expresses what our "self" is. If the will has already surrendered to God, it means that our "self" has surrendered to God and is no longer the master. Our self and spiritual life stand in opposition to each other. When the self is demolished, the spiritual life will surely grow. When the self remains strong, the spiritual life will surely suffer loss. Hence, we can know a person's life just by looking at his will. However, the same is not true of the feeling because when the emotion has the most wonderful feeling, the believer can still be full of self—wanting to entertain and please the self.

Therefore, a believer who sincerely seeks progress should not be deceived into thinking that his feeling is his life, eagerly cherishing a feeling of happiness. Instead, he should ascertain whether or not his will has been fully surrendered to God. It makes no difference whether he feels happy or not. God wants us to live by faith. He may want to see us living simply by faith and being satisfied simply by doing His will without the consolation of our feeling for a long time. Are we willing? We should be happy because we have done the will of God, not because we feel happy. His will should suffice to make us happy.

MAN'S DUTY

When a believer is regulated by a life of feeling, he neglects his duty towards others. A life of feeling has self as the center. Therefore, it cannot be concerned with the needs of others. A believer must have the faith and the will to carry out his duty. Responsibility has no regard for feeling. Our duty towards others is fixed. Our duty towards our work is also fixed. These cannot change according to how we feel. A duty must be performed according to principles; it cannot change according to how we feel.

When a believer merely understands a truth in his feeling, he will not carry out his duty. He is so happy during his time of fellowship with the Lord; therefore, he is desirous of such times. When a believer has experienced the happiness of a pleasant feeling, his greatest temptation is to be alone with the Lord to enjoy this happiness throughout the day, without taking care of all the other things around him. He dislikes his work because temptations and difficulties in his work are inevitable. He feels that he is so holy and victorious when he is face to face with the Lord. However, once he performs his daily duties, he finds himself just as defeated and filthy as before. Therefore, he wants to escape from his duties in the hope of being able to stay in the Lord's presence so that he can be holy and victorious for a long time. He considers his duties as worldly things which he, as a holy and victorious person, should not be concerned with. He is very desirous of a time and place to have fellowship with the Lord, but he detests his duties because they frustrate his happiness. He does not care for the need and welfare of others because he seeks after a time and place to fellowship with the Lord. Parents who bear this attitude fail to take good care of their children; likewise, slaves fail to serve their master faithfully. To them these things are worldly, and it is all right not to care about them since they are seeking after something more spiritual.

The reason for this is that the believer is not yet living by faith. Therefore, he is still after "self-nourishment." Since he is not yet fully in union with God, he can only commune with God at a *particular* time and in a *particular* place. He has not learned to look to the Lord by faith in all things and work together with Him. He still does not know how to be in union with the Lord in the trivial matters of daily living. His experiences of God have been confined solely to the feeling. Therefore, he loves to pitch a tent on the mountain and dwell with the Lord for a long time, but he does not want to come down from the mountain to cast the demons out.

Believers should know that the highest life of a Christian can never contradict the duties of his human living. When we read the Epistles to the Romans, Colossians, and Ephesians, we can see how a believer must fulfill his human duties. The highest life of a Christian is not expressed only at a particular time or a particular place. If so, this life would be rather ordinary. Instead, it can be fully expressed at any time and in any place. It makes no difference whether one is doing housework, preaching, or praying. The life of Christ can be manifested in every kind of activity.

All our dissatisfaction over our present position and all our reluctance to perform the duties associated with this position are the result of living by our emotion. We resist because the happiness we desire is not found in these things. However, our life is not for happiness. So why do we seek happiness? The life of feeling requires us to disregard our duties. The life of faith is not so. Our love for God does not require us to forsake our duties towards our friends and our enemies. If we are in union with God in all things, we know what our proper duties towards every person are and how to fulfill them.

DOING GOD'S WORK

To reject the emotional life and live wholly by faith is the most important requirement for doing God's work. Emotional believers are *useless* in God's hand. Those who live by their feeling know how to enjoy happiness but not how to work. They are not yet qualified to work. They are people who live for themselves; they have not lived for God. Only those who live for God can work for God. What does this mean? Does it mean that all the work of an emotional believer is not counted?

A believer must arrive at the state of living by faith before he can have the reality of working for God and truly be an instrument in His hand. Otherwise, his objective is to obtain happiness, whether physical or emotional. When he is unhappy, he wants to quit. He works for the feeling and quits for the feeling. His heart is full of self-love. When God puts him to work in a field which is full of emotional and physical suffering, he feels sorry for himself and refuses to go on. The work of Jesus is a work of the cross; the work of a believer is also a work of the cross. What is there to be happy about? It would be very difficult for God to gain true workers if we do not deliver our emotion and self-love fully to death.

Today God needs a group of people to be His workers who are willing to follow Him to the end. Too many Christians can work for the Lord when the work is flourishing, when the work suits their interests, and when their feelings are not hurt. However, when the cross comes, demanding them to die and requiring them to hold on to God by faith, without the help of any good feelings, they refuse to go on. The work which is truly accomplished by God will definitely have results. However, can anyone, after receiving God's command to work for eight to ten years, faithfully continue on without seeing any result, just because it is God's command? How many Christians work simply because God commands them to do so? How many work for results? God needs believers of faith to work for Him because all His work has eternity in view. Because His work bears an eternal nature, it is difficult for those who live in time to perceive and understand. Those who live according to feeling cannot be included in this kind of work because there is nothing to please their feeling. If the death of the cross does not deeply deal with their self to the point that they do not keep anything for themselves, then as far as God's work is concerned, they can only follow the Lord to a certain point and no further. God needs men to work for Him who have been completely broken and who are willing to follow Him unto death.

FIGHTING AGAINST THE ENEMY

A believer who lives by his feeling is even less useful in spiritual warfare because spiritual warfare involves attacking the devil through prayer. This is certainly a work of self-denial. How great a suffering this is! There is nothing in this work that makes the self happy. Rather, it is a pouring out of one's self-life for the Body of Christ and for the kingdom of God. To resist and wrestle in the spirit is hard to bear! If the spirit bears an unspeakably heavy burden for God's sake, what is there to be happy about? If all our strength is directed against the evil spirits, how can that be enjoyable? This is a warfare of prayer. Yet for whom do we pray? It is not for ourselves but for God's work. This kind of prayer is for warfare. It is not as enjoyable as our usual emotional prayer. What is comfortable about travailing by prayer in our soul for the saints, destroying and establishing by prayer? Spiritual warfare does not cause the flesh to be happy unless we are fighting in our imagination.

When an emotional believer fights against Satan, he is easily defeated. When he attacks Satan by prayer, Satan uses his evil spirit to attack the believer's feeling. He makes the believer feel that warfare is hard and prayer is dry. When the believer feels sorrowful, tasteless, dark, and dry, he ceases to fight. Hence, an emotional believer cannot fight Satan. Satan only has to attack his feeling, and he will not be able to withstand. If the feeling has not gone through death, it gives Satan ground every time. Each time he opposes Satan, Satan only has to attack his feeling to defeat him. If we have not overcome our feeling, how do we expect to overcome Satan?

Therefore, spiritual warfare requires a person to have an attitude of death to his feeling and to live by faith alone. This kind of person is able to endure the pain of being alone. He is able to fight the enemy without seeking man's acceptance and companionship. He is able to go on in spite of any feeling of suffering. He does not care if he is dead or alive; he only cares for how God leads. This kind of person bears no self-interest, aspiration, or preferences. He has already committed his self to death and fully lives for God. This kind of person does not blame or misunderstand God but loves all of God's ways. He can fill the breach. Although it seems that God has deserted him and that there is no one to help him, he can still face the opposition alone. This kind of person can be a prayer warrior to defeat Satan.

REST

When a believer has gone through all of the Lord's dealings, he will enter into a life of faith. This life of faith is none other than a true spiritual life. When a believer arrives at this stage, he will have a life of rest. The fire of the cross has already eliminated his greedy heart. He has learned his lesson. Now he knows that only God's will is of any value; whatever else he may naturally desire is not the highest, nor do they match the highest life. Now he is happy to lose everything. Whatever the Lord thinks should be withdrawn, he gladly allows the Lord's hand to take away. The sighing, bitterness, and sorrow produced from his hoping, seeking, pursuing, and struggling are gone. He knows that the highest life is to live for God and obey His will. Although he has lost everything, he is satisfied because God's will is accomplished. Although there is nothing for him to enjoy, he yields to the arranging hand of God. It matters not what he encounters as long as God is pleased. This is perfect rest; nothing outward can stir him.

Now the believer is living by the will (the will that is in union with God); his will is full of the strength of the spirit which rules over his emotion. His life is peaceful, steady, and at rest. The former life of ups and downs is gone. However, we should not take this to mean that he will never again be regulated by his emotion, because this kind of sinless perfection is not possible unless one enters heaven. However, if we compare his present condition to the past, we can say that he is at rest and steady. Even though the former confusion is definitely gone, he will occasionally be affected by his emotion. Therefore, he needs to watch and pray.

Neither should we think that it is no longer possible for him to feel happy or sad. There is not such a thing; unless our organ for emotion is destroyed, our feeling still remains. Our emotion will still feel sorrow, darkness, and dryness. However, all these only affect the outward man; it does not affect the inward man because there is a clear separation between our spirit and soul. Therefore, no matter how much the soul suffers outwardly or is confused, our spirit remains peaceful and secure as though nothing has happened.

When the believer's life reaches this stage of rest, he realizes that all the loss he suffered for the Lord before has been replaced. At this time, he has gained God. Hence, everything of God is also his. Now in God, he can properly enjoy the things which He withdrew before. At that time, God caused him to experience sorrow and hardship because his soul-life was the mastermind in all things. He had many loves and pursuits in himself; he even sought what was outside of God's will. This independent action had to be dealt with by God. Since he has lost the self and lost his soul-life, he can enjoy God's happiness in a proper position and within a proper boundary. Only now has he learned to have a proper relationship with God's happiness in God. The heart which fervently sought things for the self is dead. He accepts everything which he receives with thanksgiving. Whatever is not given to him, he does not demand just for the sake of happiness.

When believers have reached this stage, they are counted as having reached a pure stage. Pureness means that there is no mixture involved. Whatever is mixed is not pure. According to the Bible, impureness is filthy. When a believer has not yet reached this stage, he does not have a pure life. Why? Because there is mixture in his life. He lives for God, but he also lives for himself. He loves God, but he also loves himself. His intention is for God, but he also has selfish motives for his own glory, happiness, and comfort. This is a defiled life. He lives by faith, but he also lives by feeling; he walks according to the spirit, but he also walks according to the soul. Although the place which he reserves for himself is not big, it is enough to make his life impure. Only that which is pure is clean; anything mixed with a foreign object is defiled.

When a believer has gone through the thorough work of the cross, he arrives at a life of pureness. Everything is for God, everything is in God, and God is in everything. There is nothing for the self. Even the desire to make the self happy is gone. The self-love of the emotion has been put to death. His only objective in life is to do the will of God. As long as God is pleased, nothing else matters. His unique objective is to obey God; how he feels is not important. This is a pure life. Although God grants him peace, comfort, and joy, he no longer enjoys these things for the sake of satisfying his desire. He views all things in God. His soulish life has been terminated. God has given him a spiritual life that is pure, restful, real, and trusting. God destroyed him, but God also has established him. Everything soulish has been destroyed; everything spiritual has been established.